Number Two: The Texas A&M University Economics Series

e the parameters for a "constitution of freedom"? In the final two sections of the book the author xamines the economic applications of constitu- onal contract and the prospects for a free society.

MES M. BUCHANAN is University Distinguished Profes- r and General Director of the Center for Study of blic Choice, Virginia Polytechnic Institute and State niversity. He is author of several books on economics d on social philosophy, including *The Limits of Lib- ty: Between Anarchy and Leviathan* and, with Gordon llock, *The Calculus of Consent: Logical Foundations* *Constitutional Democracy.*

Texas A&M University Press

College Station, Texas   77843

BN 0-89096-038-0

Freedom in
Constitutional Contract

Perspectives of a Political Economist

By

JAMES M. BUCHANAN

TEXAS A&M UNIVERSITY PRESS

College Station and London

Library of Congress Cataloging in Publication Data

Buchanan, James M
    Freedom in constitutional contract.

    (Texas A & M University economics series; no. 2)
    Bibliography: p.
    Includes index.
    1. Social contract. I. Title. II. Series:
Texas. A & M University, College Station. Texas A & M
University economics series; no. 2.
JC336.B8   301.5'92   77-89513
ISBN 0-89096-038-0

Manufactured in the United States of America

FIRST EDITION

Contents

PART IV. ECONOMIC APPLICATIONS

PART V. PROSPECTS

Preface

THIS book is written by an economist, but its subject matter is not "economics" in the ordinary use of that term. It is motivated by the conviction that the perspectives of an economist are valuable in the discussion of basic issues of social philosophy. The separate parts of the book are closely connected in that each essay represents an effort to clarify particular aspects of what I hope is an integrated and internally consistent position. To some extent the book may be described as my response to the several intellectual and philosophical challenges that have been advanced in opposition to the constitutionalist-contractarian construction.

Individuals can secure and retain freedom in constitutional contract; they cannot do so in any other way. This statement summarizes my argument in this book and elsewhere. But what sort of freedom? What kind of constitutional contract? These are relevant and important questions, but they are not answered here. Before we can begin to approach such questions, it is necessary to lay out the ground rules for discourse, and it is to this purpose that my efforts here are devoted. A genuine constitutional dialogue must take place in the remaining decades of this century if America is to remain a free society. If these essays can bring such dialogue closer to realization and/or assist in clearing away unnecessary barriers to understanding, my objective will be met. I noted above that this book reflects responses to challenges. In a different but related sense, this book represents necessary ground-clearing on my own part before an attempt to participate more specifically in constitutional reform.

The separate parts of this book were written over the course of several years. I am indebted to my colleagues at the Center for Study of Public Choice for advice and encouragement throughout the period, and especially to Professor Gordon Tullock, whose criticism serves always to keep my philosophical proclivities in bounds. The National Science Foundation provided research support during the preparation of several parts of the book.

Mrs. Betty Tillman Ross has, once again, helped me to keep things in order. Quite apart from her direct assistance in manuscript preparation, her understanding of my utility function has allowed her to protect me from many of the inefficient intrusions of modern academia.

Several of the chapters represent revisions of papers that have been previously published. Permission to reprint these has been granted by holders of the copyright in each case. "A Contractarian Perspective on Anarchy" is reprinted by permission of the editors and publishers of *Nomos*, the yearbook of the American Society for Political and Legal Philosophy. "Law and the Invisible Hand" is reprinted by permission of the publisher from *The Economics of Interaction of the Law*, edited by Bernard Siegan (Lexington, Mass.: D. C. Heath & Co., Lexington Books, 1977). "Good Economics—Bad Law," which was originally published in *Virginia Law Review* 60 (Spring, 1974): 483–492, is reprinted by permission of the publisher, Fred B. Rothman. "Before Public Choice," which was initially published in *Explorations in the Theory of Anarchy*, edited by Gordon Tullock, pp. 27–38, is reprinted by permission of the Center for Study of Public Choice, Virginia Polytechnic Institute and State University.

"Politics, Property, and the Law," which first appeared in *Journal of Law and Economics* 15 (October, 1972): 439–452, is reprinted by permission of the University of Chicago Law School. "Student Revolts, Academic Liberalism, and Constitutional Attitudes," from *Social Research* 35, no. 4 (Winter, 1968): 665–680, is reprinted with permission of the editor and of the New School for Social Research. "The Samaritan's Dilemma" was initially presented at the Conference on Altruism and Economic Theory, Russell Sage Foundation, New York, in March, 1972, and was published in *Altruism, Morality, and Economic Theory*, edited by E. S. Phelps, pp. 71–86,

© 1975 Russell Sage Foundation. "A Hobbesian Interpretation of the Rawlsian Difference Principle," first published in *Kyklos* 29 (1976): 5–25, is reprinted with permission of *Kyklos*.

I am indebted to Sage Publications for permission to reprint "The Relevance of Pareto Optimality" from the *Journal of Conflict Resolution* 6 (December, 1962): 341–354. I am also indebted to the American Economic Association for permission to reprint two papers presented at annual meetings of the association. The first, "Political Constraints on Contractual Redistribution," initially published in *American Economic Review* 64 (May, 1974): 153–161, was written jointly with the late Winston C. Bush. I appreciate the permission of his widow, Mrs. Winston C. Bush, to include this paper in this volume. The second paper is "A Contractarian Paradigm for Applying Economic Theory," which appeared in *American Economic Review* 65 (May, 1975): 225–230. North Holland Publishing Company gave its permission to reprint "Taxation in Fiscal Exchange" from the *Journal of Public Economics* 6 (Fall, 1976): 17–29. This paper was originally presented at the International Seminar on Public Economics in France in January, 1975.

Three separate chapters of the book were originally published in *Ethics,* and I appreciate the permission of the University of Chicago Press to reprint them here. They are "Politics and Science," *Ethics* 77 (July, 1967): 303–310; "Ethical Rules, Expected Values, and Large Numbers," *Ethics* 76 (October, 1965): 1–13; and "Pragmatic Reform and Constitutional Revolution," *Ethics* 79 (January, 1969): 95–104. The last of these articles, which is chapter 19, was written jointly with Dr. Alberto di Pierro, and I am particularly grateful to my coauthor for allowing me to include it as part of the argument of this book.

Four other chapters are revisions of papers originally prepared for presentation to conferences. They are "Notes on Justice in Contract," presented at the Conference on Justice, Ohio University, in July, 1976; "Ethical Rules, Expected Values, and Large Numbers," presented at the Conference on Reason, Values, and Political Principle, Pomona College, Claremont, California, in March, 1977; "Democratic Values in Taxation," presented at the Conference on Democratic Values in Taxation, Racine, Wisconsin, in October,

1974; and "Criteria for a Free Society: Definition, Diagnosis, and Prescription," initially presented under the title "The Constitution of Freedom" in a plenary lecture at the Alpbach European Forum, Alpbach, Austria, in September, 1976.

Freedom in Constitutional Contract
Perspectives of a Political Economist

Introduction

THE political economy within which we live, work, and play is exceedingly complex. My role, as a social scientist-cum-philosopher, is to cut through the jungle that describes perceived reality and to impose conceptual order. This effort has the dual purpose of providing a better understanding of what we observe and of laying down some basis for improvement. As I personally conceive this role, the social productivity of abstract analysis is high.

My favorite style of art is abstract impressionism. I enjoy seeing the imagination of the artist constrained within the limits of an object's essential elements while roaming free of most detail. Neither Mark Rothko nor Andrew Wyeth captures my fancy; Nicolas de Staël does. Abstract impressionism contains both positive and normative features, if I may be allowed to mix scientific methodology with art form. The artist who succeeds captures the basic elements of that which he paints while at the same time idealizing those elements into forms that are normatively more satisfying than photographic reality. Something like this process must also characterize the work of anyone who succeeds in expressing his social philosophy. At one level the discussion must be grounded in widely recognizable features of social interaction. The human beings who make up the community must be those persons we might meet instead of those imaginary beings who roam through the hobbit worlds of J. R. Tolkien. At the same time, however, the social philosopher must try to describe the behavior of these real persons in pure, and hence imaginary, settings from which may be removed many of the "noisy" and inessential features of the social process available for direct observation. Within these imaginary settings the explanation of social interaction must be positive if it is to seem at all convincing. But the choice of settings is necessarily normative, in implication if not in intent.

In his great book *The Wealth of Nations* Adam Smith offered a positive explanation of how an economic system would work under the motive force of individual self-interest, freed from the petty regulations of politics but still constrained within an appropriate set of laws and institutions. But Smith developed this explanation of an alternative social order for the purpose of drawing a favorable contrast with that order (or disorder) that he observed. I refer to Smith here by way of an attempted indirect explanation of my own efforts, in this book and elsewhere. In several forms and with varying emphases I am trying to sketch out features of a "social constitution" that seems plausibly attainable for a society of persons whom I can recognize as my fellow human beings.

Some of the institutions of my own imaginary world are visible to anyone's mind's eye; some have been proximately realized in the historical past; some seem descriptive of present-day patterns; glimpses of others are in an attainable future. But there also remain institutions of social order that I discuss which are foreign to the conceptions of modern man, including my colleagues in the academy. My task becomes that of explanation to those who commence in disbelief. I must try to convince the skeptical that the constitutionalist-contractarian blueprint does offer a basis for constructing a society within which persons can remain free.

"Explanation" embodies both analysis and persuasion. An acceptable analysis must be consistent with the laws of social interaction that inform human attitudes.[1] Analysis remains unpersuasive that requires the instrumental use of unrecognizable abstractions. This is one of the many persistent difficulties with Marxian analytics. The class-struggle abstraction is unnatural to the attitudes of most Americans. Analysis that seems to depend on class identification and class action is likely to be ruled out of bounds, quite independently of any empirical testing of its implied hypotheses.

By contrast and comparison, Adam Smith's butcher and baker can be recognized as our neighbors, despite the distance of two centuries.

---

[1] Cf. Michael Polanyi, *Knowing and Being, especially* chap. 14.

The butcher who seeks to turn an honest profit on his sales instead of one who acts to advance the cause of meat cutters everywhere becomes the basis for an abstracted analysis that can be persuasive. Once we so much as acknowledge that the unit of consciousness is the human being (that it is Buchanan and not "society" who writes this sentence), explanation of interaction among separate persons by a model of self-interested motivation necessarily becomes acceptable to a degree. This is not to suggest that self-interest as commonly understood, or even utility maximization in its broadest sense, can support the explanatory burden placed upon it by the most extreme of modern "economist imperialists." My claim here is much less sweeping. I do no more than suggest the appropriateness of the self-interest abstraction *as a part* of any purported explanation of social reality. This position allows me to accept, with Aristotle and everyone else, that man is, indeed, a social animal and also to accept, with Adam Smith, an important role in human action for sympathy with fellow beings.

Let me return to comparison with *The Wealth of Nations*. Adam Smith described the working of an economy that did not exist but that could have existed. His explanation was persuasive because his readers could recognize that the alternative he described was within the realm of the possible. The explanation-persuasion was a necessary precursor of general public support for constructive reforms—for acquiescence in the natural developments that the budding industrial revolution promised as well as for the explicit dismantling of governmental restrictions. What I have tried to do, in this book and elsewhere, is to outline, imperfectly and indirectly, features of a constitutionalist-contractarian order that should be within the possible, but that cannot be secured without, first, understanding and, second, constructive change. The market economy, basically as described by Adam Smith, is a necessary part of the social order—indeed, perhaps its most important part. But the economy cannot function *in vacuo*; it must be incorporated in, and must be understood to be incorporated in, a structure of "laws and institutions."

Modern economists have grossly neglected the constitutional-institutional or framework requirements for the operation of an economic system. This neglect has been accompanied by a comparative failure of those who are not economists to understand fully how the organization of the economic system can influence the opportunities for freedom of choice. If asked to state an instrumental purpose for the analysis in this book, I should respond in terms of these two areas of critical importance. I hope to cause economists, both those who specialize in formal theory and those who directly participate in policy formation, to think more about the "laws and institutions" within which the economy that they analyze operates. But I also hope to widen understanding of the fundamental principles of economic order among social scientists and social philosophers generally. I can do so only by demonstrating that the perspectives of a political economist can be of value in the discussion of political theory in its broadest sense.

At the beginning of this introductory chapter I stated that I conceive my own role to be directed toward imposing conceptual order on the institutional complexities that we observe. This conception requires a theory of social interaction. The economist, equipped with a well-established theory of market exchange, has a relatively easy time of it compared to those who attempt to bring legal-political institutions into a comparable explanatory structure. Relatively speaking, it is simple to derive a "logic" for most of what we see occurring in the strictly economic aspects of reality, in those aspects where men and women are behaving in the "ordinary business of life." It is immensely more difficult to derive a comparably persuasive "logic" for much of what we seem to see in the legal and political arena, in politics, broadly defined.

In an earlier book, *The Calculus of Consent*, Gordon Tullock and I tried to examine what we called the "logical foundations of constitutional democracy." Using straightforward economic methods, we derived a conceptual structure of political order from individual utility maximization that was not, descriptively, much different from that which seems to have informed James Madison and his colleagues and from that which was at least promised by the operation of the Constitution of the United States. The book "explained" many elements of what we observed in the institutions of constitutional democracy in America. The analysis did impose an order on historical reality, and in so doing it may have countered, at least to a degree, some of the criticisms of the American political heritage that have arisen largely from a failure of understanding.

The successful reception of *The Calculus of Consent*, along with its continuing influence, suggests that our positive analysis was persuasive within limits. But the deficiencies of that work lay in the ability of the analysis to explain too much. I have found it difficult to discriminate adequately between those observations of political-constitutional change that reflect merely the logical consequences of the underlying constitutional structure and those that reflect departures from and/or perversions of that structure. Much of what we have observed since 1960 has seemed to be in violation of a normatively superior constitutional order that "almost was" and still "might have been" descriptive of the United States. This apparent violation prompted efforts to "explain" what seemed to be happening, again in terms of a theory of interaction. To an extent, my later book, *The Limits of Liberty: Between Anarchy and Leviathan*, represented my own contribution to an ongoing explanatory elaboration. Included in that elaboration are the extremely important positive theories of bureaucracy and regulation.[2]

As the institutional reality that we observe becomes less and less "efficient" in the sense of reflecting that which might have emerged from genuine social contract, the logical structure, or order, that our positive analysis isolates and identifies loses its normatively desirable properties. The role of the modern analyst becomes more and more akin to that of Adam Smith in his attack on the mercantile system. Existing institutions are positively analyzed, with the intended or unintended result of drawing an unfavorable contrast with the workings of an alternative order that is normatively preferred.

To accompany the analysis of existing institutions, we need an analysis of those institutions that might be, and work here may proceed at several different levels. The philosopher may try, in a manner like that of John Rawls,[3] to define the abstract "principles" of justice, liberty, or security that must characterize the social interaction process. Alternatively, the social philosopher may attempt, more ambitiously, to describe in some detail the working properties of his idealized society in the hope that his analysis will be sufficiently persuasive to

[2] Some of the basic contributions here are Gordon Tullock, *The Politics of Bureaucracy*; William Niskanen, *Bureaucracy and Representative Government*; and Albert Breton, *The Economic Theory of Representative Government*.

[3] John Rawls, *A Theory of Justice*.

convert others to make the changes toward this ideal. Such a third-century Adam Smith has not yet shown himself on the intellectual horizon, and the task may be well beyond the genius of modern man. Finally, the social scientist–cum–philosopher may concentrate his efforts in the more limited sense of developing a set of critical attitudes about social process that seem to be prerequisite to any generalized dialogue on constitutional reform.

It will be evident that the separate essays in this book fall broadly into this third level of discourse. In part one the discussion includes criticisms of alternative paradigms that seem inconsistent with a recognizably desirable constitutional order of society. The essays in part two are devoted more specifically to an articulation of a constitutionalist-contractarian attitude, along with some treatment of the limits of the basic contractarian position. Part three includes several discussions of a theme that has been too much neglected—that which concerns the problem of insuring that persons and groups will act in accordance with the rules. Several economic applications of extensions of the constitutionalist-contractarian position are introduced in part four, including some discussion of the "fiscal constitution." In work currently in progress I hope to develop some of these ideas more fully. Finally, in part five of this book I offer both a diagnosis of the current condition of "constitutional anarchy" and a summary of my own prescriptions for reform.

I am modest in my claims. If my general explanatory arguments are persuasive, some progress toward extended discussion of constitutional reform should be guaranteed. In such a discussion, more specific suggestions for practical policy steps should emerge. In competitive sports the mental attitude of a team is commonly described as being "up" or "down" for a game. If my efforts here and elsewhere are successful, perhaps the attitudes of legal-political-social-economic philosophers will shift to make them "up" for the process of constitutional criticism, reevaluation, and reform that must take place, and soon, if Americans are to remain free citizens.

PART I

ANARCHY, LAW, AND THE INVISIBLE HAND

1

A Contractarian Perspective
on Anarchy

Two-Stage Utopia

I HAVE often described myself as a philosophical anarchist. In my conceptualized ideal society individuals with well-defined and mutually respected rights coexist and cooperate as they desire without formal political structure. My practical society, however, moves one stage down from the ideal and is based on the presumption that individuals could not attain the behavioral standards required for such an anarchy to function acceptably. In general recognition of this frailty in human nature, persons would agree to enact laws, and to provide means of enforcement, in order to achieve the closest approximation to the ideally free society that is possible. At this second level of norms, therefore, I am a constitutionalist and a contractarian: constitutionalist in the sense that I recognize that the rules of order are, and must be, selected at a different level and via a different process than the decisions made within those rules, and contractarian in the sense that I believe that conceptual agreement among individuals provides the only benchmark against which to evaluate observed rules and actions taken within those rules.

This avowedly normative construction enables me to imagine the existence of an ideal social order inhabited by real persons, by men and women that I can potentially observe. In moving from stage one, where the persons are themselves imaginary beings, to stage two, the persons become real, or potentially so, while the rules and institutions of order become imaginary. But I must ask myself why I consider the second stage to be an appropriate subject for analysis and discussion whereas the first stage seems methodologically out of bounds, or at least beyond my interest. Presumably the distinction here must rest on the notion that the basic structure of order, "the law," is itself chosen, is subject to ultimate human control, and may be changed as a result of deliberative human action. By contrast, the fundamental character traits of human beings either cannot be, or should not be, manipulated deliberately. In other terms, attempts to move toward an idealized first-stage order may require some modification of human character, an objective that seems contrary to the individualistic value judgments that I make quite explicit. On the other hand, attempts to move toward a second-stage ideal require only that institutions be modified, an objective that seems morally and ethically acceptable.

As a preliminary step I have called for the adoption of a "constitutional attitude," a willingness to accept the necessity of rules and an acknowledgment that choices among rules for living together must be categorically separated from the choices among alternative courses of action permitted under whatever rules may be chosen. But what happens if I should be forced, however reluctantly, to the presumption that individual human beings, as they exist, are not and may not be capable of taking on such requisite constitutional attitudes? In this case my treatment of an idealized constitutionalist-contractarian social order becomes neither more nor less defensible than the discourse of those who go all the way and treat genuine anarchy as an ideal. Yet somehow I feel that my discussion of idealized social order is more legitimate, more productive, and less escapist than the comparable discussion of the libertarian anarchists, perhaps best exemplified here by Murray Rothbard.[1] I shall return to this proposition below, and I shall attempt an argument in defense.

The Logic of Authority

Before I do return to my proposition, however, I want to examine one possible consequence of abandoning the constitutionalist-contractarian perspective. If we say that persons are simply incapable of

---

[1] Murray Rothbard, *For a New Liberty*. See also David Friedman, *The Machinery of Freedom*. I shall not discuss those putative anarchists who fail to see the internal contradiction between anarchy and socialism. The absurdity of such juxtaposition should be apparent without serious argument.

adopting the requisite set of constitutionalist attitudes, which is another way of saying that they are incapable of evaluating their own
long-term interests, we are led, almost inexorably, to imposed authority as the only escape from the genuine Hobbesian jungle. Anyone
who takes such a position, however, must acknowledge that a "free
society," in the meaningful sense of process stability, is not possible.
The analysis turns to alternative criteria for authority, both in terms
of the basic objectives to be sought and in terms of the efficiency
properties of structures designed to accomplish whatever objectives
might be chosen. But whose values are to be counted in deriving such
criteria? We have, in this setting, already rejected the individualistic
base, at least in its universalized sense, from which such criteria
might be derived. But if only some persons are to be counted, how do
we discriminate? Of necessity, the treatment of the idealized limits to
authority must be informed by the explicit or implicit value norms of
some subset of the community's membership. In the extreme, the
value norms become those of the person who offers the argument,
and his alone.

Most discussion of social reform proceeds on precisely this fragile
philosophical structure, whether or not the participants are aware of
it. When an economist proposes that a particular policy measure be
taken—for example, that the ICC be abolished—he is arguing that
his own authority, backed presumably by some of the technical analysis of his professional discipline, which had its own implicit or built-
in value norms (in economics, Pareto efficiency), is self-justificatory.
But since different persons, and groups, possess different norms,
there is no observed consensual basis for discriminating between one
authority and another. The linkage between the consent of individuals and the policy outcomes is severed even at the purely conceptual
level and even if attention is shifted back to basic rules of order.

The implication of all this is that the authority which emerges
from such a babel of voices, and from the power struggle that these
voices inform and motivate, carries with it no legitimacy, even in
some putative sense of this term. The authoritarian paradigm for the
emergence and support of the state lacks even so much as the utilitarian claims made for the basic Hobbesian contract between the individual and the sovereign, whoever that might be. There can be no
moral legitimacy of government in this paradigm, no grounds for

obligation to obey law, no reasons for the mutual respect of individuals' boundaries or rights.

If most persons, including most intellectuals and academicians, view government in this perspective, and more importantly, if those who act on behalf of government view themselves in this manner, both the libertarian anarchist and the constitutionalist-contractarian exert didactic influence in their attempts to expose the absence of moral underpinnings. But does not such activity, in and of itself, reduce to nihilism under the presupposition that universalized individual values are not acceptable bases for moral authority? If individuals are not capable of acting in their own interest in the formulation of social institutions, both the anarchist and the contractarian may be deemed genuinely subversive in their "as if" modeling of society— in their establishment of normative standards for improvement that are empirically nonsupportable. The activity in question weakens the natural subservience to the existing authority, whoever that might be, and may disrupt social order without offering redeeming elements that might be located in some constructive alternative.

Individualistic Norms

These are questions that the libertarian anarchist and the contractarian must ask and somehow answer to their own satisfaction. I pose these questions here in part for their own intrinsic interest and importance but also in part because they place the libertarian anarchist and the constitutionalist-contractarian squarely on the same side of the central debate in political philosophy, the debate that has gone on for several centuries and that promises to go on for several more. Both the libertarian anarchist and the constitutionalist-contractarian work within the individualistic rather than the nonindividualistic framework or setting.[2] I use the term *nonindividualistic* instead of *collectivist* explicitly here because I want to include in this category the transcendent or truth-judgment paradigm of politics, a paradigm

---

[2] This is recognized by Plattner when he places John Rawls, an avowed contractarian, and Robert Nozick, almost a libertarian anarchist, in the same category "on the deepest level." Against both Plattner advances the transcendentalist view of politics as supraindividualistic. See Marc F. Plattner, "The New Political Theory," *The Public Interest* 40 (Summer, 1975): 119–128, notably p. 127.

that may produce either collectivist or noncollectivist outcomes at a practical level.

I want to argue first that it is normatively legitimate to adopt the individualistic model, regardless of empirical presuppositions, and second that within this model, broadly defined, the constitutionalist-contractarian variant is superior to the libertarian-anarchist variant. It is morally justifiable, and indeed morally necessary, to proceed on the "as if" presumption that individuals, by their membership in the human species, are capable of acting in their own interest, which they alone can ultimately define. Empirical observation of human error, evaluated *ex post*, can never provide a basis for supplanting this "as if" presumption, because there exists no acceptable alternative. If persons are considered to be incapable of defining and furthering their own interests, who is to define such interests and promote them? If God did, in fact, exist as a suprahuman entity, an alternative source of authority might be acknowledged. But failing this, the only conceivable alternative authority must be some selected individual or group of individuals, some man who presumes to be god, or some group that claims godlike qualities. Those who act in such capacities and who make such claims behave immorally in a fundamental sense: they relegate other members of the species to a value status little different from that of animals.

The primary value premise of individualism is the philosophical equality of men as men despite all evidence concerning inequalities in particular characteristics or components. In thinking about men, we are morally obligated to proceed as if they are equals, as if no man counts for more than another. Acceptance of these precepts sharply distinguishes the individualist from the nonindividualist. But we must go one step further to inquire about the implications of these precepts for social order. It is at this point that the libertarian anarchist and the constitutionalist-contractarian part company, but philosophically they have come a long way together, a simple statement but one that is worthy of emphasis.

Anarchy and Contractual Order

The issue that divides the anarchist and the contractarian is "conjecturally empirical." It concerns the conceptually observable structure of social order that would emerge if men could, in fact, start from scratch. Would they choose to live in the idealized anarchy, or would they contractually agree to a set of laws, along with enforcement mechanisms, that would constrain individual and group behavior? This question cannot actually be answered empirically because, of course, societies do not start from scratch. They exist in and through history, and those elements of order that may be observed at any point in time may or may not have emerged contractually.

It is at this point that the constitutionalist-contractarian paradigm is most vulnerable to the criticisms of the anarchist. How are we to distinguish between those elements of social order, those laws and institutions, which can be "explained" or "interpreted" (and by inference "justified") as having emerged, actually or conceptually, on contractual precepts and those which have been imposed noncontractually (and hence, by inference, "illegitimately")? If the contractual paradigm is sufficiently flexible to explain all observable institutions, it remains empty of discriminant content, quite apart from its possible aesthetic appeal.

Careful use of the model can, however, produce a classification that will differentiate between these two sets of potentially observable institutions. For example, the existence of unrestricted political authority in the hands of a political majority could never be brought within contractarian principles. Persons who could not, at a time of contract, predict their own positions would never agree to grant unrestricted political authority to any group, whether it be a duly elected majority of a parliament, a judicial elite, or a military junta. Recognition of this simple point is, of course, the source of the necessary tie-in between the contractarian paradigm and constitutionalism.[3] But what are the constitutional limits here? What actions by governments, within broad constitutional authority, may be thrown out on contractarian precepts?

Arbitrary restrictions or prohibitions on voluntary contractual agreements among persons and groups, in the absence of demontrable spillover effects on third parties, cannot be parts of any plau-

---

[3] For an elaboration of the underlying theory, see James M. Buchanan and Gordon Tullock, *The Calculus of Consent: Logical Foundations of Constitutional Democracy.*

sible "social contract." For example, minimum-wage legislation and most restrictions on entry into professions, occupations, types of investment, or geographical locations could be rejected, as could all discrimination on racial, ethnic, and religious grounds. This is not to suggest that the appropriate line is easy to draw and that borderline cases requiring judgment are absent. More importantly, however, the classification step alone does not justify the institutions that remain in the potentially allowable set. To conclude that an observed institution may have emerged, conceptually, on generalized contractarian grounds is not at all equivalent to saying that such an institution did, in fact, emerge this way. Many, and perhaps most, of the governmental regulations and restrictions that we observe and that remain within possible contractarian limits, may, in fact, represent arbitrary political impositions which could never have reflected generalized agreement.

Consider a single example, that of the imposition in 1974 of the speed limit of fifty-five miles per hour. Where can we classify this observed restriction on personal liberties in terms of the contractarian paradigm? Because of the acknowledged interdependencies among individual motorists, in terms of safety as well as fuel use, it seems clearly possible that general agreement on the imposition of some speed limit might well have emerged, and fifty-five miles per hour might have been within reasonable boundaries. But whether or not the fifty-five-miles-per-hour limit, as we observe it, in fact would have reflected a widely supported and essentially consensual outcome of some referendum process cannot be determined directly. The observed results could just as well reflect the preferences of members of the governmental bureaucracy who were able to exert sufficient influence on the legislators who established the limit.

Constitutional Contract

If we look too closely at particular policy measures in this way, however, we tend to overlook the necessary differentiation between the constitutional and the postconstitutional stages of political action. Should we think of applying contractarian criteria at the postconstitutional level at all? Or should we confine this procedure to the constitutional level? In reference to the fifty-five-miles-per-hour limit, as long as the legislature acted within its authorized constitutional powers, which are themselves generally acceptable on contractarian grounds, the observed results in any one instance need not be required to meet conceptual contractarian tests.

At this juncture the contractarian position again becomes highly vulnerable to the taunts of the libertarian anarchist. If specific political actions cannot be evaluated per se, but must instead be judged only in terms of their adherence to acceptable constitutional process, the basic paradigm seems lacking in teeth. Improperly applied, it may become an apology for almost any conceivable action by legislative majorities or by bureaucrats acting under the authorization of such majorities, and even strict application finds discrimination to be difficult. This criticism is effective, and the contrasting stance of the uncompromising libertarian anarchist is surely attractive in its superior ability to classify. Since to the anarchist all political action is illegitimate, the set of admissible claims begins and remains empty.

The constitutionalist-contractarian can and must retreat to the procedural stage of evaluation. If his hypotheses suggest that particular political actions, especially over a sequence of isolated events, fail to reflect consensus, he must look again at the constitutional authorizations for such actions. Is it contractually legitimate that Congress and the state legislatures be empowered by the Constitution to impose speed limits? What about the activities of the environmental agencies, acting as directed by Congress? What about the many regulatory agencies? Such questions as these suggest that the constitutionalist-contractarian must devote more time and effort to attempts to derive appropriate constitutional limits, notably with respect to the powers of political bodies to restrict economic liberties. Furthermore, the many interdependencies among the separate political actions, each of which might be plausibly within political limits, must be evaluated. Admittedly, those of us who share the constitutionalist-contractarian approach have been neglectful here. We have not done our homework well, and the research agenda facing us is large, indeed.

Meanwhile, we can, as philosophical fellow travelers, welcome the arguments put forth by the libertarian anarchists in condemning the political suppression of many individual liberties. We can go part of the way on genuine contractarian principles, and we can leave open many other cases that the anarchists can directly condemn. As I have noted elsewhere,[4] the limited-government ideals of the constitutionalist-contractarian may not excite the mind of modern man, and given the demonstrable overextension of political powers, the no-government ideals propounded by the libertarian anarchists may help to tilt the balance toward the individualistic and away from the non-individualistic pole.

I have acknowledged above that the anarchist critique of existing political institutions is probably intellectually more satisfying than that which may be advanced by the contractarian. But where the anarchist critique falters, and where the contractarian paradigm comes on at its strongest, is at the bridge between negative criticism and constructive proposals for change. To the libertarian anarchist, all political action is unjustified. He cannot, therefore, proceed to advocate a politically orchestrated dismantling of existing structure. He has no test save his own values, and he has no means of introducing these values short of revolution. The contractarian, by contrast, has a continuing test which he applies to observed political structure. Do these basic laws and institutions reflect consensus of the citizenry? If they do not, and if his arguments to this effect are convincing, it becomes conceptually possible to secure agreement on modification. The rules of the game may be modified while the game continues to be played as long as we all agree on the changes. But why not eliminate the game?

This question returns us to the initial distinction made between the ideal society of the philosophical anarchist and that of the contractarian. To eliminate all rules and require that play in the social game take place within self-imposed and self-policed ethical and moral standards places too much faith in human nature. Why do we observe rules, along with referees and umpires, in ordinary games? Empirical examination of such voluntary games offers us perhaps the most direct evidence for the central contractarian hypothesis that rules—laws—are generally necessary.

[4] See my review of David Friedman's book, *The Machinery of Freedom*, in *Journal of Economic Literature* 12 (September, 1974): 914–915.

Definition of Individual Rights

I could end this chapter here and remain within the limits of most discussion by economists. Traditionally economists have been content to treat exchange and contract, in all possible complexities, on the assumption that individual participants are well-defined entities capable of making choices among alternatives and in mutual agreement concerning legal titles or rights to things which are subject to exchange. The distribution of basic endowments, human and non-human, among persons has been taken as a given for most economic analysis, both positive and normative. The libertarian anarchist has gone further; in order to develop his argument that any and all political structure is illegitimate, he finds it necessary to presume that there are definitive and well-understood "natural boundaries" to individuals' rights. These boundaries on rights are held sacrosanct, subject to no justifiable "crossings" without consent.[5]

The problem of defining individual boundaries, individual rights, or, indeed, the term *individuals* must arise in any discussion of social order that commences with individuals as the basic units. Who is a person? How are rights defined? What is the benchmark or starting point from which voluntary contractual arrangements may be made?

I stated earlier that the primary value premise of individualism is the philosophical equality of men as men. Further, I stated that in thinking about men we are morally obligated to proceed as if they are equals, in that no man counts for more than another. These concepts remain, and must remain, the fundamental normative framework even when we recognize inequalities among persons in reality. The libertarian anarchist accepts this framework, but in a much more restricted application than do others who also fall within the individualistic set. The libertarian anarchist applies the norm of moral equality in holding that each and every man is *equally* entitled to have the natural boundaries of his rights respected, regardless of the fact that, among persons, these boundaries may vary widely.[6] If such

---

[5] One merit of Robert Nozick's analysis is his explicit discussion of the underlying presumptions of the "natural boundaries" model. See Robert Nozick, *Anarchy, State, and Utopia.*

[6] For purposes of discussion here I am including Robert Nozick as being among the libertarian anarchists. Although he defends the emergence of the minimal pro-

natural boundaries exist, the contractarian may also use the individual units defined by such limits as the starting point for the complex contractual arrangements that emerge finally in observed, or conceptually observed, political structures. Within the presupposition that natural boundaries exist, the differences between the constitutionalist-contractarian and the libertarian anarchist reduce to the variant hypotheses concerning the interdependencies among persons, as defined—interdependencies that could be, as noted above, subjected to testing at a conjecturally empirical level.

But do such natural limits or boundaries exist? Once we move beyond the simple rights to person in the strictly physical sense, what are the distinguishing characteristics of boundary lines? In all cases where separate individual claims may come into conflict, or potential conflict, what is the natural boundary? Robin Hood and Little John meet squarely in the center of the footbridge. Who has the right of first passage?[7]

Robert Nozick makes a bold attempt to answer such questions by referring to the process of acquisition. In his formulation the legitimacy of the boundary limits among persons depends upon the process through which rights are acquired and not on the absolute or relative size of the bundle that may be in the possession or nominal ownership of a person or group. A person who has acquired assets by voluntary transfer holds these within admissable natural boundary limits. A person who holds assets that have been acquired, by him or by others in the past, by nonvoluntary methods has little claim to include these assets within the natural limits.

What is the ultimate test for the existence of natural boundaries? It must lie in the observed attitudes of individuals themselves. Do we observe persons to act as if there are natural boundaries on the rights of others, beyond those formally defined in legal restrictions? The evidence is not all on one side here. In rejecting the extreme claims of the libertarian anarchists, we should not overlook the important fact

---

tective state from anarchy, and specifically refutes the strict anarchist model in this respect, he does provide the most sophisticated argument for the presumption of natural boundaries on individuals' rights, which is the focus of my attention here. Cf. Nozick, *Anarchy, State, and Utopia.*

[7] I use this example in several places to discuss this set of problems in my recent book *The Limits of Liberty: Between Anarchy and Leviathan.*

that a great deal of social interaction does proceed without formalized rules. For large areas of human intercourse anarchy prevails, and it works. We need no rules for directing pedestrian traffic on busy city sidewalks, no rules for ordinary conversation in groups of up to, say, ten persons, and no rules for behavior in elevators.

In the larger context, however, the evidence seems to indicate that persons do not mutually and simultaneously agree on dividing lines among separate rights. There is surely a contractual logic for at least some of the activity of the state in defining and enforcing the limits on the activities of persons. To accept this fact, however, does not imply that the legally defined rights of individuals, and the distribution of these rights, are arbitrarily determined by the political authorities. If we reject the empirical existence of natural boundaries, however, we return to the initial question. How do we define *individuals* for the purpose of deriving the contractual basis for political authority?

The Hobbesian Setting

The only alternative seems to be found in the distribution or limits on individuals' spheres of action that would be found in the total absence of formalized rules, that is, in genuine Hobbesian anarchy. There would emerge some "equilibrium" in this setting, some distribution of allowable activities among persons that could be sustained. This distribution would depend on the relative strengths and abilities of persons to acquire and to maintain desirable goods and assets. The "law of the jungle" would be controlling, and no serious effort could be made to attribute moral legitimacy to the relative holdings of persons. But this construction does have the major advantage of allowing us to define, in a conjecturally positive sense, a starting point, an "original position," from which any contractual process might commence.[8] Individuals need not be "natural equals" in this Hobbesian equilibrium, but they would still find it mutually advantageous to enter into contractual agreements that impose limits on their own

[8] In his much-acclaimed book *A Theory of Justice*, John Rawls attempts to derive principles of justice from conceptual contractual agreement among persons who place themselves in an "original position" behind a "veil of ignorance." Rawls does not, however, fully describe the characteristics of the "original position."

activities and that set up ideally neutral governmental units to enforce these limits.

The perspective changes dramatically when this essentially Hobbesian vision is substituted for the natural-boundaries or Lockean vision, or when the existence of natural boundaries to the rights of persons that would be generally agreed upon and respected is denied. In the Nozick variant of the Lockean vision, anarchy, the absence of formalized rules—the absence of law along with means of enforcement— offers a highly attractive prospect. By contrast, in the basic Hobbesian vision, or in any paradigm that is derivative from it, anarchy is not a state to be desired at all. Life for the individual in genuine anarchy is indeed predicted to be "poore, nasty, brutish, and short." The Hobbesian jungle is something to be avoided and something that people with rational self-interest will seek to avoid through general agreement on law along with requisite enforcement institutions, even if in the extreme the contract may be irreversible and Hobbes's Leviathan may threaten.[9]

Conclusions

We have here a paradox of sorts. The libertarian anarchist and the contractarian share the individualistic value premise. In addition, their diagnoses of current social malaise are likely to be similar in condemning overextended governmental authority. Further, the items on both their agendas for policy reform may be identical over a rather wide range. In their descriptions of the "good society," however, these two sets of political philosophers are likely to differ widely. The constitutionalist-contractarian, who looks to his second-stage set of ideals and who adopts at least some variant of the Hobbesian assumption about human nature, views anarchy, as an institution, with horror. To remove all laws, all institutions of order, in a world peopled by Hobbesian men would produce chaos. The contractarian must hold fast to a normative vision that is not nearly so simplistic as that which is possible either for the libertarian anarchist or for the collectivist. The contractarian seeks "ordered anarchy";

[9] The argument of the few preceding paragraphs is developed much more fully in my book *Limits of Liberty*. Also see Gordon Tullock, ed., *Explorations in the Theory of Anarchy*.

that is, a situation described as one which offers maximal freedom for individuals within a minimal set of formalized rules and constraints on behavior. He takes from classical economics the important idea that the independent actions of many persons can be spontaneously coordinated through marketlike institutions in order to produce mutually desirable outcomes without detailed and direct interference by the state. But he insists, with Adam Smith, that this coordination can be effective only if there are limits to individual actions defined by laws that cannot themselves spontaneously emerge. The contractarian position requires sophisticated discrimination between those areas of potential human activity where law is required and those areas that had best be left alone. Between the libertarian anarchist, who sees no cause for any laws and who trusts to individuals' own respect for each others' reciprocal natural boundaries, and the collectivist-socialist, who sees chaos as the result of any human activities that are not politically controlled, the constitutionalist-contractarian necessarily occupies the middle ground. His ideal world falls "between anarchy and Leviathan," both of which are to be avoided.

2

Law and the Invisible Hand

Spontaneous Order

I HAVE often argued that there is only one principle in economics that is worth stressing, and that the economists' didactic function is one of conveying some understanding of this principle to the public at large. Apart from this principle there would be no basis for general public support for economics as a legitimate academic discipline, no place for economics as an appropriate part of a liberal educational curriculum. I refer, of course, to the principle of the spontaneous order of the market, which was the great intellectual discovery of the eighteenth century.

The principle is perhaps best summarized in Adam Smith's most famous statement: "It is not from the benevolence of the butcher, the brewer, or the baker, that we expect our dinner, but from their regard to their own interest. We address ourselves, not to their humanity, but to their self-love, and never talk to them of our own necessities but of their advantages."[1] Sir Dennis Robertson put the same point somewhat differently when he said that the economists' task was that of showing how to minimize the use of that scarcest of all resources, love. And he urged his fellow economists to emit warning barks whenever they observed proposals that required love for their effective implementation.[2]

The understanding of this principle is extremely important for the shaping of attitudes toward the economic process. To those who do not understand this principle, either from a lack of formal instruction in economics (or perverse formal instruction, which is by no

[1] Adam Smith, *The Wealth of Nations*, p. 14.
[2] D. H. Robertson, *Economic Commentaries*, pp. 148–149, 154.

means uncommon) or from some failure to sense its fundamental elements from ordinary perceptions of social reality, the economy has no order. The man of habit may seldom think, but if he is forced, for any reason, to look about him, failure to understand this principle requires some resort to miracles to explain such a simple fact as the observed presence of tomato juice on his grocer's shelves each time he goes to the supermarket. In this situation the man of habit is highly vulnerable to persuasion by those who, from either ignorance or design, propose to subvert the workings of economic process. If the continuing availability of tomato juice is brought to the level of political consciousness either by chance occurrence of some exogenous event or by the deliberate effort of a demagogue, the economic illiterate would quite naturally tend to embrace governmental controls purportedly aimed at insuring stability in supply (of tomato juice or anything else). The whole *raison d'être* of economics as a discipline with some didactic purpose lies in its potential for reducing to a minimum the numbers of persons who remain illiterate in this sense.

By implication, if not directly, I have advanced here what is essentially a *political* justification for the understanding of this principle of spontaneous coordination. But there are two other, and different, justifications for understanding this principle that must be discussed. First, it has been alleged by Robert Nozick, in his much-acclaimed book *Anarchy, State, and Utopia*, that "invisible-hand explanations" of reality are intellectually and aesthetically more satisfying than alternative explanations. Nozick offers complex philosophical reasons for this allegation that I cannot fully appreciate, but the common-sense basis of his justification seems clear enough. We place positive value on those sorts of understandings and explanations that allow us to predict even when there is no prospect of control. Contrast the Newtonian (and post-Newtonian) explanations of the movements of the planets with those which required explicit intrusion of "God's will." The economic sophistication that allows us to know why the tomato juice is on the grocer's shelves and to predict what will happen if there is some increase in the demand is something of intrinsic value in its own right.

A second, and more familiar, justification for understanding the principle of spontaneous coordination lies in the efficiency applications. We know that there will be tomato juice on the grocer's shelves, but we know also that we shall get *more* tomato juice, *more* potatoes, *more* shoes—more economic value generally—if we allow market forces to operate than if we make attempts to interfere. If we can then accept aggregate economic value as an appropriate objective, an instrumental argument for understanding the coordinative principle is provided.

Or we may introduce Michael Polanyi's application of the same principle to the organization of science. If we are interested in discovering the unknown, we had best allow individual scientists free reign in their searches. The jigsaw puzzle that is confronted can best be solved by allowing different persons to look for differing sub-patterns, especially since the "big picture" has no defined borders and since no one knows what it would look like even with borders imposed.

Spontaneous Disorder

It is useful to distinguish the three justifications for understanding the principle of spontaneous coordination; we may label them the *political*, the *aesthetic*, and the *economic*. The failure to separate them may have been a source of some confusion in application. As a different example, consider not the supply of an ordinary commodity on the grocer's shelves, but the dumping of litter on the beaches near San Diego. (We assume, for now, that there is no law against dumping such litter.) We should be able to observe the result: beautiful beaches made ugly by litter. We can explain and understand this result in the selfsame way that we understand the tomato juice on the grocer's shelves. Persons do not dump litter on the beach because they are evil or malevolent. (Such people may exist, but they are surely in a tiny minority, even in the world of the late 1970's.) Persons dump litter on the beach because to do so is in their own self-interest, which may be either narrowly or broadly defined. This reason does not imply that the persons who dump litter do not value a clean beach more highly than a littered beach; almost all will do so. But the private, personalized costs of cleaning up their own litter are probably greater for most persons than the differential value of the marginal change in the total appearance of the beach that their own activity can produce. In a large-number setting, the change in the total amount of littering brought about by the change in behavior of one person may be relatively insignificant. Hence, it may be to each person's interest to continue to litter while deploring the overall appearance of the beach.

This is, of course, a familiar example to economists—an example of external diseconomies, of the generation of public bads, of a generalized prisoners' dilemma. Some economists would go on to suggest that the observed results arise because of the absence of property rights in the commonly used resource, the beach. If this scarce resource were assigned to some person or group, it would then be in their interest to maintain standards of cleanliness, to internalize the externalities, and in so doing to insure economic efficiency. My purpose here, however, is not to discuss the particulars of this example or to raise the more general issues concerning the uses to which various constructions of "market failure" have been put. My purpose is the quite different one of illustrating that "invisible-hand explanation" may be as applicable to "orders" that are clearly recognized to be undesirable as to those that are recognized to be desirable. We have explained the observed pattern of litter on the beach by looking at the behavior of persons, each of whom is maximizing his own utility. Out of this behavioral interaction a result emerges, an order of sorts, which was not designed by anyone. It was not intended by any of the actors in the process.

We may now apply our three separate justifications of the basic principle of spontaneous coordination to this example. The "order" which emerges, the littered beach, has been produced by anarchy; there is no politically or governmentally orchestrated control or regulation which produces the result. We fully understand that the results emerge from the working of the "invisible hand." We can, as in the other examples, secure some satisfaction from our ability to explain these observed results so that we make them seem as "natural" as if they had been generated by rational utility-maximizing behavior on the part of the separate individuals involved in the interaction. The aesthetics of understanding the principle of order do not seem different from those present in the more familiar meat-bread-potatoes examples of Adam Smith.

An appreciation of the workings of the invisible hand also allows us to recognize that the littering of the beach will be kept within bounds, within the limits that are indeed explainable by individual utility maximization. Anarchy need not generate chaos; the public beach need not be weighted down with tons of garbage in the absence of specific regulation and control by government authorities. For any given population, and for any given set of ethical norms for behavior, anarchy in the use of the acknowledged common resource will produce some equilibrium, one that can be predicted and described in general terms by resort to the economist's set of tools.

It is in the economic instead of the aesthetic or the political characteristic that our beach littering example dramatically differs from Adam Smith's butcher, baker, and candlestick maker or from the other standard and familiar examples drawn from classical and neoclassical economics, including my can of tomato juice. In the standard examples an understanding of the principle of spontaneous coordination enables us to predict that we will get more meat, more bread, more candlesticks, and more tomato juice by allowing the forces of individual utility maximization to work independently of direct political regulation (assuming, of course, that we have a well-defined set of legally protected property rights). And if we make the widely acknowledged value judgments that more is better than less and that individuals are better able to judge their own welfare than anyone else, we can label the results to be efficient. In somewhat more technical economist's jargon we can say that the workings of the market generate Pareto-efficient results, which means that under the standard conditions postulated there will exist no possible rearrangements which could make one person better off without harming someone else.

But we cannot reach this conclusion in our beach littering example. In the equilibrium attained under anarchy, under the uninhibited and unregulated utility-maximizing behavior of persons acting each independently or separately, no single person has an incentive to change his behavior or incentive to reduce the amount of littering that he does. However, if all or even a relatively large number of persons should change their behavior by reducing the amount of littering, *everyone* might be made better off as a result. And "better off-ness" is here defined in precisely the same way as it was before, namely, by the persons themselves. Each person who uses the beach may find himself with more utility after the general change in behavior than before. And no one would find himself with less utility than before the change. This is merely another way of saying that the results produced by the operation of the invisible hand, by the independent and separate utility-maximizing behavior of persons, are not necessarily efficient in the economic sense. The principle of spontaneous coordination, properly applied to our beach littering example, allows us to understand and to explain the possible economic inefficiency that would characterize the anarchistic equilibrium just as it allowed us to understand and to explain the possible economic efficiency of the anarchistic equilibria (with well-defined property rights) in the market examples drawn from Adam Smith. The principle of spontaneous order, as such, is fully neutral in this respect. It need not be exclusively or even primarily limited to explanations of unplanned and unintended outcomes that are socially efficient.

The Order of Law

So much for a very sketchy capsule summary of the elementary principles of theoretical welfare economics. This is all by way of introducing my basic purpose, which is that of examining the potential applicability of the principle of spontaneous coordination to human activities that are not normally classified as "economic"—activities that are not normally discussed in terms of the production, exchange, and trade of "goods" or "bads." More specifically, I want to look carefully at the emergence and evolution of "the law," which I define here broadly to include the whole set of legal institutions. I want to discuss the applicability of the principle of spontaneous coordination to legal institutions and its implications for legal reform, notably for constitutional change. My discussion and analysis will be critical of the position that seems to be taken by Professor F. A. Hayek, a distinguished Nobel laureate in economics and a social and legal philosopher whose ideas I respect and admire.[3]

---

[3] The Hayek position is expressed most fully in *Law, Legislation, and Liberty*, Vol. 1, *Rules and Order*. My criticism is based on what I interpret to be the basic thrust of Hayek's argument, gained from a careful reading of his book. In particular places Hayek seems to concede many if not all of the points that may be advanced in opposition. My purpose here is not one of exegesis, but instead one of offering constructive criticism.

In his specific attribution of invisible-hand characteristics to the evolution of legal institutions, Hayek seems to have failed to separate properly the positive and the normative implications of the principle. Interpreted in a strictly positive sense, the principle of spontaneous coordination can do much to add to our understanding of legal institutions. But this understanding and explanation can be equally helpful in assessing the efficient and inefficient elements of the order that we may observe, actually or conceptually. "The law" as it exists can probably be classified as some admixture of the bread and meat examples of Adam Smith and the beach littering example that I introduced earlier. In order to derive normative implications, we must carefully discriminate. The forces of social evolution alone contain within their workings no guarantee that socially efficient results will emerge over time. The historically determined institutions of legal order need not be those which are "best." Such institutions can be "reformed," can be made more "efficient." The discussions of such potential reforms should, of course, be fully informed by an understanding of the principle of spontaneous order. But warnings against unnecessary and ill-timed interferences with legal institutions should not extend to the point of inhibiting us against efforts at improvement, which seems to me to be the position Hayek's argument forces upon us.

I shall elaborate on this argument in several stages. A basic point that I stress in almost all discussion is the necessity of recognizing that "we start from here." Any evaluation or analysis of social institutions must commence with the status quo for the evident reason that it describes that which exists. For present purposes there exists some body of law; there is in being a set of legal rules, legal institutions, that may be described. A major part of law school training is indeed little other than the transmission of this description.

And it is surely appropriate for qualified scholars to devote intellectual energies to what may be called the "positive history" of these institutions. In such a history some understanding of the principle of spontaneous order can be helpful. The legal historian who searches for some explicit or planned design in the existing structure, in whole or in every part, is surely destined for frustration. In a very important sense, as Hayek stresses, law "grows"; it is not "made." The legal historian must explain the sources of this growth as best he can, and by resorting to invisible-hand explanations he can add clarity and understanding. But certain parts of the law are also "made" and have been explicitly designed for the accomplishment of particular purposes. The historian must classify the elements of law into these two sets. Explanation and classification—perhaps the work of the positive historian is complete when he has done these tasks.

For those who seek to evaluate the existing structure of law, however, the records of the positive historian offer little more than preliminary inputs. Return to the beach littering example and suppose that a careful history "explains" the absence of either a set of behavioral standards or more formally imposed constraints on private behavior. Population growth alone might explain why those behavioral standards that were deemed appropriate a half-century past may be inappropriate at the present. But what is the conceptual basis upon which an evaluative judgment of "inadequacy" or "undesirability" may be established? How can the analyst attribute "inefficiency" to the results that he observes when the historian has explained how these results have emerged?

It is at this point that Hayek's argument seems misleading. He seems to suggest that those institutions that have evolved spontaneously, through the independent responses of persons to the choices that they faced, embody efficiency attributes. But as the littering example is designed to demonstrate, an explanation of the results by the operation of invisible-hand responses need not carry with it normative overtones.[4] But how can norms be introduced? It is here that my own position becomes what Hayek would call *constructivist*, a term that he uses pejoratively. In order to distinguish my position from constructivism of the idealist type, however, I should add the word

---

[4] My position seems to be close to that taken by Ernest Gellner in a lengthy critique of W. V. Quine. For example, I fully share the views expressed in the following: "The pragmatist picture is of an on-the-whole sound and healthy evolutionary progression. The facts of the case are quite different. Neither life in general, nor mankind or its cognitive history in particular, are on some sound, reliable rails or path. Moreover, those two stories (biology and history) should not be assimilated to each other; the mechanisms of natural selection and evolution, and those of cultural transmission and accumulation, are so different from each other (and no doubt contain enormous differences internally) that no purpose is served by treating them as one plot, even if they were both and all of them sound and trustworthy—which they are not" (Ernest Gellner, "The Last Pragmatist: The Philosophy of W. V. Quine," *Times Literary Supplement*, July 25, 1975, p. 853).

contractarian. My answer to the question posed is straightforward. We may evaluate any element of the existing legal structure in terms of its possible consistency with "that which might emerge" from a genuine "social contract" among all persons who are involved in the interaction.[5] This test applies equally to those elements of legal structure that may have evolved without conscious design or intent and to those elements which may have been quite explicitly "laid on" for the achievement of a particular purpose at some time in the past. The evaluative analyst must test all "law" on such "as if" contractarian criteria. But from such tests he can do nothing except advance hypotheses of possible failure. His understanding of the principle of order allows him to hypothesize that all of the persons who use the beach would agree on some rule that would constrain their littering behavior, or would agree on a change in the law that is in existence with respect to littering behavior. The ultimate test of his hypothesis is observed agreement on the change suggested.[6]

I am not sure how Hayek would classify this basically contractarian position that I have sketched. It seems clearly to fall within the constructivist category in the sense that it does "provide a guideline for deciding whether or not existing institutions were [are] to be approved."[7] But the position is not at all rationalist in the sense that rationality norms, as such, are applied to the group. If properly qualified and interpreted, the contractarian position offers a plausibly acceptable alternative to both Hayek's implicit attribution of efficiency to whatever institutions emerge from an evolutionary process and to the rationalist conception which posits the existence of a group mind. Hayek's criticisms of the latter position, which I fully share, seem to overlook the contractarian alternative, and his strictures may be taken, perhaps misleadingly, to apply equally to the contractarian construction.[8]

[5] My position is developed in some detail in my book *The Limits of Liberty: Between Anarchy and Leviathan.*

[6] The basic methodological position outlined here is discussed more fully in my paper "Positive Economics, Welfare Economics, and Political Economy," *Journal of Law and Economics* 2 (October, 1959): 124–138.

[7] Hayek, *Rules and Order,* p. 10.

[8] I say "perhaps misleadingly" here because in the preface to *Law, Legislation, and Liberty,* vol. 2, *The Mirage of Social Justice,* Hayek states that he considers his own objectives to be closely related to those of John Rawls, as expressed in the

To imply, as Hayek seems to do, that there neither exists nor should exist a guideline for evaluating existing institutions seems to me to be a counsel of despair in the modern setting. There are, of course, many elements of the existing legal structure that would, without doubt, qualify as efficient in the technical Pareto sense; this would be true with respect to those elements that might have evolved in some evolutionary process and in the absence of any design, and those elements that might have been explicitly selected. There need be no relationship between the historical origins of a legal institution and its current efficiency properties. The latter relate exclusively to the institution's ability to command assent in comparisons with effective alternatives that might be suggested. In every case, the "as if" contractarian test must be applied, and existing institutions should be provisionally classified as "possibly efficient" only after meeting such a test. Note that efficiency in this restricted sense is not at all comparable to any concept of efficiency that may be defined with respect to the utility function of a particular individual or even of a group of individuals. That which is Pareto-efficient is that upon which all persons assent, at least to the extent that they fail to agree on any particular change.

Hayek properly stresses that many institutions that have emerged without conscious design are, nonetheless, efficient in the sense defined. But he fails to note that they must be subjected to the same test as those which are to be classified as inefficient.[9] There are surely many elements of legal structure that may be provisionally classified as inefficient in the Pareto sense. For them, explicit and deliberately designed proposals of reform can be, and should be, advanced by those whose competence offers them an understanding of the principle of spontaneous coordination. Framework proposals for change can be, and should be, constructed and then presented for possible approval or disapproval by the members of the relevant public, the

---

latter's *A Theory of Justice*. The fact that Rawls is an avowed contractarian suggests that Hayek may not apply his constructivist-rationalist criticisms to the contractarian approach, properly interpreted.

[9] In her summary paper on Hayek's work, Shirley Letwin suggests that Hayek does allow for "inefficient" outcomes under spontaneous adjustments. See Shirley Letwin, "The Achievements of Hayek," in *Essays on Hayek*, ed. Fritz Machlup, pp. 147–170.

participants in the interaction. The economist can, and should, suggest the enactment of a rule, a law, that would impose fines on persons who litter the beach, a rule that is deliberately constructed for the attaining of an end result, the cleanliness of the beach.

This example may, however, be somewhat misleading for two reasons. First of all, the example is deliberately designed to suggest that *all* persons can be made better off by a simultaneous and fully symmetrical change in behavior, and without the necessity of introducing more complex compromises, compensations, multidimensional exchanges, political logrolling, or side payments. Even for most strictly economic examples things are not likely to be nearly so simple as in the beach littering case. Consider a situation in which the participants are not symmetrically engaged in the activity that creates potentially undesirable results. Consider mining activity in the desert. A few persons secure gains from undertaking this activity; to them the expected private benefits exceed the expected private costs. Many other persons, the set of nonminers, may be damaged slightly by the defacing of the desert that mining necessarily involves. Assume that there is in existence no law against mining and that the desert is not privately owned. Is the observed result inefficient or efficient? The economist who seeks to reach a provisional or hypothetical judgment here must reckon the costs that would be imposed on those who are now miners, whose behavior would necessarily be constrained by a new law, against the benefits or gains that would be promised to nonminers by the possible change in the level or type of mining activity. If the existing situation, with no law, is considered to be inefficient, there must be some set of compensations possible which could "pay off" or "bribe" the persons who are engaged in mining to induce them voluntarily to modify their behavior.

This example is considerably more complex than the simple beach littering case, but neither example presents difficulties in defining the end results to be evaluated. A second source of misconception may arise from these strictly economic examples, however, precisely because of the apparent ease with which the end objectives are defined. For the more general elements of legal structure, the definition of an objective may itself be one of the most difficult steps in the process. Consider, as a familiar but highly useful example, the rules for ordinary games. Whether by some evolutionary and unplanned process or by deliberate invention, an existing game is defined by its rules in being. Are these rules efficient in the orthodox Pareto sense? How can we apply the "as if" contractarian test? Would the players generally agree on any change?

This problem poses conceptual difficulties because it becomes almost impossible to specify the objective that might be sought through changes to the rules. There is nothing approximately akin to "cleanliness" or "natural beauty" here. Criteria of "fairness" may be adduced, but what can "fairness" mean independently of agreement?[10] The criteria for improvement of the rules that define the general game are necessarily more internalized by the participants than are those of the beach littering example. In the latter example there is apparently an agreed-on standard of valuation (a clean beach is better than a dirty one) which the observing analyst can call upon in his development of suggested hypotheses for change. The tests of the hypotheses are identical: the agreement among participants. But the task of the analyst in advancing reform proposals is conceptually more difficult in the one case than in the other; the constitutional analyst must be considerably more sophisticated in his prognoses than the economic analyst who advances suggestions for economic policy changes.

My argument may be broadly accepted, but there remains the question: Why is a scholar with the sophistication of Hayek led to attribute efficiency to the results of the social evolutionary process, an attribution that makes such results analogous with those that emerge from the operation of markets *within* a defined legal framework? Failure to understand the principle in the latter case has led, and will lead, to many ill-conceived and damaging interferences through the intrusion of political, governmental controls. But are not these intrusions themselves a part of general social evolution? How can Hayek adduce norms that will allow him to adjudge such interferences to be "out of bounds," while elevating the overall structure to a position

---

[10] Hayek notes that no one has probably succeeded in explicitly articulating the rules that define "fair play" (Hayek, *Rules and Order*, p. 76). This comment is in apparent contrast to the economist's articulation of the conditions that define efficiency, as normally understood. Even here, however, the contrast is not so great as it might seem, since the economist's criterion, like that of the observer of other social games, must ultimately reduce to agreement among participants.

that should not be called into question by potential constructivists? Surely Hayek must acknowledge that the rules that *emerge* (those that need not be "constructed") to constrain market adjustments may themselves be inefficient. But what is his own test? While he seems to allow for reform, for "legislation" to correct for evolutionary aberrations, he offers no criteria for judgment. Hayek is, I think, led into what we must classify finally as a logically inconsistent position because of his implicit fear that politically orchestrated changes must, in most cases, produce social damage. He has been, I think, over-zealous in transferring his wholly justified criticism of those who have failed to understand the workings of the invisible hand in the operation of markets, *constrained by law*, to the unjustified and partially contradictory criticism of those who seek to evaluate the emergence and operation of law itself in constructivist, rationalist terms.

Nomos and Thesis

In my discussion to this point I have not distinguished between *nomos* and *thesis*, to introduce Hayek's terminology for the "law of liberty" and the "law of legislation," respectively. Basically, my criticism of the invisible-hand or evolutionary criteria for evaluation applies equally to both types of law, but it may be useful to outline Hayek's own distinction here. His emphasis is on *nomos*, that body of law that emerges from the separate decisions of judges in a process of spontaneous adjustment.[11] The evolution of the English common law is his historical model, and the implication is clear that the re. sults that emerge from this process are somehow assumed to be efficient and that attempts to interfere with these results are likely to be harmful. As my argument has indicated, I see no reason to expect that the evolution of law made by independent judges insures efficiency or optimality.[12] Hayek elevates this set of legal institutions as

---

[11] Bruno Leoni, in *Freedom and the Law*, has also analyzed judge-made law in a model of adjustment analogous to the working of a competitive market order.

[12] Richard Posner is more specific in his claim to the effect that the decisions made under common law rules are guided by considerations of economic efficiency. See his *Economic Analysis of Law*. For my own criticism of Posner's argument, see chapter 4 below. Posner's claim is, however, less sweeping than Hayek's in one sense. Posner argues that the evolution of the common law has insured the satisfaction of criteria of economic efficiency, defined in the narrow sense. While he

prior to and conceptually different from legislation, which he defines as designed or constructed rules that direct the activities of governments. He has relatively little to say about criteria for evaluating legislation, which does not emerge from the invisible-hand process.[13] It is nonetheless clear that he assigns "legislation," which would include constitutional law, to a relatively insignificant role in the whole legal structure. *Nomos*, the law of liberty, "lawyer's law," Hayek strongly suggests, exists independently of and prior to legislation.

Hayek's emphasis becomes almost the inverse of my own at this point. In a positive, empirical sense many of our social and legal institutions have grown independently of design and intent. But man must look on *all* institutions as potentially improvable. Man must adopt the attitude that he can control his fate. He must accept the necessity of choosing. He must look on himself as man, not another animal, and upon civilization as if it is of his own making.[14] In some final analysis, Hayek's position may be taken to reflect a basic European attitude which is sharply different from the American. The European classical liberal, who is well represented by Hayek, can and perhaps should stress the evolutionary sources of many of the institutions that stand as bulwarks of individual freedom. The American cannot, and should not, neglect the fact that his own heritage of freedom, although owing much to its European antecedents, was deliberately constructed in large part by James Madison and his compatriots. Theirs were no invisible hands. They set out to construct a constitutional framework for the "good society," which they defined implicitly as "free relations among free men." For two centuries their

implies that this evolution has also been socially desirable, he does not specifically make this the only criterion for the broader "social efficiency."

[13] I presume Hayek will deal with legislation more fully in the projected third volume of *Law, Legislation, and Liberty* which is not yet published.

[14] I make this statement in order to contrast it explicitly with the following by Hayek: "Freedom means that in some measure we entrust our fate to forces which we do not control; and this seems intolerable to those constructivists who believe that man can master his fate—as if civilization and reason itself were of his making" (Hayek, *Law, Legislation, and Liberty*, II, 30). Of course Hayek would acknowledge that some aspects of civilization are of man's making, just as I would necessarily acknowledge that some aspects emerge from the "growthlike" processes of social evolution. What is important, however, is the difference in emphasis or thrust here, a difference that has important implications for the development of attitudes toward the potentialities for social reform.

construction has stood the test.[15] But who would dare, in 1977, to suggest that constitutional improvements are not possible, that the observed erosion of our traditional liberties cannot be reversed by deliberately designed reforms motivated by something akin to the initial Madisonian vision? Americans, because they are Americans, must place their faith in their ability to impose rules of law upon themselves rather than in the rules of law that the historical process imposes upon them.

[15] Defenders of the evolutionist position may argue that Madison and his colleagues did little more than write down the widely accepted and well-understood English law and that explicit construction was minimal. Nonetheless, the consciousness that they were constructing the legal framework for the new nation seems clearly to have been present in the minds of the founding fathers.

3

Good Economics—Bad Law

ONE of the most interesting developments in American higher education over the past decade has been the emerging recognition by lawyers that an understanding of elementary economic principles is a vital component in their professional equipment. This recognition has prompted the current quest by law schools for economists close enough to the institutional world to offer practical assistance. The law school of the University of Chicago occupies a unique place in this development. Its heritage of resident economists—Henry Simons, Aaron Director, Ronald Coase (along with their economics department colleagues, notably George Stigler and Gary Becker)—has begun to pay dividends, and Chicago-style lawyer-economists—Gordon Tullock, Henry Manne, Richard Posner—have been in the forefront of the law-economics intersection. Posner's book is the most comprehensive attempt to marry these two sometimes contrary approaches to social interaction.[1]

In assessing Posner's book, I shall conduct the following mental experiment. I assume that Posner's book is widely adopted as textual material in first-year law courses. I assume, further, that the students are well motivated, diligent, and intelligent and that they permanently retain the elementary economic principles that Posner teaches.[2] What will be the effects on those lawyers who later find themselves

[1] Richard A. Posner, *Economic Analysis of Law.*

[2] Empirical studies concerning retention of economic principles after graduation suggest that this is, indeed, a heroic assumption. These studies have suggested that exposure to basic economics has little, if any, discernible effect on attitudes toward important economic issues only a few years after the learning experience. Perhaps it is plausible to say that budding young lawyers would be more professionally motivated. And, in addition, the elementary economics that they would learn from Posner

in positions of decision-making power as judges, as legislators, as administrators, or as legal scholars and educators who will themselves write other books and train still other lawyers?

The results of my mental experiment may be summarized briefly. Considered on a case-by-case basis, legal decisions would indeed be improved if those charged with authority should be made cognizant of economic principles. By accepting *pragmatic* criteria, the intrusion of economics into law gets, and deserves, high marks. Good economics, Chicago-style, which is what Posner teaches, is better than no economics or the bad economics picked up all too readily from the charlatans and the journalists on the fringes of the academy.

But the application of good economics (or bad) takes place within a legal setting. If this setting is considered invariant, pragmatic criteria are, of course, controlling. If, however, broader *philosophical* criteria are introduced, the law itself must be evaluated, and good economics applied wthin a bad or misguided conception of legal process need not promote the structural, procedural changes that may be urgently required. It is in this respect that Posner's work fails my test. The jurisprudential setting or framework within which his whole economic analysis of law is placed does not seem to have been critically examined.

I shall try to defend this "good economics—bad law" theme in the two sections that follow. As I am a professionally trained economist who shares a Chicago heritage (preempirical), ordinary prudence would perhaps suggest that I place primary critical attention on the economic analysis, per se, and that I acquiesce on the embodied conception of legal process, presumably on the grounds that the latter is best left for the lawyers to criticize. But law is far too important to be left to the lawyers, especially since lawyers come increasingly to man the corridors of Leviathan.

The Economics of Law

Posner's procedure is to apply hard-nosed, and often quite sophisticated, price theory to a long series of topics, all of which fall within

---

would be superior in content to that taught in the average university course in the subject.

the legal lexicon. Chapters are devoted to property, contracts, crimes and torts, monopoly, antitrust activity, labor, public utilities, price controls, corporations, capital markets, income distribution, taxes, poverty, federalism, and racial discrimination, along with less specifically "economic" subject matter. Posner's overriding purpose is to demonstrate that economic principles can offer guidelines for the legal resolution of conflicting claims, for the enactment of new legislation, and for the interpretation of existing statutes. Why does economics offer such valuable assistance here, aside from the trivial acknowledgment that more information is always better than less? At this point care must be taken to distinguish between positive economic analysis and the advancement of the efficiency norm that is often associated with this analysis. The latter, which involves an explicit value judgment, need not accompany the former. Posner does not fully appreciate this potential separability, and the efficiency criterion is too enthusiastically endorsed. Indeed, he is forced to justify abrogation of this criterion only by resort to an indirect reinstatement. For ordinary crimes—theft and rape, for example—he is somewhat reluctantly willing to allow unconditional legal deterrence independently of "maximum value" on the grounds that potential transactions costs between criminal and victim are low. Hence, freely negotiated exchanges or market allocation can be presumed to be an effective substitute for litigation. That is to say, if the benefits secured by the potential rapist exceed the losses suffered by the potential victim, mutual gains from exchange should exist, and such trades should take place. Posner is trapped into this argument, which to me approaches absurdity, because of his insistence on the relatively unlimited applicability of the maximum-value or efficiency criterion. He seems quite unwilling to acknowledge that law is to be enforced because it is law, sometimes quite independently of external economic considerations.

Despite the questionable normative status assigned to maximum value or efficiency, Posner's results can be interpreted to make them more generally acceptable. Maximum value need not be adopted as the end objective. It may, instead, be assessed instrumentally in terms of its relatively greater consistency with precepts of social order, with precepts of observable legality—precepts that are more in keeping with law's functional role. Posner recognizes this more general conception when he states: "If the law fails to allocate responsibilities between the parties in such a way as to maximize value, the parties will, by an additional and not costless transaction, nullify the legal allocation."[3] In somewhat broader and less emphatic terms, this statement can be interpreted as a lawyer's version of one of the most basic of all economic principles: when mutual gains are present, parties will be motivated to initiate trades with a view to capturing the potentially realizable surplus value. Attempts to shut off or to forestall trade when mutuality of gain exists encourage costly evasions. The very legality of society itself may be seriously eroded if those who make collective decisions fail to understand this elementary consequence of the economists' teaching.

An example lies close at hand, one to which Posner's analysis and approach could be readily applied. Faced with a disruption in the normal channels of fuels supply, and especially in the face of a rapidly increasing demand for energy, many American politicians (most of whom are lawyers) in late 1973 commenced to talk seriously about the prospects of imposing mandatory controls over the allocation of supplies and about the subsequent necessity of rationing heating oil and gasoline among potential demanders. The chaos that any full-scale attempt to introduce such "solutions" must create could be understood and predicted by the decision maker trained on Posner's book who retained his critical facilities. In predicting the stress put on social order by a regime of controlled prices and rationed allocations, this lawyer (be he judge, legislator, bureaucrat, or presidential adviser) need not place an overriding value on economic efficiency per se, but his elementary understanding of positive economic analysis would cause him to recognize more fully the genuine social costs of any such policy.

With such knowledge the decision maker should be motivated to search for and to support institutional alternatives which generate less social tension, less evasion of postulated standards of conduct, and more general adherence to legal norms. Law and legislation that is thoroughly informed by good economics will be based on an understanding of the market's function in maintaining social order, which is *not* primarily that of insuring efficiency or maximizing value as

[3] Posner, *Economic Analysis of Law*, p. 99.

measured in market-determined prices. (The efficiency norm may, of course, assume secondary importance in its own right.) The market economy's sociopolitical function is that of *minimizing* the necessity of resorting to internal ethical constraints on human behavior and/or external legal-governmental-political restrictions. To the extent that men are allowed freely to trade, conceived in the broadest possible sense of the term, there is little need for the preacher or the administrative authority. In the example noted, if market pricing is allowed and encouraged to ration limited fuel supplies among potential users, the success of exhortations to voluntary behavior aimed at meeting "social needs" need not be of critical importance. Nor, when such exhortations fail, need they be replaced by overt legal restrictions on behavior, restrictions that will invite evasion and that will serve to penalize those who are law-abiding and those who are unclever law violators while benefiting those who are successful in accomplishing mutually gainful "trades" despite the artificial institutional barriers.

The distributional consequences of pure market pricing in the face of unanticipated reductions in normal supplies of a vital commodity may be deemed undesirable; the efficiency guaranteed by market pricing need not be the only criterion for policy. Good economics will, however, offer guidelines even to the lawyer-legislator who places distributional equity very high on his personal value scale. He may opt in favor of legislation that would introduce what is essentially a double currency in the allocation of limited supplies; individuals might be assigned specific ration points (although the criteria for determining the allocation must be largely arbitrary). As long as these ration points may themselves be freely traded, and market prices for them established, major social disruption may be avoided. Efficiency in allocation will be insured simultaneously with the attainment of any distributive result that may be desired by the decision takers.

I have discussed the fuels allocation problem both for its policy relevance and for an illustration of how good economics might greatly facilitate the making of public decisions, independently of the choice of ultimate social objectives. Posner's book would provide the lawyer-cum-politician with the basic economic analysis required here, although his attempt to be inclusive in his array of applications tends to distract attention away from the central principle that is embodied almost universally. This is not to suggest that Posner's book will fully substitute for more rigorous and careful economics texts and that the lawyer who is trained on this book need not seek out the advice and counsel of the professionally trained economist. Posner does make errors, most of which are relatively minor and not worth noting here. In addition, his discussion of specific topics (for example, taxation) is sometimes unsophisticated. There is one ambiguity that warrants correction. Posner appears to confuse the productivity of resources in securing and maintaining monopoly positions, resources devoted to monopolizing, with the productivity of resources in producing outputs in industries that are monopolized. The social productivity of the first of these investments is clearly negative; the social productivity of the second is higher than that of comparable resources in competitive industries.

A more important limitation is that imposed by the strict Chicago economics that Posner espouses. At the outset of his book (page x) he dismisses modern welfare economics, which he calls "Pareto optimality and the like," as vocabulary and jargon, something to be carefully distinguished from "positive economic analysis." But it is precisely the problems posed in modern welfare economics that force the economist to come to grips with the basic issues in political and legal philosophy. As the discussion in the following section will suggest, a failure to appreciate these issues is the major criticism to be levied against Posner's book as a whole, and that failure might well have been avoided by a willingness to move beyond the provincialism of post-Knightian Chicago economics into the sometimes murky waters of "Pareto optimality and the like."

Legal Norms

There is a normative theory of law in Posner's book over and beyond the series of economic applications. Posner's interpretation of legal history suggests that the common law, as it has developed, has been at least indirectly guided by the efficiency criterion of orthodox economists, a criterion which assumes special significance in Posner's scale of values, as I have previously noted. By implication, therefore, judge-made common law is superior to legislation, the decisions that emerge from the activities of politicians. This theory bears an apparent resemblance to that advanced by the late Bruno Leoni,[4] whom Posner does not cite. Leoni argued persuasively for the superiority of "law" over "legislation," developing in the process the interesting analogy between the structure of law, the legal order, that emerges from the separate decision making of independent judges (governed by precedent but without the uniformity imposed by any "supreme" court) and the spontaneous economic order that emerges from the separate decision making of independent demanders and suppliers, each of whom acts on the basis of the limited information set that he confronts. The result, in both cases, is an order willed by no single decision maker.

Leoni's distinction between law and legislation is not, however, that which is suggested in Posner's work. Leoni's categorization grew out of a profound, philosophically based conservatism grounded on a sharp functional differentiation. The object of the never-ending search by loosely coordinated judges acting independently is to find "the law," to locate and to redefine the structure of individual rights, not *ab initio*, but in existing social-institutional arrangements. The working of law, as an activity, is not guided by, nor should it be guided by, explicit criteria for "social improvement." Law, in this vision, is a stabilizing institution which provides the necessary framework within which individuals can plan their own affairs predictably and with minimal external interferences. To Leoni, legislation is functionally different in that its very purpose must be one of securing or implementing explicit social or collective objectives. This is the process through which politically organized groups of persons supply "public goods" to themselves.

One need not share Leoni's basic distrust of politicians and ordinary political processes to appreciate the relevance of the categorical distinction that he made. Nonetheless, an absence of this appreciation mars Posner's work, with the consequence that the implied theory of law becomes quite different from that of Leoni, which I have summarized briefly. In his array of economic applications Posner appears to offer potential advice and counsel to future judges and legislators alike. But lawyers finding themselves in the role of jurists should act differently from lawyers-cum-legislators. The divergent choice set-

---

[4] Bruno Leoni, *Freedom and the Law.*

tings suggest that criteria for "good" decisions would be identical only by accident.

For the legislator, the solid economics which Posner teaches can be of great assistance. Regardless of social objectives, the public goods that he conceives himself to be promoting or producing through new or amended legislation, knowledge of the economic effects of alternative proposals will be helpful in constructing potentially workable schemes for change.

For the jurist economics should have relatively little comparable value, save in the pragmatic sense noted earlier and elaborated below. Faced with the necessity of resolving a conflict among parties over the appropriate delineation of rights, should the judge invoke the efficiency criterion of the economist either directly or in an instrumental sense? If he is to invoke *any* extralegal criteria, a case might be made for the economic, as I have tried to do in the first section of this paper. But is it not "bad law" to suggest that the judge be guided in his decision making by criteria other than those offered in the existing institutional setting that he confronts? Precedent, custom, tradition, expected ways of doing things, predicted patterns of behavior—these intralegal criteria provide ample searching ground for the imaginative jurist even in hard cases; these criteria are wholly consistent with the functional role of the jurist.

An example may be helpful. Monopoly is a recognized source of inefficiency in an economy, with relatively few offsetting social virtues. It becomes appropriate for the legislator, informed by this knowledge, to consider and possibly to support, antimonopoly statutes. If he is successful in the complex set of political negotiations that characterizes representative legislative assemblies, such statutes may finally be enacted into law. And the law so enacted that emerges from a legislature composed of economically sophisticated lawyer-politicians will be "better" than that which emerges from a legislature that is peopled by unsophisticated lawyer-politicians. Suppose now, however, that no antimonopoly statute exists and that none has ever existed. A disgruntled consumer-purchaser brings suit against a producing and selling firm that is alleged to have attained a monopoly position, an allegation that is factually supportable although no overt predatory action vis-a-vis other firms, existing or potential, is in evidence. Should the judge, informed by economic principle, effectively change the basic law in order to promote efficiency? Posner would apparently have the judge outlaw monopoly in such a situation (see his pages 20–30) on the grounds that the transactions costs barrier would inhibit the effective organization of potential purchasers who could, if organized, strike a bargain with the monopoly firm. The existence of major thresholds of transactions costs may be acknowledged in such cases, but without the justification of explicit judicial intrusion into the legislative process. The situation calls for legislative action, the role designed for and fulfilled by politicians who putatively represent the interests of all parties in the community, potential consumers and producers alike.[5] It seems self-evident to me that the judge should not change the basic law because by such behavior he would be explicitly abandoning the role of jurist for that of legislator. He would be "making law," and regardless of the criteria which guide his decisions, his action is unbounded by the complex pull and haul of representation among separate interests, the very center of democratic process. In saying that the jurist should enforce existing law instead of enacting new legislation, I am, of course, aware of the absence of any firm dividing line between these activities in any empirical or descriptive sense. I also recognize that the hierarchical structure of the American court system promotes instead of retards judicial intrusion into legislative process. My emphasis is on the desirability of imposing, despite the practical difficulties that may be confronted, the conceptual abstraction which sharply separates these two activities.

Unfortunately, Posner's failure to make the vital distinction between the two functional roles that lawyers often occupy in politics is not something uniquely attributable to him. Relatively few scholars in our law schools and universities, and still fewer persons among working politicians and jurists, seem to retain the understanding of *constitutional* democracy which rests directly on the conceptual separation between the rules within which collective decisions are to be made—the constitution—and the making of decisions within those rules, presumably to produce or promote "public good."[6]

---

[5] For an elaboration of my position in the context of Coase-like examples, see my paper "The Institutional Structure of Externality," *Public Choice* 14 (Spring, 1973): 69–82.

[6] This distinction is elaborated in James M. Buchanan and Gordon Tullock,

Recognition of this weakness gives me pause in what could otherwise be an unqualified endorsement of the developing interface between law and economics. If lawyers and law schools seek to introduce more economic theory into their training in order to become more informed potential legislators and advisors to legislators, my support remains unqualified and enthusiastic. If, however, they seek to become and to train potential jurists who are instructed to have no qualms about legislating for us all, the pragmatic improvements that result might forestall instead of hasten the changes in jurisprudential attitudes that are essential for a return to operative constitutional democracy. My mental experiment leads me to think about the potential excesses of a "Posner court" in the 1980's and 1990's guided by its extralegal criterion of "maximum value." Would such a court be comparable to the Warren court in the generation of social unrest and disorder? Is "maximum value" a more acceptable extralegal criterion for judicial decision than "social justice"? The opportunity costs of introducing more sophisticated economics into legal training may be measured in the lost opportunities for attaining a better appreciation of fundamental constitutional precepts. On balance, "good political and legal philosophy" would surely hold its own against "good economics," if indeed this could be the choice of alternatives. Unfortunately, given that the mind set in modern academia probably precludes the teaching of "good legal philosophy" anywhere, the "good economics," which tenuously holds on even if in isolation from mainstream ideology, should dominate the alternatives in any practical curriculum decision.

The Calculus of Consent: Logical Foundations of Constitutional Democracy. In *The Limits of Liberty: Between Anarchy and Leviathan* I have examined more specifically the necessity of role separation between those who act for the "Protective State," the jurists, and those who act on behalf of the "Productive State," the legislators.

4

The Libertarian Legitimacy
of the State

I WAS somewhat disturbed by the widespread reception of Robert Nozick's much-acclaimed book by the intellectual-academic community in the United States.[1] I was concerned lest Nozick should succeed or appear to succeed in tying together a libertarian position with an entitlement theory of distributive justice. This tie-in, should it be accomplished, would discredit, and substantially destroy, the moral appeal of the basic libertarian position. It would leave those of us who remain steadfastly libertarian, but who refuse to base precepts of justice on some chance distribution of endowments, without an intellectual constituency and with a continuing challenge to defend our position against charges of internal inconsistency or outright contradiction. These early fears were, I think, unfounded, because the weakness in Nozick's construction becomes increasingly apparent on critical reflection. The nonentitlement libertarian need not be forced into intellectual retreat by Nozick, whose effort may be viewed, on later evaluation, as an interesting digression on the continuing discourse stimulated in large part by the acclaimed, if widely misinterpreted, work of Nozick's colleague John Rawls.[2]

Nozick's central concern is the moral legitimacy of state or governmental control over the lives of individuals. He looks about him, as indeed anyone must, and sees a maze of quite arbitrary interven-

[1] Robert Nozick, *Anarchy, State, and Utopia.* For my early reaction, see the review article "Utopia, the Minimal State, and Entitlement," *Public Choice* 23 (Fall, 1975): 121–126.

[2] See John Rawls, *A Theory of Justice.*

tions, both regulative and redistributive, which are seldom called into question at the most fundamental philosophical level. Rather than directing his considerable intellectual energies toward the margins of Leviathan's existing reach, Nozick chooses to go back to essentials. He properly defines the first question in political philosophy to be that concerning the very existence of anything that might be called a state.

The Minimal State

This approach leads him to examine, first, the arguments of those who reject the moral legitimacy of any state. His first explicit objective is, therefore, to demonstrate that a minimal state will qualify as morally legitimate, a demonstration that is specifically aimed at undermining the opposing claims of the libertarian anarchists (notably Murray Rothbard).[3] Nozick derives this minimal state by means of what he calls an "invisible-hand explanation." Through a series of ordinary marketlike exchanges a dominant protective firm or association will emerge, selling its services (protection for persons and property) to individuals who will look upon its activities as no different than the activities of butchers, bakers, and candlestick makers.

In order to understand why Nozick devotes a major share of his book to this complex conceptual derivation, which may seem bizarre, it is useful to review briefly the position of his implicit adversary, the libertarian anarchist. This anarchist is a peculiarly American breed, an anarchist who allows for private property rights and for market exchange and who extends his defense of laissez-faire even to the supply and competitive organization of the policing function. There is no state in his idealized conception of the world, and there are competing firms which offer policing services available to all.[4] Nozick accepts this paradigm, but he recognizes the inherent instability of the system. What will happen when clients of one agency or association are damaged by clients of another agency or claim to be dam-

[3] Murray Rothbard, *For a New Liberty.*

[4] For a summary discussion of the history of these ideas, see Laurence Moss, "Private Property Anarchism: An American Variant," in *Further Explorations in the Theory of Anarchy,* ed. Gordon Tullock, pp. 1–33.

aged? Conflicts may occur, and one agency will win. Persons who have previously been clients of losing agencies will desert and commence purchasing their protection from winning agencies. In this manner a single protective agency or association will eventually come to dominate the market for policing services over a territory. Independent persons who refuse to purchase protection from anyone may remain outside the scope of the dominant agency, but such independents cannot be allowed to punish clients of the agency on their own. They must be coerced into not punishing. In order to legitimize this coercion, these persons must be compensated, but only to the extent that their deprivation warrants.

The dominant protective agency, as derived from this construction, will maintain domestic tranquility. Persons and possessions will be secure against aggression. The agency will, however, have all of the characteristics of a protective or "night watchman" state, and it might as well be labeled as such. But what is the value of this derivation? How is Nozick's derivation superior to the more familiar and more straightforward contractarian one, which requires only that persons agree to establish a protective state? I shall return to this question, but it will be useful first to summarize Nozick's subsequent application of his minimal-state derivation.

He is concerned to show that the minimal state, so derived, is legitimate, while at the same time showing that no extensions beyond these limits are legitimate. Without the latter purpose, the complex analysis of the minimal state would hardly seem worth the bother. Nozick's direct target in the second of these aims would seem to be the massive governmental apparatus that we observe, although his intellectual target is the construction of John Rawls, who derives "principles of justice" on basic contractarian grounds. Although the argument is not explicitly developed, Nozick apparently feels that any resort to contractarian norms opens up the prospect of justification for almost unlimited coercive action on the part of government. Presumably he would reject the attempted use of the contractarian model to classify legitimate and illegitimate spheres of collective or governmental action. I shall return to this central issue, but only after some treatment of Nozick's own derivation of principles of justice, the derivation that is central to his critique of Rawlsian norms.

Distributive Justice

Nozick is highly critical of all end-state or patterned conceptions of distributive justice. In this his argument seems wholly convincing. We cannot infer "injustice" from any examination of end-state results. Any attribution surely depends on the process through which an observed result or sequence of results is generated. An observed pattern of absolute equality could scarcely be classified to be "just" if we know that this result has been achieved by mutual theft. Nozick, who is exceptionally good with examples, offers his Wilt Chamberlain story to demonstrate this principle. He first allows his reader-critic to postulate his own idealized end-state distribution, be it absolute equality or anything else, with basketball player Wilt Chamberlain being among the members of the group. Nozick then asks us to evaluate the results that will emerge when many persons express their desires to see Wilt Chamberlain play basketball and voluntarily purchase his services. In the process, Chamberlain secures an income of $250,000 annually, much more than anyone else in the community, and in the process the initially postulated ideal distribution is, of course, violated. But can Chamberlain's earnings be adjudged unjust when the process which has generated the result seems clearly to be unobjectionable?

The example seems convincing, but an apparently slight modification will change its implications dramatically. Suppose now that Chamberlain is not a member of the community initially, and instead assume that he lives alone on an island off the coast, unable to market his potentially valued services unless he secures an immigration visa. His alternative prospects are worth only $1,000 in real value. Chamberlain will pay up to $249,000 for the privilege of selling his superior and highly valued athletic skills to members of the community. The initial members of the community may collect and distribute these rents among themselves, equally or in any one of many other ways. Or, if swept by generosity, they may even return to Wilt Chamberlain a pro rata share of his rental value, a value generated by his opportunity to sell his services to members of the community.

A second and different example that does not involve the question of initial membership in the community may be helpful. Consider a group of twenty fishermen, each with his own boat and equipment. These people differ in talents and also in their willingness to work hard, and on any particular day they will also differ in luck. It could be predicted that the distribution of the total fish catch among the twenty men would exhibit inequalities among differing individuals. Contrast this case with a setting in which the twenty fishermen combine to charter a large boat with accompanying gear, with each man assuming some assigned station on the boat throughout the day. As in the other case, there will be differences in catch among the separate fishermen. But the argument for some explicit social or group redistribution in the second case seems overwhelmingly stronger than in the first case. In the second case the individual fisherman, *on his own*, may be able to secure only a very small fraction of the income that he might be able to secure as a member of the larger group effort. The social product of the jointly used capital, the large boat, may loom large relative to the social product of the individual fishermen, taken separately and independently.

The difference between the first and second cases in either of our two examples here isolates a profound gap between Nozick's position and that of someone who acknowledges the productivity of the whole set of laws and institutions that describes an observed social order. Nozick explicitly accepts as his starting point a Lockean state of nature, a situation in which there are well-defined and generally accepted natural limits to person and possessions. By inference, although he does not directly discuss this point, Nozick suggests that the economic value of a person's total endowment is modified by the shift from anarchy to the minimal state only by the reduction in predation. There are no gains from social interdependence as such.

The conceptual validity of this whole framework depends critically on the acceptability of the initial situation. If we can jump over, or assume away the basic set of issues that arise in attempting to define and to describe an initial distribution of individuals' "rights," "boundaries," or "limits," most of the problems disappear. There should be relatively little quarrel with Nozick's Wilt Chamberlain example, as he has posed it. The end-state results, whatever they might be, that emerge from the ordinary market process should be acceptable both because the process itself seems unobjectionable and because the initial-state situation is explicitly defined to be acceptable. Nozick

imposes the process onto an initial situation that is defined to eliminate problems of regress. But this imposition tends to distract attention from the direct interrelationship that is all-important. Nozick
does not fully resolve the question: What happens when a fully
acceptable process is superimposed onto an initial distribution that
embodies none of the attributes of desirability such as justice or fairness?[5] In this case it becomes much more difficult to sort out the two
elements of the interaction.

This question has been a source of continuing confusion in the
socialist critique of market organization. Much of that critique has
concentrated on the undesirable qualities of the distributive results
that emerge from market process, with the implications that those
results thereby imply a condemnation of the workings of market exchanges. But the argument is confused because it fails to make the
necessary distinction between the initial or premarket distribution of
endowments or capacities among persons and the postmarket results,
a distinction that reflects the workings of the voluntary exchange
process. The socialist critique should be directed not at the market
process at all, but at the initial distribution of premarket endowments
and capacities. The market process, per se, generates *mutual* gains to
all participants, surely a desirable attribute under widely divergent
ethical standards.[6]

Nozick's argument seems to me to confuse the issue here through
his exclusive insistence on process as opposed to end-state results.
Much of the apparent criticism of end states is indirectly aimed at the
preprocess situation instead of the process as such, at the preprocess
distribution of endowments or capacities instead of the market organization. Nozick, of course, fully recognizes the dependence of his
whole structure on some satisfactory resolution of the "starting point"
problem. And it is here that he explicitly invokes his "entitlement"
criterion for justice. By this criterion, a person's holdings are just provided only that they have been acquired justly, that is, by an acceptable
process. Hence, in the example, Wilt Chamberlain's holdings of

---

[5] Nozick recognizes this question in his discussion of possible rectification of
entitlements that were acquired unjustly, but his treatment of it remains ambiguous.

[6] I have discussed this basic distinction in some detail in my paper "Political
Equality and Private Property: The Distributional Paradox," in *Markets and Morals*,
ed. G. Dworkin, G. Berwent, and P. Brown.

$250,000 are just because, as postulated, he has acquired them through a process of voluntary sale of services which others value highly.

But something seems amiss here. Recall that Chamberlain was assumed to start from an initial situation in which the distribution was adjudged to be just, a preexchange distribution of endowments deemed acceptable. *All* persons secure gains from the exchange process in which Wilt Chamberlain supplies his services to willing purchasers. *All* members of the community are made "better off," by their own expressions of preference, than they would have been had the exchange not taken place. But there may well exist many alternative trading arrangements under which Chamberlain's services might be made available to the members of the community and in which *all* persons, including Chamberlain, would benefit, that would involve differing distributions of the rental value of his scarce talents. In our earlier variation on Nozick's example Chamberlain secured only slightly more than $1,000, while the community's remaining members shared the $249,000 in any one of a large number of ways.

Let us change our earlier variation on Nozick's example to allow Chamberlain to be a member of the community from the outset. Now suppose that through a wholly voluntary set of agreements all prospective purchasers of Chamberlain's services appoint a single agent to deal with Chamberlain. As a result, he agrees to provide services for, say $10,000, with the rental value of $240,000 being available for general distribution to all consumers.[7] What would be Nozick's reaction to this end result? There has been no coercion; hence, he would have to imply that the holdings that are observed are just. But this set of entitlements would be quite different from those which suggest that Chamberlain get $250,000. Must we conclude from this modified example that the entitlement theory or criterion of justice allows almost any one of many possible end states to be classified as just? This much Nozick will accept, but will he accept the further implication that the processes of acquisition which pass muster are themselves almost open-ended? Surely if end states as widely variant as the two we have postulated can be reached by fully acceptable proc-

---

[7] A real-world example is offered in the United States by the National Collegiate Athletic Association, which effectively prevents university and college athletes from securing more than a small fraction of their full rental values.

esses, the content of the entitlement theory of justice seems minimal.

How would Nozick respond to this charge? He could hardly call upon the forces of his minimal state to coerce prospective purchasers so that the appointment of a single bargaining agent would not be allowed. Freedom of association is surely to be allowed in Nozick's utopia. Yet if this much is admitted, the end-state results may describe almost any conceivable pattern of distribution, depending on the institutions of voluntary exchange that emerge from personal interactions. No one set of institutions would seem to warrant priority over any other on Nozick's criterion.

Would there be any set of conditions under which an entitlement theory, properly applied, would indicate that Chamberlain must retain the full amount of his rental value, the $250,000 in Nozick's original example? This question gets me back to my alternative example of the twenty fishermen, each of whom operates his own boat and equipment. If social interdependence is not, in itself, of economic value, there is no way in which the owner of a valued resource or talent can be made to surrender some portion of rental value unless he is coerced. If, in fact, Chamberlain's opportunities to earn real income on his own and outside the market nexus provided to him by the community approach or equal those opportunities which operation inside that nexus offers him, there is no rental value which is unique to the community as such. Chamberlain would, in this case, be able to secure the full value of his services merely by threatening to withdraw them and operating on his own, as his own economy.[8]

This reasoning suggests the general principle that a person's minimally guaranteed holdings under the effective operation of a minimally-protective state will be definitionally equivalent to those holdings that he can enforce in an n-person noncooperative game. Should Chamberlain's services be withdrawn from the market nexus, the value of total product in the economy falls by $250,000, and production on his own can replace only $1,000 of this amount. But is the

---

[8] This is, of course, the idea behind the solution concept of the core in n-person game theory. In our example if Chamberlain can earn as much on his own, completely outside the economic nexus, as he can within the community, the distribution according him the full rental value, and only this distribution, qualifies as a core solution. On the other hand, if he has no opportunities outside the economic nexus, *any* distribution of the rental value satisfies core requirements.

$249,000 rental value properly attributable to Chamberlain, personally, or to the cooperative setting within which his valued services are made available to others in the community? The so-called entitlement criterion for justice in holdings tells us nothing here, and Nozick acknowledges that in many cases the criterion must allow for widely divergent end-state results, any one of which may be equally deserving to be called just.

Social Rent

If we carry this line of argument just one step further, however, we must recognize that a person's ability to subsist literally on his own outside the modern economic nexus may be absent. In such case *any* return, *any* income share above zero, requires the cooperation of others as provided by the possibility of participation in an interdependent economy. In this context, therefore, any income share, and, by implication, every income share, whether it be from the sale of labor services, from the sale or lease of capital assets, or from anything else, is "social rent," which may be divided or distributed any number of ways, any one of which may be justified on entitlement grounds. Care must be taken at this point to distinguish the notion of social rent defined here from the more familiar categories of rent normally discussed in economic theory. All income becomes "social rent" if individuals have no option except to remain within the interdependent economy. This rule does not, however, imply that all income or even a large portion of it is purely "Ricardian rent." Differing patterns of distributing income among persons may modify the allocation of resources among uses within the economy, and considerations of efficiency would normally be expected to emerge to place bounds or limits on the set of potentially admissible distributions. But the explicit introduction of efficiency norms would require something other than a minimally protective state. Within the structural confines of Nozick's analysis, therefore, the designation of all, or substantially all, income as "social rent" seems necessary.[9]

[9] This is not the place to discuss the concept of "social rent" in greater detail. The concept is obviously related to the whole theory of competitive and monopoly governmental structures and to the notion of "voting with the feet" by migration among governments.

This problem of indeterminacy does not concern Nozick, because his underlying presumption seems to be that something akin to a competitive market order will emerge naturally or spontaneously under the operation of the minimally protective state almost independently of either the starting point or the underlying technological characteristics of the society. Hence, the end-state distribution to which the entitlement criterion is applied becomes something that approximates a marginal productivity imputation, as it is traditionally defined in economic theory. Somewhat indirectly, therefore, Nozick's entitlement conception becomes a vehicle for reviving the argument that attributes ethically desirable properties to the distributive outcomes of a competitive market order.

Laws and Institutions

There are two basic problems with this underlying presumption, the first of which arises out of Nozick's minimal-state limits while the second of which is more traditional. In the first place, Nozick's construction does not allow for laws and institutions that are deliberately designed to promote competitive and deter noncompetitive contractual agreements among parties. Freely associating individuals, within the confines of the minimally protective state, may exchange restrictive as well as productive agreements. Despite the dreams of some of the more enthusiastic laissez-faire theorists, and despite the acknowledged role of the state historically in restricting competition, there seems to be no grounds for the faith that the "natural" forces at work in an economy will insure a workably competitive order, independently of specific institutional arrangements designed to promote this end. There will, of course, be pressures to undermine any restrictive agreements that emerge. But in a world of rapidly changing technology, the distributional gains from the attainment and operation of monopolistic and cartellike agreements may attract significant resources into the invention and implementation of such agreements, even when it is fully recognized that state protection is wholly absent.[10]

---

[10] On the points made in this paragraph, see Frank H. Knight, *Risk, Uncertainty, and Profit*, p. 193.

A second and more familiar difficulty lies in Nozick's implicit bridge between a workably competitive economic order, with its implied marginal productivity distribution of income shares, and the ethical legitimacy of this distribution, even if it is accomplished indirectly through the process-oriented entitlement criterion. Even if the first problem noted above is wholly neglected, and even if we assume that a workably competitive economy will tend to emerge and be maintained under the legal framework of Nozick's minimally protective state, the range of end-state distributive results that might fall within this domain is wide, indeed. The fortunes of the Rockefeller family would be as "just" as the chance rewards of the peculiar talents of professional athletes and entertainment celebrities. On careful examination, Nozick's argument seems to prop up a highly questionable criterion of distributive justice. If "entitlement" is defined to allow almost any conceivable end-state result to emerge and to be legitimatized, Nozick probably would have been on stronger grounds to make his argument explicitly in terms of the justice of the status quo.[11]

The alternative route that might have been taken is to acknowledge that the minimal state alone will not insure the workability of a competitive economic order and that even should it do so, there might be limits beyond which the distributive results would prove unacceptable. This route would, however, introduce explicit discussion of the design of the laws and institutions along with their possible contractual derivation from the constitutional stage of agreement among persons. This route is, of course, the way that both John Rawls and I have proceeded. Rawls attempts to derive "principles of justice" from the contractual process that takes place when persons choose among and agree upon alternative institutions from behind the "veil of igno-

---

[11] Although I have not evoked criteria of "justice," I have argued that because the status quo distribution of rights offers the only conceivable starting point for improvement or reform, attempts should be made to work out mutually agreeable contracts which insure to *all* participants a position at least equal to that enjoyed at the starting point. See my *The Limits of Liberty: Between Anarchy and Leviathan.* Hayek makes the different, but related, point that attempts to achieve what he calls the "mirage of social justice" may be condemned as likely to do more harm than good, without, however, attributing "justice" to that distribution of rights which is observed to exist at any point in time. See F. A. Hayek, *Law, Legislation, and Liberty,* vol. 2, *The Mirage of Social Justice.*

rance."[12] In his conception, any institution that emerges from such a contractual process is "just." In this construction, process serves much the same function as it does in Nozick's more limited analysis, and it is difficult to understand why Nozick places such importance on the process through which holdings are acquired by persons and rejects categorically the possibility that through wholly voluntary process these same persons may agree to operate within defined rules and institutions, which may well include some that restrict the range of possible distributive outcomes. Admittedly, Rawls himself creates considerable confusion and ambiguity in his own discussion by moving beyond process through which rules are chosen and attempting to specify the content of the rules themselves. It is not my purpose here, however, to elaborate on the Rawlsian construction.

My point is mainly that of emphasizing the use of process, as opposed to end-state results, in both Nozick's and Rawls's constructions. For Rawls, as for contractarians generally, that which emerges from contractual agreement is just, and such rules and institutions might, in fact, range from something akin to the Rawlsian difference principle on the one hand to some Nozickian defense of emerging entitlements on the other. Nozick, by comparison, makes no attempt to discuss the process of choosing institutions. Instead he suggests that *any* end-state result that emerges from a just process is itself just, but this conception is restricted to a postconstitutional or postrule level of consideration. Nozick simply does not allow for a process through which laws, rules, and institutions are explicitly chosen by members of the group. And by implication he does not allow for a method through which existing laws, rules, and institutions may be evaluated with a view toward possible reform or improvement. In this sense, therefore, Nozick leaves aside or ignores most of the problems that concern Rawls and that have concerned other social philosophers through the ages.

Nozick's whole attempt must, I think, be judged a failure.[13] Nonetheless, I can appreciate both the problem that he tried to resolve and the immensity of the task. It may be helpful for me to put

12 Rawls, *Theory of Justice.*

13 For a comparable conclusion by one of his peers within philosophy, see the outstanding review article by Josiah Lee Auspitz, "Libertarianism without Law," *Commentary* 60 (September, 1975): 76–84.

the problem in my own personal terms. I find myself being required, by force of law, to give up a large share of my annual income, almost all of which is labor income or salary, to the support of the state, which I feel powerless to control. My vote will not affect the governmental decisions that are relevant for my position. At first glance I seem to be in the last stage of Nozick's "Tale of the Slave."[14] Much of the government's activity is clearly illegitimate by my own standards of evaluation. But I cannot, with Nozick, go all the way and classify all government beyond protection of life and property as illegitimate for the reasons indicated. In attempting to do this, I run squarely into the Hobbesian problem. What is mine and thine? I recognize that I cannot subsist without the cooperation of my fellows; I do not possess an effective option of withdrawing completely from the economic nexus. Hence, independently of the continuing social contract, as represented in the whole legal-constitutional-political-economic structure, I cannot enforce a claim to that particular share of income or property which I currently command.

But that which I can enforce is vitally important, and recognition of this fact allows me to resolve Nozick's "Tale of the Slave" to my own satisfaction. I can enforce those elements of income or utility that I can secure by my total or partial withdrawal from the economic nexus. Even if potential emigration is neglected, I can reduce my income tax liability by not earning income, to the extent that I choose. In so doing I am effectively opting out of the system. And as long as I retain this option, I cannot classify myself as a slave subject to the will of the bureaucratic-demagogic master that modern democratic process seems to represent. The critical step toward becoming a slave would be that which denies me this option, which either imposes a tax on my potential earning power or requires that I do forced labor for the collectivity. Nozick's "Tale of the Slave" is cleverly presented, but it tends to be misleading because Nozick does not make the categorical distinction that I have noted here. In his last stages of the tale he does not indicate whether or not the collectivity retains the power to require labor on the part of the individual, a power that is categorically distinct from the power to impose taxes on earnings from

[14] Nozick, *Anarchy, State, and Utopia*, pp. 290–292.

labor.[15] In his more general discussion Nozick does not appear to think that such a distinction is significant.[16]

The failure to make this distinction, if it should come to characterize the attitudes of many people, can have tragic consequences. If modern Americans and Western Europeans come to view the exactions of the modern welfare state as not different in kind from those depicted in Solzhenitsyn's *Gulag Archipelago*, the subsequent alienation can itself become a force for reducing the distinction in fact. We cannot, and we should not, try to escape from our own responsibility for controlling the Leviathans that we have allowed to grow, only in part as a result of our own creation. Nozick's noble but misguided effort to brand all extensions of state power beyond minimal state limits as illegitimate may backfire if the effects should be those of reducing our willingness to take on such a responsibility. *Some* extensions of state power are more illegitimate than others. The contractarian-libertarian can at least try to establish plausibly acceptable criteria for discrimination.

[15] Conscription is, therefore, categorically different from a personal income tax, although the difference tends to be overlooked by economists who analyze conscription as form of tax. The fact that in the United States conscription has been imposed suggests that in some potential sense American citizens may not be beyond the confines of Nozick's stages of slavery. On the other hand, the fact that the draft did, during the Vietnam war, arouse opposition that was demonstrably different from that aroused by punitive income taxation suggests that American citizens do make the distinction.

[16] Indirectly, Nozick's descriptions of Utopia as a world of competing clubs embodies limits on "social rents" and, hence, on the degree of governmental power over the individual. I have not examined the relationship between this description of Utopia and the more general norms of justice advanced by Nozick, nor does he develop this relationship in detail. Such an effort would, nonetheless, seem to represent a useful extension.

5

Politics and Science

KNOWING of my admiration for both men, a colleague called to my attention Frank Knight's 1949 critique of Michael Polanyi's *Science, Faith, and Society*.[1] The republication of Polanyi's monograph in 1964 contained a new introduction by the author, but no reference was made to Knight's fundamental criticism. Because the issue raised by Knight seems too important to be ignored, there is perhaps some justification in my attempt to restate the difference between these two scholars in my own terms. This justification is strengthened by the continuing relevance of the issue at stake, especially with reference to the general methodological setting for modern political science.

As Knight notes at the outset of his review, Polanyi's implied equation of science and social order represents an interesting inversion of the more familiar, and hopefully discredited, view that sociopolitical problems are similar to scientific problems in that scientific method is required for their solution. For Polanyi, orthodox scientific method, as many persons think and talk about it, does not characterize scientific process. Scientific problems as well as social problems, or indeed all problems, involve *personal evaluation*. Knight offers his normally persuasive "yes, but . . ." type of criticism to this elevation of intuitive perception (as opposed to observation) as a predominant role in scientific discovery. Within limits he broadly accepts Polanyi's theory of scientific progress.

The differences between these two social philosophers are indeed profound, but any treatment of such differences would be misleading if it were not prefaced by an emphasis of their agreement on many

[1] Frank Knight, "Virtue and Knowledge: The View of Professor Polanyi," *Ethics* 59 (July, 1949): 271–284.

issues. Knight accepts, again within limits, Polanyi's eloquent defense of freedom in the scientific community. More importantly for my purposes here, both Knight and Polanyi assign a major role to the spontaneous coordination process represented by market exchange broadly conceived in the social constitution for their "good societies." Both generally and in particulars they share an avowed opposition to the authoritarian state, and both openly support individual freedoms defined in terms of classical liberalism.

What is at issue between Knight and Polanyi is the legitimacy of the same defense of freedom in science and in the political order. Is social organization like scientific organization? Can norms or principles for organization that seem demonstrably appropriate for the community of science be extended by analogy and analysis to the social or political order? Both directly and by implication if not by major emphasis Polanyi's answer to these questions is affirmative. Knight's response is an emphatic no. In essence, Polanyi seems to say: "Have respect for truth, and you shall be free." Knight seems to respond by saying: "But sociopolitical questions cannot be answered by 'true' or 'false.' Things are not nearly so simple as that." Michael Polanyi, the optimist, confronts Frank Knight, the pessimist. They look at political process through quite different windows.

The waning prospects for advancing toward the social order that both Knight and Polanyi seek (or even preserving the achievements made) may depend critically on some reconciliation of their opposing views—or if not reconciliation, at least mutual understanding. Modern liberalism advances, and confusedly oversteps itself, often on the basis of arguments that are at least akin to Polanyi's. Classical liberalism retreats and reduces itself to negativism in the process, often on the basis of arguments that may be interpreted as inarticulate expressions of the Knightian conception of social order.[2]

The Jigsaw Puzzle

To Polanyi, a distinguished physical scientist in his own right, science is analogous to the continual filling in and expansion of a

---

[2] It must be emphasized here that neither Polanyi nor Knight is responsible for the extensions suggested, directly or indirectly. In fact, the very reasonableness of

gigantic, never-ending jigsaw puzzle.[3] No single scientist need know what the final picture may look like, and the prevailing interpretation of the big picture may change progressively through time. Scientific effort consists in searching out pieces or shapes that fit from among an infinite variety of possibilities, and a scientific discovery consists in the initial intuitive perception of a relevant shape or pattern. On this vision of scientific process Polanyi bases his argument for the freedom of individual scientists to seek out and look for shapes and patterns as their own professional consciences dictate. The jigsaw analogy is indeed convincing, and its organizational implications are clear. The most efficient means of organizing many people in the solving of a single puzzle is to allow each one to conduct his own private search among the whole jumble of pieces. Planning from above in such puzzle solving is obviously nonsensical. And although the analogy must be used with some caution, much the same can be said for the organization of science and scientific endeavor. The planned or centrally directed organization of science aimed at accomplishing specific social goals can only stifle the general progress of science itself.

Truth in Science

There is no important difference between Knight and Polanyi on the latter's argument in defense of scientific freedom or even on the broad conception of what scientific progress represents. Slight difference arises, however, in their implied conceptions of "truth" in science, and this difference, in turn, becomes important, indirectly, in the extension of the reasoning to political order. To Polanyi truth is derived from an existential reality remaining to be discovered even if it is outside the scientist's current perception, and progress in science takes place through ever-improving glimpses of this reality. In its fullness or completeness, this reality may never be grasped, and scien-

---

each of their own positions is helpful in providing a base for reconciliation of the more rigid extremes.

[3] For an explicit discussion of this analogy, see Michael Polanyi, "The Republic of Science" (lecture delivered at Roosevelt University, Chicago, January 11, 1962), pp. 6–8.

tific development may modify existing conceptions, even to the extent of discarding old prints and replacing them with new ones. In the process, however, there is an avowed faith in the existence of the reality which any picture or model more or less successfully represents.[4]

In an instrumental sense Knight's view of scientific truth is similar, but conceptually there seems to be an important difference. Although he remains far from accepting a purely relativistic position, Knight refrains from either asking or answering the question concerning the existence of some ultimate and unchanging reality. "Truth" is measured only by agreement or consensus among informed persons, despite the acknowledged questions that this definition begs. Whether or not there is reality behind the models becomes essentially an irrelevant question. In this Knightian context the pictures, the models of science, are "true," at any given epoch, within the relatively absolute limits defined by general agreement among the informed. These models, these pictures, change through time, sometimes dramatically and ofttimes slowly. "Truth," as such, changes in the process, and there is no finality in revelation, even in some utopian future state. On balance, this Knightian position, if I have interpreted it correctly, depends critically on the emergence of "relatively absolute absolutes" in scientific truth as in everything else. Despite the convergence of the two positions in a practical sense, the tolerance limits are somewhat broader in Knight's conception of truth than in Polanyi's. To Polanyi, progress toward the unveiling of a yet undiscovered reality is shown to be more efficient if individual scientists are allowed freedom of search, of exploration. One of his provocative lectures is entitled "A Society of Explorers," a title that in itself is revealing. The defense of scientific freedom becomes *instrumental*; ultimately, the aim is efficiency in science, in discovery of truth itself. By contrast, Knight's position must produce, finally, a defense of scientific freedom that is grounded on the ever-present relativism of even the most widely acknowledged "truths." Prag-

---

[4] "The first step is to remember that scientific discoveries are made in search of reality—of a reality that is there, whether we know it or not. The search is of our own making, but reality is not" (Michael Polanyi, "The Creative Imagination," mimeographed [Oxford, April, 1965]).

matically, as suggested above, both scholars agree on the organization of science. Both agree that science "works better" if it is organized on the basis of free individual decisions.

Truth in Politics

My attempted summary sketch of Knight's and Polanyi's differences in the conception of scientific truth is perhaps sufficient to introduce their more profound differences in the conception of political truth. These latter differences are, of course, the main subject of Knight's paper. Only by some general understanding of the role that truth plays in their conception of scientific process can the widely differing assessments of these two respected philosophers for the prospects for political freedom be appreciated.

What is political decision? Presumably, like all decisions, it results from a choice among alternatives, a choice that must be binding on all members of the body politic. How can this kind of decision be compared with a scientific decision (explanation)? Presumably, in science a decision results from a choice among alternative explanations of phenomena, and this decision is not considered to be final until all, or substantially all, qualified members of the scientific community accept it. Once this stage is reached, the chosen explanation becomes binding in the paradigmatic sense. The similarities as well as the differences between the two cases become clear in this summary. One difference arises immediately. In politics decisions are made, and implemented, *before* general agreement is attained. Results are binding by force of the decision, not by prior agreement by force of reasoned argument. Nonetheless, the similarities are also striking, provided that the underlying alternatives for choice are themselves comparable in the two cases. If, in point of fact, a political decision can be represented as a choice among alternative explanations of "reality," there will be, *ex post*, one "best" choice, which, within limits, can be appropriately labeled to be the "true." Given this classical conception of politics, which continues to dominate a large part of modern political science, the Polanyi extension is helpful and revealing. Political choices are essentially "truth judgments," and the rules for choosing among alternatives are, or should be, based on norms for efficiency in arriving at "truth" in some quasi-scientific sense of this term. Free and open discussion, toleration of dissenting opinion—these become but features of a total process of producing political truth efficiently.

The truth-judgment model of politics need not be accepted. There may be no best alternative upon which all members of the group should agree, even given full knowledge. The question of politics may remain one of choice, and individuals may differ in their evaluations of the alternatives. These differences may be inherently personal and subjective, and they may be irreducible to agreed-on objective standards. Political choice, in this alternative vision, becomes a necessary means of reconciling different individual and group evaluations, not a means of producing truth at all. Hopefully, or better, ideally, general agreement can be attained after sufficient discussion, exchange, compromise. But even should full unanimity be observed in support of some multidimensioned outcome, a "true" judgment cannot be said to have been produced. The terms are simply not applicable in the realm of discourse that we use to discuss politics.

If politics is not aimed at the discovery of truth in any sense comparable to that of science, agreement among individuals cannot be expected to emerge as a result of free and open discussion. Enlightenment does not necessarily produce unanimity, and it is essentially a false hope that so elevates sweet reason. Politics becomes the process through which divergent interests are compromised. Politics is the collective counterpart to individual choice and nothing more. As an individual I may choose to paint my house either white or red. There are certain physical constraints within which my choice must lie, but given these, I can choose among alternatives in accordance with my own tastes or values. It becomes highly questionable, if not improper, to say that my selection of white as the color for my house is true while the alternative red is false. This use of terms would be equally questionable even if all of my neighbors, as well as the architectural color consultants, agree that white is aesthetically the more satisfying color. The analogy used here threatens to open up the age-old issue of truth in art, which I do not choose to and shall not consider.

Politics, in this interpretation which I attribute to Knight and which I share with him, becomes the collective counterpart to my choice of paint color. There are some things that men must do collectively instead of individually for simple reasons of efficiency.

Group choices must be made. Once we confront group choice, however, we encounter the prospect of individual disagreements on the
ordering of alternatives. Is the collective house to be painted red or
white? It is likely that some members of the group will prefer one
color and some the other. Politics is the process through which the
initial preferences are expressed, discussed, compromised, and, finally,
resolved in some fashion. Resolution may, however, amount to an
overruling of some preferences in favor of others. Political order or
stability requires, of course, that those whose preferences are over-
ruled acquiesce in the collective outcome. It does not require that their
tastes be modified to prefer the chosen outcome or that, once they
fully understand the alternatives, they will necessarily prefer what is
chosen for them. Indeed, it is precisely the presence of dissent in the
face of decision that separates genuinely democratic politics from
politics of the brainwashing variety.

Individuals differ one from the other even if they are equally informed. Economists summarize this quality by saying that utility
functions differ. Individuals rank "goods" (or "bads") differently.
But "goods" (or "bads") can be either private or public. In my own
utility function, a biennial trip to Europe stands much higher than the
biennial purchase of a new automobile. In the utility function of my
colleague, this order is reversed. We are different. In my own utility
function, federal government outlay on the space program stands
higher than federal outlay on the poverty program. In the utility
function of my colleague, this order is reversed. There seems to be
little, if any, difference in these two cases except that which dictates
that we both accept some politically determined result in the latter
mix of public goods. Acceptance does not, however, imply agreement, and no particular mix emerges as the "true" one.[5]

In the politics discussed here, Knight's basic criticism of Polanyi's

[5] The discussion here is confined to political issues upon which disagreement
can be interpreted in the two alternative ways suggested. Much the same analysis
can be extended to issues in normative ethics, and indeed, the discussion of disagreement by Charles L. Stevenson in *Ethics and Language* closely parallels that
presented here. Stevenson's distinction is between disagreement in *belief* and disagreement in *attitudes*. Essentially, he seeks to clarify the ambiguities arising when
this distinction is not made explicit, and on balance he takes what would be, in the
argument of this paper, a position close to that advanced by Knight, as I have
interpreted the latter.

position seems surely to be correct. Contrast the sketch of political choice advanced here with scientific choice. In the latter, alternative explanations are possible for a single set of phenomena, and at the initial stages of inquiry scientists may express wide disagreement. The process of scientific discovery is, in itself, a narrowing of the areas of this disagreement. Possessing a common reference system and acknowledging common standards for evaluation, scientists are engaged in a continuously developing process of rejecting "false" explanations and replacing them with "true" ones. Here, "truth" is appropriately measured by agreement, and the term is, in itself, meaningful. This is not, of course, to deny that there does not remain "taste" or "valuation" in science at all levels. Scientific disagreements are not, however, primarily disagreements on values. They are disagreements on facts, on analysis, on interpretation—disagreements that will progressively disappear as the field of knowledge widens. Pragmatically, science proceeds "as if" its practitioners are explorers discovering existential reality, and the metaphysical questions about this reality itself need not be raised at all.

Justice and the "Good Society"

A part of politics is surely the grubby, quasi-corrupt, day-to-day settling of intergroup, interpersonal claims. It is, and must be, pressure-group politics with the pork barrel and the wheeler-dealers as vital elements. But is that all there is to politics? Is there not some place left for the classical quest after justice, after the organizing principles of the "good society"?

Some reconciliation of the Knight and Polanyi positions becomes possible if attention is shifted to the different politics embodied in these questions. Earlier, politics, as implicitly defined, involved the production of public goods. But we can define another stage of political choice. Politics can be considered as the choice of rules by which men live together. We are deep in the cardinal sin of using the same word, *politics*, to mean two quite different things, and indeed, this double use has been one of the major sources of modern confusion. I shall, from this point, refer to this higher-stage, rule-making politics as "constitutional" politics, which will appropriately distinguish it from the mundane stage of politics in the ordinary meaning. It is one of the many tragedies of twentieth-century liberalism that the importance of distinguishing between these two stages has now been almost wholly forgotten.

Consider now constitutional politics, the problems of choice among rules. Here, the alternatives are rules or institutions within which both private-goods and public-goods choices shall be made by persons acting singly or in groups. Constitutional rules constrain both private individual choice and collective political behavior. Rules prohibiting theft prevent my taking my neighbor's property, and rules prohibiting arbitrary discrimination prevent my being taxed for public goods while my neighbor goes scot-free.

What can we say about the process through which such rules are chosen? Does it resemble science? Or is it, at an admittedly different level, similar in kind to the ordinary operational choice of public "goods" already discussed?

The appropriate location for genuine constitutional choice seems to be somewhere between the limits imposed by the choice among scientific explanations on the one hand and the choice among alternative publicly supplied goods on the other. There may be differences in individual evaluations of alternative rules—differences that may, in one sense, reflect basic value orderings. To this extent agreement will not be produced by open discussion. Something more than evaluation is involved in many cases, however. Individual differences may be based, to a large extent, on differing predictions about the working properties of the alternative rules under consideration. Within these limits meaningful discussion and analysis can take place, and the careful assessment of alternative models can closely resemble scientific process of the standard sort.

The useful analogy for constitutional choice is found in the choice of rules for a standard parlor game. Prospective players engage in a discussion of these rules before play actually starts, and after play has commenced this discussion continues concerning possible changes in the rules adopted. In such a context, what is the purpose or objective sought by the players? It is not, and cannot be, the advancement of their own differential interests, the single player's own preferred good, because when the rules are chosen there must remain great uncertainty about how particular rules will advance particular interests. The inherent uncertainty that surrounds constitutional choice among rules makes individual behavior necessarily different from that which may be observed in situations where private interests are readily identifiable. The individual, as a prospective player, will prefer that set of rules which he predicts will make for a "better" game, a game that is "fair," "efficient," "interesting." These terms reduce to the same descriptive content in this particular choice setting.

Consider now the problem of reaching group agreement on a set of rules, a set that applies to all participants in the game. Different persons will initially possess somewhat differing versions of their ideal game. Discussion can proceed, however, and disagreement can be narrowed, because argument can be based not on personal values but on predicted working properties of alternative rules. Such discussion, to the extent that it is open and free, can squeeze out major areas of discord; disagreement may remain after full discussion, but this situation will be scarcely different from that of science, since basic value differences remain even in the consensus that science seeks, and secures, as it progresses.

The shift of attention from the level of operational decision to that of constitutional decision restores, to an extent, Polanyi's analogical tie between science and the social order. Care must be taken at this point, however, to keep the major differences that remain clearly in mind. Let us limit consideration to genuine constitutional decisions, the choices among alternative political rules. As suggested, there are important elements of similarity between the process of discussion, selection, and agreement on such rules and the process of free scientific discovery. But there are also important differences, and these are based in the fundamental objectives that are implicit in each of the two processes. Science represents a process of exploration and discovery, and success is measured by agreed-on criteria of truth. Pragmatically, we are convinced by the force of scientific argument. Scientific proof can be established; propositions can be refuted. Within limits that can be defined in advance and with reasonable precision, radiation treatments can retard cancer. Christian Science cannot do so, within equally defined limits.

Compare this scientific procedure with the choice of a set of rules for political order, a constitution. Can this latter process be considered, at any level, as one of discovery or exploration seeking the "true"? Admittedly, this conception has been held by political philosophers throughout the ages. The good society has been sought as if it were unique. But is this conception legitimate, or is it wholly misleading?

It seems clear that feedback effects of error cannot work in constitutional politics as they can in science. Assume, for current argument, that there does exist one uniquely best set of rules for organizing social interaction and that general agreement on this set as best would, in fact, be attainable in some *ex post* global settling of accounts. Rules must be chosen, however, without a vision of this final best constitution, and choice must be made among several alternatives. Suppose that an error is made and that, initially, rules are chosen that are inconsistent with those that should be embodied in the good society. How will this error make itself known to those individuals, of necessarily limited vision, who must live by the rules that they have chosen? What external observations can reveal to persons that they are involved in a game that is being played under a second-best or *n*th-best set of rules? Contrast this position with that faced by the reasonably intelligent savage engaged in a rain dance; he can, by using his senses, observe that the dance does not bring the rain. Of course, such distinctions and comparisons should not be pushed too far, but their existence must be recognized.

The "best" social order is simply that which works "best." However, only one set of rules can be tried at one time, and experiments must be long-range to be at all revealing. No alternative explanations are, therefore, likely to be directly observable, unless we allow for cross-cultural comparisons on the one hand and historical observations on the other. Again by contrast, the rainmaker's dance can be observed alongside the cloud seeding experiments of the trained meteorologist. Alternative scientific experiments are possible within the limited observation pattern of individuals, and choice can be made among them on the basis of such observation and not on the basis of a mere comparison of conceptual alternatives.

Is There One "Good Society"?

A more fundamental difference between politics and science, even at the level of selection among constitutional rules, involves the uniqueness of solution. This issue relates to the conception of scientific truth, discussed earlier, but additional complexities are also present. In one sense science is discovery, and this definition, in itself, implies the uniqueness of that which is found, the object of search. Pragmatically, the issue of truth in science can proceed as if the underlying reality is unique.

When these conceptions are extended from science to social order, to politics, however, major questions arise. If politics at the constitutional level involves a process of discovery and exploration analogous to that of science, must we assume that there is a unique explanation, a unique set of rules which defines the elements of good society and which, once discovered, will come to be generally accepted by informed and intellectually honest men? Is there such an end to the rainbow in political philosophy after all? Is there a single best set of rules for organizing men politically, a set that can be continually if never completely discovered like the big jigsaw puzzle of science, provided only that there is maintained a free and open discussion of alternatives and that allowance is made for provisional trial and error, for experiment, for science transferred to social systems?

To some omniscient being of a different and higher order of intelligence than man, to a being who can view man's interactions one with another solely in terms of his own evaluative criteria, the answer may be in the affirmative. But to man himself the existence of such singularity in solution seems highly dubious. Values would seem to differ, and perhaps widely, even among enlightened men, and different men will tend to value different rules. My ideal "good society" need not be identical with yours in general or in its particulars even if we fully agree on the working properties of the alternative rules under discussion.

Polanyi, the distinguished physical scientist, seems to opt for an affirmative answer, as is perhaps understandable. In science, man becomes as God in his vision of the natural universe. By extension, God, observing man, can see the reality of social order. And notably, Polanyi allows God a role, and it is not distorting his approach to say that he conceives discovery in the political-social realm as the revelation of God's design. In relatively sharp contrast, Knight remains highly dubious about God, and he is unwilling to go beyond man's own competence to judge on the basis of his own criteria. At this level men place values on different things. "Science" and "politics" remain poles apart, even when we have reduced politics, to the maximum extent that is possible, to the long-range continuing search for a set of constitutional rules.

Political Science

If I have interpreted them correctly, the differences between Knight and Polanyi seem to be intrinsically important, but their relevance to social thought generally is much wider than specific concentration on the ideas of these two scholars alone might suggest. At issue, finally, is the whole conception of political process. Throughout the ages political philosophers have taken the Polanyi side of the argument, and this includes even those who have been the most vociferous in their denunciations of "science," as such, in politics. The Polanyi conception belongs squarely in the idealist tradition of political philosophy, a tradition from which modern political science, as a discipline, is only now beginning to emerge. For the most part politics has been conceived as a process of arriving at truth judgments. This conception is well illustrated by a recent argument of a leading American political scientist. In a volume devoted to "rational decision," Professor Harvey C. Mansfield, Jr., suggested that rational decision tends to be prevented from emerging in politics because of the necessity for compromise of divergent interests.[6]

This truth-judgment conception of politics may be accompanied, as is the case with Polanyi, by an eloquent defense of individual freedom based on the continuing and inexhaustible processes of discovery, on the provisional nature of all truth that is found, and upon the efficiency in exploration that only such freedom can insure. Unfortunately, however, the truth-judgment conception need not carry such a defense of individual freedoms as its accompaniment. The conception lends itself more or less naturally to what amounts to an attitude of basic intolerance on the part of those who hold that certain political "truths" have already been discovered.[7] Implicitly, those

---

[6] Harvey C. Mansfield, Jr., "Rationality and Representation in Burke's 'Bristol Speech,'" in *Rational Decision*, Nomos Ser. No. 7, ed. Carl J. Friedrich, esp. pp. 197ff.

[7] Polanyi seems to recognize this point in quite a different context: "On the grounds of the discipline which bound him to the quest of reality, he [the scientist] must claim that his results are universally valid. . . . To claim universal validity for

persons claim the "right" to impose "truth" on those who refuse, with apparent ignorance, stubbornness, or blindness, to recognize error. Members of the recalcitrant minority, those who reject the "truth" that politics reveals, become first cousins of the rainmaker, and they tend to be treated with similar scorn. This attitude of intolerance seems especially to characterize the liberal of the modern American left who dominates the academic setting and to whom there must always exist a set of prevailing "truths," politically determined, from which open dissent becomes, somehow, "immoral."

The philosophical gap between this idealist conception of politics and the alternative conception, here attributed to Knight, is wide indeed. Politics, in the latter, becomes at best some attempt to compromise issues among individuals and groups with admittedly different values. There are no "truths." The implicit tolerance that this position must embody is self-evident. The defense of individual freedom is here noninstrumental. It is based, finally, on a recognition and acceptance of the value of individual values.

---

a statement indicates merely that it *ought* to be accepted by all" ("The Creative Imagination," p. 19).

PART II

THE STRUCTURE OF SOCIAL CONTRACT

6

Before Public Choice

Contractarian Explanation

A contract theory of the state is relatively easy to derive, and careful use of this theory can yield major explanatory results. To an extent, at least, a "science" exists for the purpose of providing psychologically satisfying explanations of what men can commonly observe about them. Presumably we "feel better" when we possess some explanatory framework or model that allows us to classify and interpret disparate sense perceptions. This imposition of order on the universe is a "good" in the strict economic sense of this term; men will invest money, time, and effort in acquiring it. The contract theory of the state, in all of its manifestations, can be defended on such grounds. It is important for sociopolitical order and tranquility that ordinary men explain to themselves the working of governmental process in models that conceptually take their bases in cooperative instead of noncooperative behavior. Admittedly and unabashedly, the contract theory serves, in this sense, a purpose or objective of rationalization. We need a "logic of law," a "calculus of consent," a "logic of collective action," to use the titles of three books that embody modern-day contract theory foundations.[1]

Can the contract theory of the state serve other objectives, whether these be normative or positive in character? Can institutions which find no conceivable logical derivation in contract among cooperating parties be condemned on other than strictly personal grounds? Can alleged improvements in social arrangements be evaluated on anything other than contractarian precepts, or, to lapse into economists'

[1] See Gordon Tullock, *The Logic of Law*; James M. Buchanan and Gordon Tullock, *The Calculus of Consent: Logical Foundations of Constitutional Democracy*; and Mancur Olson, *The Logic of Collective Action*.

jargon, on anything other than Paretian criteria? But even here, are these criteria any more legitimate than any others?

In earlier works I have tended to go past these fundamental questions. I have been content to work out, at varying levels of sophistication, the contractarian bases for governmental action, either that which we can commonly observe or that which might be suggested as reforms. To me this effort seemed relevant and significant. "Political economy" or "public choice"—these seemed to be labels assignable to honorable work that required little or no methodological justification. It was only when I tried to outline a summary treatment of my whole approach to sociopolitical structure that I was stopped short. I came to realize that the very basis of the contractarian position must be examined more thoroughly.

We know, factually and historically, that the "social contract" is mythological, at least in many of its particulars. Individuals did not come together in some original position and mutually agree on the rules of social intercourse. And even had they done so at some time in history, their decisions could hardly be considered to be contractually binding on all of us who have come behind. We cannot start anew. We can either accept the political universe or we can try to change it. The question reduces to one of determining the criteria for change.

When and if we fully recognize that the contract is a myth designed in part to rationalize existing institutional structures of society, can we simultaneously use the contractual derivations to develop criteria for evaluating changes or modifications in these structures? I have previously answered this question affirmatively, but without proper argument. The intellectual quality as well as the passionate conviction of those who answer the question negatively suggest that more careful consideration is required.

How can we derive a criterion for determining whether or not a change in law, or, if you will, a change in the assignment of rights, is or is not justified? To most social scientists change becomes desirable if "I like it," even though many prefer to dress this reason up in fanciful "social welfare function" or "public interest" semantics. To me, this stance seems to be pure escapism; it represents retreat into empty arguments about personal values which spells the end of rational discourse. Perhaps some of our colleagues do possess godlike qualities, or at least think that they do, but until and unless their godliness is accepted we are left with no basis for discourse. My purpose is to see how far we can rationally discuss criteria for social change on the presumption that no man's values are better than any other man's. Is agreement the only test? Is the Wicksellian-contractarian-Paretian answer the only legitimate one here? If so, are we willing to accept its corollaries? Its full implications? Are we willing to forestall all social change that does not command unanimous or quasi-unanimous consent?

Provisionally, let us say that we do so. We can move a step beyond, while at the same time rationalizing much of what we see, by resorting to "constitutionalism," the science of rules. We can say that particular proposals for social change need not command universal assent provided only that such assent holds for the legal structure within which particular proposals are enacted or chosen. This reasoning seems to advance the argument; we seem to be part of the way out of the dilemma. But note that this argument provides us with no means at all for evaluating particular proposals as "good" or "bad." We can generate many outcomes or results under nonunanimity rules. This explains my initial response to the Arrow impossibility theorem and to the subsequent discussion. My response was, and is, one of no surprise at the alleged inconsistency in a social decision process that embodies in itself no criteria for consistency. This also explains my unwillingness to be trapped, save on rare and regretted occasions, into positions of commitment on particular measures of policy on the familiar efficiency grounds. We can offer no policy advice on particular legislative proposals. As political economists we examine public choices; we can make institutional predictions. We can analyze alternative political-social-economic structures.

The Notion of Fair Rules

But what about constitutional change itself? Can we say nothing, or must we say that at this level the contractarian (Wicksellian, Paretian) norm must apply? Once again, observation hardly supports us here. Changes are made, changes that would be acknowledged to be genuinely "constitutional," without anything remotely approaching unanimous consent. Must we reject all such changes out of hand, or can we begin to adduce criteria on some other basis?

Resort to the choice of rules for ordinary parlor games may seem to offer assistance. Influenced greatly by the emphasis on such choices by Rutledge Vining, I once considered this analogy to be the key to genuinely innovative application of the contractarian criteria. If we could, somehow, think of individual participants in a setting of complete uncertainty about their own positions over subsequent rounds of play, we might think of their reaching genuine agreement on a set of rules. The idea of a "fair game" does have real meaning, and this idea can be transferred to sociopolitical institutions. But how far can we go with it? We may, in this process, begin to rationalize certain institutions that cannot readily be brought within the standard Wicksellian framework. But can we do more? Can we, as John Rawls seems to want to do in his monumental *A Theory of Justice*, think ourselves into a position of original contract and then idealize our thought processes into norms that "should" be imposed as criteria for institutional change? Note that this is, to me, quite different from saying that we derive a possible rationalization. To rationalize, to explain, is not to propose, and Rawls does not emphasize this quite critical distinction. It is one thing to say that, conceptually, men in some genuinely constitutional stage of deliberation, operating behind the veil of ignorance, might have agreed to rules something akin to those that we actually observe, but it is quite another thing to say that men in the here and now should be forced to abide by specific rules that we imagine by transporting ourselves into some mental-moral equivalent of an original contract setting where men are genuine "moral equals."

Unless we do so, however, we must always accept whatever structure of rules that exists and seek constitutional changes only through agreement, through consensus. It is this inability to say anything about rules changes, this inability to play God, this inability to raise himself above the masses, that the social philosopher cannot abide. He has an ingrained prejudice against the status quo, however it may be defined—understandably so, since his very role, as he interprets it, is one that finds itself only in social reform. (Perhaps this role conception reflects the moral inversion that Michael Polanyi and Craig

Roberts note: the shift of moral precepts away from personal behavior aimed at personal salvation and toward moral evaluation of
social institutions.)

Escape from the Hobbesian Jungle

Just what are men saying when they propose nonagreed changes
in the basic structure of rights? Are they saying anything more than
"this is what I want and since I think the state has the power to impose it, I support the state as the agency to enforce the change"? We
may be able to get some handles on this very messy subject by going
back to Hobbes. We need to examine the initial leap out of the
Hobbesian jungle. How can agreement emerge? And what are the
problems of enforcement?

We may represent the reaction equilibrium in the Hobbesian
jungle at the origin in the diagrammatics of Fig. 1. If we measure
"B's law-abiding behavior" on the ordinate and "A's law-abiding
behavior" on the abscissa, it is evident that neither man secures advantage from "lawful" behavior individually and independently of
the other man's behavior. (Think of "law-abiding" here as "not-
stealing.") Note that the situation here is quite different from the
usual public goods model in which at least some of the "good" will
tend to be produced by one or all of the common or joint consumers
even under wholly independent adjustment. With law abiding as the
"good," however, the individual cannot, through his own behavior,
produce to increase his own utility. He can do nothing except provide
a "pure" external economy; all benefits accrue to the other parties.
Hence, the independent adjustment position involves a corner solution at the origin in our two-person diagram. But gains from trade
clearly exist in this Hobbesian jungle, despite the absence of unilateral action.

It is easy enough to depict the Pareto region that bounds potential positions of mutual gains by drawing the appropriate indifference contours through the origin as is done in Fig. 1. These contours indicate the internal or subjective rates of trade-off between
own and *other* law abiding. It seems plausible to suggest that the
standard convexity properties would apply. The analysis remains
largely empty, however, until we know something, or at least postu-

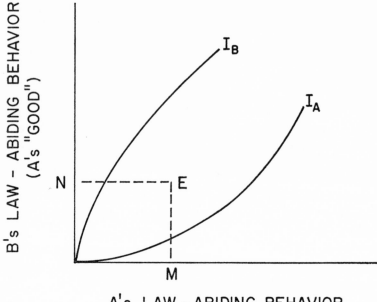

Fig. 1

A's LAW - ABIDING BEHAVIOR
(B's "GOOD")

late something, about the descriptive characteristics of the initial position itself. And the important and relevant point in this respect is
that individuals are not equal, or at least need not be equal, in such
a setting, either in their relative abilities or in their final command
over consumables.[2] To assume symmetry among persons here amounts
to converting a desired normative state, that of equality among men,
into a fallacious positive proposition. (This is, of course, a pervasive
error, and one that is made not only by social philosophers. It has
also had significant and pernicious effects on judicial thinking in the
twentieth century.) If we drop the assumption of equality or symmetry, however, we can say something about the relative values or
trade-offs between the relative "haves" and "have-nots" in the
Hobbesian or natural adjustment equilibrium. For illustrative purposes
here, think of the natural distribution in our two-person model as
characterized by A's enjoyment of ten units of "good," and B's enjoy-

[2] The formal properties of the "natural distribution" that will emerge under
anarchy have been described by Winston Bush in his paper "Individual Welfare in
Anarchy," in *Explorations in the Theory of Anarchy*, ed. Gordon Tullock, pp. 5–18.

ment of only two units. Both persons expend effort, which is a "bad" in generating and in maintaining this natural distribution. It is this effort that can be reduced or eliminated through trade—through agreement on laws or rules of respect for property. In this way, both parties can secure more "goods." The posttrade equilibrium must reflect improvement for both parties over the natural distribution or pretrade outcome. There are prospects for Pareto-efficient or Pareto-superior moves from the initial no rights position to any one of many possible posttrade or positive rights distributions.

Let us suppose that agreement is reached; each person agrees to an assignment of property rights, and, furthermore, each person agrees to respect such rights as are assigned. Let us suppose, for illustration, that the net distribution of goods under the assignment is fifteen units for A and seven units for B. Hence, there is a symmetrical sharing of the total gains from trade secured from the assignment of rights. Even under such symmetrical sharing, however, note that the relative position of B has improved more than the relative position of A. In our example A's income increases by one-half, but B's income increases more than twofold. This relative increase suggests that the person who fares relatively worse in the natural distribution may well stand to gain relatively more from an initial assignment of rights than the person who fares relatively better in the pretrade state of the world.

Agreement is attained; both parties enjoy more utility than before. But again the prisoner's dilemma setting must be emphasized. Each of the two persons can anticipate gains by successful unilateral default on the agreement. In Fig. 1, if E depicts the position of agreement, A can always gain by a shift to N, if this shift can be accomplished; similarly, B can gain by a shift to M. There may, however, be an asymmetry in prospective gains from unilateral default on the rights agreement. The prospective gains may well be higher for the person who remains relatively less favored in the natural distribution. In one sense, the vein of ore that he can mine by departing from the rules through criminal activity is richer than the similar vein would be for the other party. The productivity of criminal effort is likely to be higher for the man who can steal from his rich neighbor than for the man who has only poor neighbors.

This dilemma may be illustrated in the matrix of Fig. 2, where the initial pretrade or natural distribution is shown in cell IV and the posttrade or positive rights distribution is shown in cell I. Note that, as depicted, the man who is relatively poor in the natural equilibrium, person B in the example, stands to gain relatively more by departing unilaterally from cell I than does person A. Person B could, by such a move, increase his quantity of goods from seven to twelve, whereas person A could only increase his from fifteen to seventeen. This example suggests that the relatively rich person will necessarily be more interested in policing the activities of the poor man, as such, than vice versa. This fact is, of course, widely accepted. But the construction and analysis here can be employed for a more complex and difficult issue that has not been treated adequately.

Shifts in Natural Distribution

Assume that agreement has been attained; both parties abide by the law; both enjoy the benefits. Time passes. The rich man becomes lazy and lethargic. The poor man increases his strength. This change modifies the natural distribution. Let us say that the natural distribution changes to a ratio of six to six. The rich man now has an overwhelmingly more significant interest in the maintenance of the legal status quo than does the poor man, who is no longer poor in terms of natural ability. The initial symmetry in the sharing of gains between the no-trade and the trade positions no longer holds. With the new natural distribution, the rich man secures almost all of the net gains.

		B	
		ABIDES BY LAW	OBSERVES NO LAW
A	ABIDES BY LAW	I 15, 7	II 6, 12
	OBSERVES NO LAW	III 17, 3	IV 10, 2

Fig. 2

The example must be made more specific. Assume that the situation is analogous to the one examined by Winston Bush. The initial problem is how the manna which drops from the heavens is to be divided between the two persons. The initial natural distribution is in the ratio of ten to two, as noted. Recognizing this fact along with their own abilities, A and B agree that by assigning rights they can attain a fifteen-to-seven ratio, as noted. Time passes, and B increases in relative strength, but the "goods" are still shared in the fifteen-to-seven ratio. The initial set of property rights agreed to on the foundations of the initial natural distribution no longer reflects or mirrors the existing natural distribution. Under these changed conditions, a lapse back into the natural equilibrium will harm B relatively little, whereas A will be severely damaged. The poor man now has relatively little interest in adherence to the law. If this trend continues and the natural distribution changes further in the direction indicated, the poor man may even find himself able to secure net advantages from a lapse back into the Hobbesian jungle.

The model may be described in something like the terms of modern game theory. If the initial natural distribution remains unaltered, the agreed-on assignment of rights possesses qualities like the core in an n-person game. It is to the advantage of no coalition to depart from this assignment or imputation if the remaining members of the group are willing to enforce or to block the imputation. No coalition can do better on its own, or in this model, in the natural distribution than it does in the assignment. These corelike properties of the assigned distribution under law may, however, begin to lose features of dominance as the potential natural distribution shifts around "underneath" the existing structure of rights, so to speak. The foundations of the existing rights structure may be said to have shifted in the process.

This analysis opens up interesting new implications for net redistribution of wealth and for changes in property rights over time. Observed changes in claims to wealth take place without apparent consent. These may be interpreted simply as the use of the enforcement power of the state by certain coalitions of persons to break the contract. They are overtly shifting from a cell I into a cell II or cell III outcome in the diagram of Fig. 2. It is not, of course, difficult to explain why these coalitions arise. It will always be in the interest of

a person, or a group of persons, to depart from the agreed-on assignment of claims or rights, provided that he or they can do so unilaterally and without offsetting reactive behavior on the part of the
remaining members of the social group. The quasi-equilibrium in
cell I is inherently unstable. The equilibrium does qualify as a position in the core of the game, but we must keep in mind that the core
analytics presumes the immediate formation of blocking coalitions.
In order fully to explain observed departures from the status quo we
must also explain the behavior of the absence of the potential blocking coalitions. Why do the remaining members of the community
fail to enforce the initial assignment of rights?

The analysis here suggests that if there has been a sufficiently
large shift in the underlying natural distribution, the powers of enforcing adherence on the prospective violators of contract may not
exist, or, if they do exist, these powers may be demonstrably weak-
ened. In our numerical example, B fares almost as well under the new
natural distribution as he does in the continuing assignment of legal
rights. Hence, A has lost almost all of his blocking power; he can
scarcely influence B by threats to plunge the community into Hobbesian anarchy even if A himself should be willing to do so. And it
should also be recognized that "willingness" to enforce the contract
(the structure of legal rules, the existing set of claims to property)
is as important as the objective ability to do so. Even if A should be
physically able to enforce B to return to the *status quo ante* after some
attempted departure, he may be unwilling to suffer the personal loss
that might be required to make his threat of enforcement credible.[3]
The law-abiding members of the community may find themselves in
a genuine dilemma. They may simply be unable to block the unilateral violation of the social contract.

In this perspective, normative arguments based on "justice" in
distribution may signal acquiescence in modifications in the existing
structure of claims. Just as the idea of contract itself has been used to
rationalize existing structure, the idea of "justice" may be used to
rationalize coerced departures from contract. In the process, those
who advance such arguments and those who are convinced may "feel
better" while their claims are whittled away. This reasoning, I think,

---

[3] For a more extensive discussion of these points, see chapter 12 below.

explains much attitudinal behavior toward redistribution policy by specific social groups. Gordon Tullock has, in part, explained the prevailing attitudes of many academicians and intellectuals.[4] The explanation developed here applies more directly to the redistributionist attitudes of the scions of the rich, for example, the Rockefellers and the Kennedys. Joseph Kennedy was less redistributive than his sons; John D. Rockefeller was less redistributive than his grandsons. We do not need to call on the psychologists, since our model provides an explanation in the concept of a changing natural distribution. The scions of the wealthy are far less secure in their roles as custodians of wealth than were their forebears. They realize perhaps that their own natural talents simply do not match up, even remotely, to the share of national wealth that they command. Their apparent passions for the poor may be nothing more than surface reflections of attempts to attain temporary security.

The analysis also suggests that there is a major behavioral difference fostered between the intergenerational transmission of non-human and human capital. Within limits, there is an important linkage between human capital and capacity to survive in a natural or Hobbesian environment. There seems to be no such linkage between nonhuman capital and survival in the jungle. From this it follows that the man who possesses human capital is likely to be far less concerned about the "injustice" of his own position, less concerned about temporizing measures designed to shore up apparent leaks in the social system, than his counterpart who possesses nonhuman capital. If we postulate that the actual income-asset distribution departs significantly from the proportionate distribution in the underlying and existing natural equilibrium, the system of claims must be acknowledged to be notoriously unstable. The idle rich, possessing nonhuman capital, will tend to form coalitions with the poor that are designed primarily to ward off retreat toward the Hobbesian jungle. Such coalitions can take the form of the rich acquiescing in and providing defense for overt criminal activity on the part of the poor, or the more explicit form of political exploitation of the "silent majority," the constituency that possesses largely human instead of nonhuman capital.

[4] See Gordon Tullock, "The Charity of the Uncharitable," *Western Economic Journal* 9 (December, 1971): 379–391.

This description has some empirical content in the 1970's. But what can the exploited groups do about it? Can the middle classes form a coalition with the rich, especially when the latter are themselves so insecure? Or can they form, instead, another coalition with the poor, accepting a promise of strict adherence to law in exchange for goodies provided by the explicit confiscation of the nonhuman capital of the rich? (Politically, this might take the form of confiscatory inheritance taxation.) The mythology of the American dream probably precludes this route from being taken. The self-made, the *nouveaux riches*, seek to provide their children with fortunes that the latter accept only with guilt.

All of this suggests that a law-abiding imputation becomes increasingly difficult to sustain as its structure departs from what participants conceive to be the natural or Bush-Hobbes imputation, defined in some proportionate sense. If the observed imputation, or set of bounded imputations that are possible under existing legal-constitutional rules, seems to bear no relationship at all to the natural imputation that men accept, breakdown in legal standards is predictable.

Where does this leave us in trying to discuss criteria for improvement in rules, in assignments of rights, the initial question that was posed in this paper? I have argued that the contractarian or Paretian norm is relevant on the simple principle that "we start from here." But "here," the status quo, is the existing set of legal institutions and rules. Hence, how can we possibly distinguish genuine contractual changes in law from those which take place under the motivations discussed above? Can we really say which changes are defensible "exchanges" from an existing status quo position? To the extent that property rights are specified in advance, genuine "trades" can emerge, with mutual gains to all parties. However, to the extent that existing rights are held to be subject to continuous redefinition by the state, no one has an incentive to organize and to initiate trades or agreements. This amounts to saying that once the body politic begins to get overly concerned about the distribution of the pie under existing property rights assignments and legal rules, once we begin to think either about the personal gains from law breaking, privately or publicly, or about the disparities between existing imputations and those estimated to be forthcoming under some idealized anarchy, we are necessarily precluding and forestalling the achievement of potential structural changes that might increase the size of the pie for *all*. Too much concern for "justice" acts to insure that growth will not take place, and for reasons much more basic than the familiar arguments about economic incentives.

In this respect, the late 1970's seem a century, not a mere decade and a half, away from the early 1960's, when the rage was all for growth, and the new-found concern about distribution had not yet been invented. At issue here, of course, is the whole conception of the state, or of collective action. I am far less sanguine than I once was concerning the possible acceptance of the existing constitutional-legal framework. The basic structure of property rights is now threatened more seriously than at any period in the two-century history of the United States. In chapter 12 I develop the hypothesis that we have witnessed a general loss of strategic courage, brought on in part by economic affluence. But there is more to it. We may be witnessing the disintegration of our effective constitutional rights, regardless of the prattle about "the constitution" as seen by our judicial tyrants from their own visions of the entrails of their sacrificial beasts. I do not know what might be done about all this, even by those who recognize what is happening. We seem to be left with the question posed at the outset: How do rights reemerge and come to command respect? How do laws emerge that carry with them general respect for their legitimacy?

7

Politics, Property, and the Law

WARREN SAMUELS has used the fascinating case of *Miller et al.* v. *Schoene*[1] as a vehicle for presenting his interpretation of the inter-relationships between politico-legal and economic processes.[2] I share with Samuels the methodological conviction that only by moving beyond the narrowly conceived limits of economic theory and into the examination of the political, legal, and social constraints within which economic actions are bounded can we hope to unravel much of the confusion that currently describes the discussion of concrete policy issues. I differ profoundly with Samuels, however, on the theory of politics, property, and law that his interpretation implies. The central arguments in *Miller et al.* v. *Schoene* may be examined from quite a different conception of the functional role of judicial process, of legislation in democracy, and of the appropriate means or instruments through which tolerable efficiency can be attained in a regime of economic interdependency. Classificatory labels are subject to over-simplification, but for purposes of casual identification my approach is that of the political economist who interprets Paretian criteria in essentially Wicksellian terms and who can be described, somewhat more broadly, as falling within what has been called the "Virginia school."[3]

[1] 276 U.S. 272 (1928).

[2] Warren J. Samuels, "Interrelations between Legal and Economic Processes," *Journal of Law and Economics* 14 (October, 1971): 435–450.

[3] Mancur Olson and Christopher Clague, "Dissent in Economics," *Social Research* 38 (Winter, 1971): 753.

The Argument Summarized

The following excerpts from Samuels's paper summarize the facts:

> *Miller et al.* v. *Schoene* is a case which involves red cedar and apple trees and their respective owners; and cedar rust, a plant disease whose first phase is spent while the fungus resides upon its host, the chiefly ornamental red cedar tree, which is not harmed by the cedar rust. The fungus does have a severely adverse effect upon the apple tree during a second phase, attacking its leaves and fruit. The legislature of the state of Virginia in 1914, passed a statute which empowered the state entomologist to investigate and, if necessary, condemn and destroy without compensation certain red cedar trees within a two-mile radius of an apple orchard. . . . [P. 436]

> *Miller et al.*, plaintiffs in error in the instant case, unsuccessfully brought suit in state courts, and sued to reverse the decision of the Supreme Court of Appeals in Virginia. The arguments for the plaintiffs in error were basically simple and direct, as well as of profound heuristic value. Their main contention was that the legislature was, unconstitutionally in their view, attempting to take or destroy their property to the advantage of the apple orchard owners. [Pp. 436–437]

In Samuels's interpretation, the Virginia legislature, and ultimately the Supreme Court, "had to make a judgment as to which owner would be visited with injury and which protected" (p. 439). The legislature chose to favor the apple growers and to penalize the owners of the red cedar groves. The courts upheld the legislature in this action. According to Samuels, the result was an "effective new law of property" (p. 439). An unforeseen and unpredicted natural event, the emergence of red cedar rust, necessitated state intervention and state decision one way or the other.

The implications of this conception are sweeping, and Samuels makes his position explicit. When previously existing rights to property are challenged by any party, the state, acting through its legislative-cum-judicial arms and agencies, must, willy-nilly, make a choice among conflicting claimants. Presumably, the state will be guided in its deliberations and in its decision by the relative pressure of divergent economic interests responsibly exerted. Samuels places his trust in the emergence of the measurably superior benefit even without the necessity of compensation. It is apparent that Samuels's approach offers a significant role for the cost-benefit analyst, who may, presumably, measure relative monetary values independently of distributional consequences and whose results will be, or should be, used by the legislator-cum-judge in his attempt at reaching a "correct" decision.

Legal Rights and Trading Opportunities

My major quarrel with Samuels does not, however, center on the difficulties in reconciling outcomes of a collective decision-making process with those that might be classified as "efficient" by some idealized economic observer. My complaint is more fundamental. Samuels appeals too readily to state decision making, which, by its very nature, forestalls the exchange or marketlike pressures toward internalizing the interdependencies that may arise as exogenous elements modify the overall social environment. There is no guarantee that the state will select that alternative which maximizes the value of the social product, and even when this concern is dropped, there is nothing in the Samuels model which allows for the mutuality of gains that is part and parcel of an economic approach to social interaction.

The owners of adjoining plots of land coexisted peaceably before the onset of red cedar rust, a natural event that was not foreseen. There was no explicit economic interdependence between persons growing apple trees and those growing red cedar trees, and, with reference to this subset of the population, the system was on the Pareto efficiency frontier. That is, before the fungus there existed no potential trades or agreements among the apple growers and the cedar growers that remained unexploited. The subsystem was, therefore, simultaneously efficient, optimal, and in equilibrium. In this case these three terms carry essentially the same meaning.

A natural event then occurred. The new fungus did not damage the cedar trees on which it grew initially. It did subsequently threaten severe damage to the apple trees. Between the owners of apple orchards and the owners of red cedar lands arose an interdependence that did not exist before the exogenous shock. Potential gains from trade should have existed that would have allowed this new interdependence to be eliminated. Before such "trade" could have been undertaken, however, individual participants would have to have been certain of their property rights. Presumably, in the case at hand, the structure of rights in existence did not allow the apple grower to destroy the diseased cedar trees on neighboring lands. The set of "previously existing rights" presumably allowed the red cedar owners to grow diseased trees safe from molestation by damaged apple growers. This was presumably acknowledged by all parties.

This factual description of the single historical setting should not, however, be taken to imply that there was in this case, or ever is, a unique means of delineating property rights. It could have been the case that the rights of cedar growers extended only to the nurturing of undiseased trees, and/or, conversely, the rights of apple growers could have been defined in terms of the nurturing of healthy trees, which might have included the right to eliminate all neighborhood interferences. The principle to be emphasized, however, is that *some* structure, *any* structure, of well-defined rights is a necessary starting point for the potential trades that are required to remove the newly emergent interdependence. This is not to say that when the unpredicted exogenous shock occurs, the structure of rights may not contain ambiguities and possibly alternative definitions. In such case it becomes an appropriate and necessary task for the courts to lay down the precise limits of allowable actions by the parties in question. In this behavior, however, the courts are "locating the limits" that exist in the law; they are not, and they must not be seen to be, defining *new* limits or changing preexisting ones. The courts clarify ambiguities; they lend precision; they draw black and white lines in gray areas. Once they have done so, or in the absence of judicial decision when there is no imprecision, the ground is laid for the emergence of those agreements which can serve to internalize the interdependence. If there should have been some confusion over the rights of the apple growers and the cedar growers under the previously existing law, the courts, but not the legislative arm of the Commonwealth of Virginia, should have been called upon for resolution. In Samuels's account of the case, however, no dispute arose at this level; all parties were agreed on the precise structure of rights inherent in the law as it stood.

Given the acknowledgment of the content of the law of property, and given the newly emergent interdependence between the apple growers and the cedar landowners, a basis should have been laid for "trade," from which mutuality of gains might have been forthcoming. The model can be clarified if we think initially of the interaction between a single apple grower and a single cedar landowner. Once cedar rust was recognized to exist, it was to the apparent advantage of the orchard owner to initiate action to purchase or lease the adjacent cedar land, to purchase the standing cedar, or to compensate the cedar grower for cutting his trees. A region of mutual gain clearly existed, and bargains could have been struck which would have moved the solution toward the efficiency surface, possibly forestalled only by recalcitrant bargaining strategy on the part of one or both of the parties. In the trading process, of course, both parties would have secured gains over and above those secured in the postfungus disequilibrium. Mutual agreement should have signaled mutual gain.

Consider the contrast between this procedure and the one which is implicit in Samuels's discussion. In the latter case the apple grower appealed directly to the state, and the state decided just which one of the two claims was to be favored. The issue became strictly one of either-or. The problem of the informational requirements for decision immediately arises. How could the state determine which claim was of higher value? How could the damage to the apple crop be estimated against the damage to the value of the cedar trees from premature cutting? In this case, an expert, a Virginia entomologist, was called upon to make a determination. But this intrusion of the experts tends to prejudice the general argument in Samuels's favor. In most economic interdependencies there are no "experts," and there are likely to be major errors in any cost-benefit estimates. More importantly, even if the testimony of expert witnesses is introduced, who can claim that the collective decision makers will, or should, follow their advice?

Note that when the parties are allowed to bargain freely and to reach mutually satisfactory agreements, the apple grower's own assessment of probable damage to his crop becomes the measure of his own maximum payment to secure the elimination of the danger. On the other side, the cedar grower's own estimate of the value of his standing trees over and above their value as cut trees becomes the basis for his possible willingness to accept or to reject proferred compensations. The equity or inequity of compensation is irrelevant; what is relevant is the necessary place of compensation in the trading process between the two parties. Only when transfers are actually made can relative values be measured by those whose interests are directly involved.

Complex Arrangements

Whether or not the model sketched out above accurately describes the situation in *Miller et al.* v. *Schoene* is an empirical question. If the number of apple orchard owners in every fungus area was small, there should have been no action taken by the collectivity as long as we presume that the previously existing structure of rights was well defined. The efficient solution could have been depended on to emerge from the interaction between the parties in each interdependence. In the tradition of classical political economy, the forces of self-interest could have been relied on to generate an outcome that would tend to maximize the value of social product. There is no means of determining whether this solution would have resulted in the cutting of the red cedar groves or the continued infestation of the apple trees by cedar rust.

If, however, the numbers on the apple grower side of the interactions in question had been large, or beyond critical "small-number" limits, the familiar free-rider obstructions to voluntarily negotiated solutions might have arisen. In this situation there might seem to have remained a functional role for collective action. In this setting the legislative arm of the collectivity might have intervened appropriately, and it becomes possible for us to interpret the actual events of *Miller et al.* v. *Schoene* in this quite different framework.

If, for example, there had been n apple orchard owners involved in an interdependence with a single red cedar landowner, there might have been no voluntary agreement reached, despite the possibly relatively superior value of an undiseased apple yield. It might not have been to the economic advantage of any single grower to initiate agreements with the cedar landowner or to make unilateral payments to that landowner in exchange for use of the land. There would have been no means, in this case, through which the single orchardist could have *excluded* his fellows from the enjoyment of the disease reduction that his own action might have procured from the cedar landowner. Reduction in cedar rust would have been, in this situation, a purely "public good," in the modern use of this term, to the community of apple growers involved in the particular interaction. Resort to collective or joint action might have been dictated. The possible reason lies in the dual interdependencies that this setting involved: (1) that between each apple grower and the cedar grower or growers, and (2) that among the separate apple growers themselves. The first of these interdependencies could have been removed by freely negotiated trades in the absence of the second. The presence of the second or public goods interdependence, however, might well have prohibited the negotiation of a solution to the former.

The failure of negotiated settlements to emerge, however, would have been consistent with continuing inefficiency only under a particular assumption about the landownership pattern among apple growers. Only if this pattern was invariant for some reason would the public-goods dilemma have inhibited negotiated internalization. That is, if in each interaction there had been many apple growers, a number sufficient to have created a potential public goods barrier to negotiated voluntary settlements, some assumptions must be made to the effect that this number was unchangeable within certain limits. If such a restriction is not imposed on the model, mutual gains from trade would have existed among the separate orchardists, and individual owners of apple land parcels would have had incentives to merge landholdings into units sufficiently large to remove or to reduce substantially the free-rider motivation that might otherwise have inhibited direct negotiation of agreements with the owner or owners of cedar lands. The interdependencies would have been, in a nonrestricted model, removed or internalized in a two-stage process of trading agreement. In the first stage the many separate land parcels devoted to apples that were simultaneously affected by the cedar rust from a plot of trees would have been consolidated or merged under a single owner or ownership entity. In the second stage this entity would have negotiated an agreement with the cedar owner or owners concerning the elimination of the diseased trees.

The unrestricted model suggests that the publicness interaction or externality among the apple growers might itself have been internalized through consolidation of landholdings, in which case there would have remained no argument for resort to collective or state action beyond the initial definition of rights and the enforcement of contracts. This model is fully applicable, however, only when transactions costs are negligible. The concept "transactions costs" offers a generalized rubric within which many of the barriers to negotiated settlements may be placed. The point is that the interaction among the separate apple growers generated by the cedar rust might have been only one, albeit a new, dimension that had economic content. There might have been many other variables that were relevant for land consolidation. If, for example, apples had been a significant but not exclusive source of external income for a large number of family-sized farms simultaneously affected by the cedar rust from a nearby plot of cedar trees, the opportunity costs of land parcel consolidation directed at this interdependence alone might well have exceeded the benefits while at the same time the damage to the apple crop exceeded the differential value of standing over cut cedar trees.

Efficiency in Collective Response

The analysis suggests that there might have been an efficiency basis for resorting to collective or state action in the apple-cedar interaction under discussion here, but that that basis required the presence of certain narrowly defined conditions. If there were large numbers of apple growers involved in each interaction, and if transactions costs were such that voluntary agreement on land consolidation could not have been predicted to emerge, the community of all apple growers might have legitimately called on the state to resolve the dilemma in which they found themselves. Interestingly enough, the Virginia Cedar Rust Act required the petition of at least ten free-holders before the state entomologist was empowered to act. This fact suggests that the large-number condition might have been recognized to be necessary for state action by the framers of the legislation. Samuels's discussion, however, nowhere suggests that these conditions are necessary for collective intervention to be justified.

It will be useful to examine the appropriate form of collective action, however, on the assumption that these required justifications were indeed present. The state might have responded to the issue by granting to appropriately sized apple growers' cooperatives some powers of coercion over members. Normally, however, we should have expected the legislative arm of the state to consider more direct action. What is the state actually doing in such a course of action? As noted, no collective interference is warranted in the absence of a public goods interaction that persists after the appropriately negotiated adjustments in the size of the affected entities. Nonexcludability must, of course, characterize a genuine public goods setting. The state must be conceived, therefore, as offering to supply a public good, one that will be made available to all members of the large community if it is made available to any one member. The standard and familiar requirements for efficiency in the provision of such a good or service can be readily defined. Total benefits must exceed total costs, and the summed marginal evaluations over all members of the community affected must be equated with the marginal cost of provision.

The question then becomes one of implementing this set of efficiency norms through the political process. If the conditions for justifying collective interference are present, or are held to be present, how can collective action be organized to insure that the net result involves a shift toward instead of away from society's efficiency surface? It is here that Knut Wicksell offers guiding principles.[4]

We may first consider the collective decision in question as an isolated, independent event. What institutional structure for the reaching of community decisions will insure that the economy is moved toward the efficiency surface? Since there is no way of assessing the intensities of individual interests except through the revealed choice behavior of individuals themselves, a group decision rule of unanimity was suggested by Wicksell. If as much as one person in the community is harmed, there is no insurance that the damage he suffers may not outweigh the benefits or gains to all other persons in the group. The rule of unanimity is the Wicksellian equivalent of a Pareto move, and the impossibility of securing unanimous consent for any change becomes the Wicksellian criterion for classifying an attained position as Pareto optimal.

---

[4] Knut Wicksell, "New Principle of Just Taxation," in *Classics in the Theory of Public Finance*, ed. R. A. Musgrave and A. T. Peacock, pp. 72–118.

The ideal collective decision process is, therefore, an effective unanimity rule, with all members of the community participating in the choice. Cost considerations dictate departures from this ideal in several respects. Representation of individual or subgroup interests through the instrument of legislative bodies is widely accepted as a necessary practicable substitute for the fully participatory town meeting type of institutional structure. Again in some quasi-ideal limits, the members of the legislative assembly or assemblies represent, and hence act in the interests of, all citizens. The first stage in the practical implementation of the Wicksell scheme is, therefore, the application of an effective rule of unanimity in an appropriately selected legislative assembly.

With particular reference to the historical Virginia decision under discussion, we should note that collective action via the legislative body did offer an institutional means for internalizing the interdependence between the apple growers and the cedar owners. The legislative process is the instrument for reconciling the separate interests, for effecting some compromise and agreed-on solution. The legislative process, interpreted in this light, is functionally quite distinct from the judicial process. There is no role for the judiciary in the decision relating to the supply and financing of a public good. A categorical distinction must be made here, one that Samuels's treatment tends to blur over if not to disregard entirely.

Strict adherence to a rule of unanimity in a legislative body is not practicable. Wicksell himself recognized that the opportunities for strategic bargaining were too great and that these opportunities worked to make the costs of decision making excessive. Such considerations aside, however, it will be useful for our purposes to examine the type of legislative action that might have been expected to emerge under the operation of the unanimity rule in the Virginia legislature in 1914. In order to do this, let us simply assume that members of the legislative assembly did, in fact, genuinely represent all interests, and notably those of both the apple growers and the cedar owners; further, let us assume that each legislator voted strictly in terms of the estimated interests of his constituents, untainted by the strategic bargaining or holdout possibilities offered by the operation of the rule itself.

In such a setting the representatives for the damaged apple growers might have proposed that the state take action to reduce cedar rust by ordering the cutting of diseased trees in the vicinity of the apple orchards. Those legislators representing the cedar landowners would, of course, have opposed any such proposals unless compensations were paid to their constituents. In order to meet these objections, the apple-interest legislators would have then put forward alternative schemes which would have necessarily included taxes levied on their own constituents as the means of financing the compensations required to secure the acquiescence of the cedar tree growers, or, in this situation, their legislative representatives. The required compensations become, in this case, the cost of providing the collective or public good, defined as the reduction or elimination of cedar rust damage to the apple crops. As Wicksell emphasized, some such combined proposal (taxes and compensation payments) must have commanded the assent of all members of the assembly if the apple damage exceeded the damage from premature cutting of cedar. This provides the *only* test for efficiency that can be institutionalized politically. If the efficiency gains had been significant, there might have been, of course, many possible sets of taxes and compensation payments which could have secured unanimous support in the legislature. The particular proposal adopted would have depended, in part, on the simple order of presentation of the alternatives, which may have been, of course, quite arbitrarily determined.

Considered as an isolated political decision, therefore, the action of the Virginia legislature in allowing the condemnation of diseased cedar trees without compensation, and hence without taxes imposed on the prospective beneficiaries, the apple growers, violated the Wicksellian-Paretian precepts. In no way could such legislative action be interpreted as a surrogate for a voluntarily negotiated settlement among the parties at issue, with the collectivization made necessary only by the free-rider, transactions cost considerations noted. There is no means of determining, from the political-institutional record, whether the action taken was or was not efficient.

Legislation in Constitutional Limits

Our interpretation of *Miller et al.* v. *Schoene* is not complete, however, precisely because the action of the Virginia legislature cannot legitimately be considered as an isolated political event, nor can it be evaluated as such. Political choice takes place over many time periods and over several sets of alternatives in each period, covering widely divergent subject matter. Many "public goods" are supplied and financed; many proposals for collective supply and financing are rejected. As we noted above, any strict requirement of unanimity in legislative decision making would generate costly delays in reaching agreement on anything, if indeed agreement is reached at all. Historical evidence suggests that unanimity is the exception rather than the rule, and legislative bodies are constitutionally empowered to act on less-than-unanimity rules, often under some version of majority voting as embedded in a complex structure of procedure and often with certain rights of executive veto.

Any departure from strict unanimity provides an opportunity for choices to be made for the collectivity that fail to meet the Pareto efficiency criterion. This fact must be acknowledged. Nonetheless, at some constitutional stage of decision on the structure of collective decision rules themselves, the prospective inefficiencies generated by less-than-unanimity voting may be less than those predicted to be generated by the decision-making inefficiencies which the more restrictive voting rule would insure.

In this more realistic setting for legislative decision making, however, any evaluation of a single-choice action becomes much more difficult. In the Virginia case discussed, the absence of compensation to the owners of red cedar trees cannot, in itself, now be taken as clear evidence that the political process did not serve as an indirect and complex surrogate for the negotiation and settlement process among the parties. In a constitutional sense we might think of both apple and cedar growers as having acquiesced in the continuing operation of a legislative process embodying constrained majority voting, in the recognition that on occasion the economic interests of any particular subgroup in the community might be damaged, and perhaps severely. In this broader conception of collective decision making, the deliberations and choices made in a democratically selected and truly representative assembly may be interpreted as the only practicable institutional means of reconciling differences, or implementing "bargains" or "trades," in the presence of those conditions that are requisite for collective action. The interests potentially damaged, in our case those of the cedar owners, could have exercised their voting power on issues about which they were relatively indifferent in order to register their intensity of opposition to the tree cutting statute. If, in fact, the damage to red cedars should have exceeded that of infestation of the apple crop significantly, logrolling interaction in the Virginia legislature might have insured against passage of the statute in question.

As we know, however, the statute was enacted, and the cedar owners appealed to the courts, first at the state and then at the federal levels. Our question becomes: What should have been the criteria by which the courts evaluated the legislative action? In this setting, the only role of the judiciary should have been one of determining whether or not the decision taken by the legislature was made constitutionally. This determination should have involved, first, an examination of the decision rule itself, about which there apparently would have been no issue. Second, the decision might have been evaluated in terms of the precepts of the "fiscal constitution" that were implicitly if not explicitly in being.

The taxing powers of the state allow the taking of private property for public or general purposes. If we interpret the statute that allows the condemnation of trees without compensation as a tax in kind on owners of such trees, in disregard of the offsetting side of the budget account, there might have been plausible grounds for the courts to uphold the legislative action. The critical element here should have concerned the nondiscriminatory nature of the tax. Formally, however, since the "tax" was imposed on all owners of red cedar trees in two-mile radii of apple orchards, an argument could have been made that such action was nondiscriminatory over a sufficiently broad class of persons. In this context, such a "tax" on the owners of red cedar trees, on the landowners, might have been legally interpreted as no different than a tax on the owners of pool tables, playing cards, or any other of the many narrowly specified bases observed in the real world.

If the offsetting or balancing side of the budget account had been treated in isolation, the courts might also have found legitimate grounds for upholding the legislation. Representative assemblies have been empowered, constitutionally, to provide benefits to specific subgroups in the community, whether these subgroups be occupationally, geographically, industrially, or otherwise classified. Indeed, the nondiscriminatory or uniformity requirements generally held applicable to the tax side of the budget have never been applied to the public spending side.[5] Interpreted, therefore, as a specific subsidy to apple growers whose trees had been diseased, the "outlay" could have been held constitutionally valid.

On the other hand, if the two sides of the conceptualized fiscal account had been joined in the court's deliberations, the constitutionality of the Virginia legislature's action might have proved highly questionable. In this light, the action seems similar in many respects to that which evoked the Supreme Court's rejection of the original Agricultural Adjustment Administration on constitutional grounds. In *United States* v. *Butler*, the court held that the levy of a specific tax for the specific benefits of one subgroup was not a valid exercise of state power.[6]

Regardless of the court's verdict in *Miller et al.* v. *Schoene*, Samuels's interpretation of the court's action seems contrary to that which would seem appropriate under the alternative approach that I have tried to develop. It would have been illegitimate for the "Court, as part of the state, . . . [to] make a judgment as to which owner would be visited with injury and which protected" (p. 439), or "decide which party would have what capacity to coerce another." The judicial role should have been limited strictly to a determination of the constitutionality of legislative action, and it should not have included any attempt at making a judgment about the economic efficiency or inefficiency or the equity or inequity of the legislative choice actually made.

By its actual judgment it is not clear that the court exceeded the

[5] Recent court decisions with respect to differences in educational spending among differing communities within states indicate some change in legal interpretation. For a thorough discussion of the historical asymmetry in legal treatment, see David G. Tuerck, "Constitutional Asymmetry," *Papers on Non-Market Decision-Making* 2 (1967): 27–44. For a more comprehensive treatment, see Tuerck's "Uniformity in Taxation, Discrimination in Benefits: An Essay in Law and Economics," (Ph.D. diss., University of Virginia, 1966).

[6] 297 U.S. 1 (1936). Consider the hypothetical case in which cedar rust might have proved highly beneficial to apple crops but would have required investment on the part of cedar tree owners. Would the court have upheld legislation that required that such investment be made without compensation? Presumably not, yet analytically the setting seems identical with that which prevailed.

bounds of judicial propriety. The court said that "the state does not exceed its constitutional powers by deciding upon the destruction of one class of property in order to save another which, *in the judgment of the legislature*, is of greater value to the public" (my italics). In this statement the court does not seem to have considered itself to be doing what Samuels's interpretation suggests; it apparently did not attempt to inject its own standards of value measurement in determining the constitutionality of the legislation. The court's decision may have been in error in terms of consistent constitutional principles, but the error did not necessarily lie in the court's misconception of its own functional role in democratic governmental process.

Conclusions

Old arguments are important only if they shed light on matters of modern relevance. Disagreements between Warren Samuels and James Buchanan on the interpretation of *Miller et al.* v. *Schoene* might be privately but not publicly interesting if comparable conflicts are anticipated infrequently and/or those that might arise are economically insignificant. The major thrust of Samuels's paper, however, concerns the continuing ubiquitousness of such conflicts, along with their economic importance. In the vision of collective action that I have imputed to him, Samuels envisages an activist state ever ready to intervene when existing rights to property are challenged, ever willing to grasp the nettle and define anew rights which, once defined, immediately become vulnerable to still further challenges. This view projects an awesome role for the state in an environment that is subjected continuously, and necessarily, to the exogenous shocks resulting from natural phenomena, from technological change, from growth itself. Broadly conceived, something akin to cedar rust must appear every day, and in Samuels's paradigm the state must never rest. The structure of rights, as of any moment, is subjected to question, and away goes the white knight to decide whose claim shall be favored and whose rejected.

What if Mr. A simply does not like long-haired men? The presence of such men in the community harms him just as much as cedar rust harmed the apple growers. Is Mr. A then empowered to challenge the existing structure of rights that does allow men to wear their hair as they please? It matters not that "reasonable legislative-cum-judicial authorities" should always or nearly always decide in favor of the long-haired defendants. In Samuels's model the challenge itself must be appropriately processed, and each instance must be resolved on its own merits, with no apparent prejudice in favor of the "previously existing rights."

My own approach is sharply different. There is an explicit prejudice in favor of previously existing rights, not because this structure possesses some intrinsic ethical attributes, and not because change itself is undesirable, but for the much more elementary reason that only such a prejudice offers incentives for the emergence of voluntarily negotiated settlements among the parties themselves. Indirectly, therefore, this prejudice guarantees that resort to the authority of the state is effectively minimized. It insures that an efficiency basis for collective action emerges only when a genuine public goods externality arises and persists. Furthermore, this prejudice allows for a distinct and categorical separation of the legislative and judicial roles, something that is strangely absent in Samuels's vision.

Unfortunately, the theory of politics, property, and the law that is implied in Samuels's interpretation of *Miller et al.* v. *Schoene* reflects the conventional wisdom of our time. This wisdom makes the number of bills passed the criterion of legislative excellence, a criterion that is implanted in the spirit of every aspiring politician. Much more seriously, this wisdom also involves an activist federal judiciary, a judiciary that is now acknowledged to legislate and that accepts, and is seen to accept, its legislative role as such. Indeed, in Samuels's argument we may locate an apologia for the omnipresent hand of the state in all our lives, an omnipresence required by the necessary uncertainty of legal rights in a world subject to exogenous shocks. The state must adjudicate all conflicting claims, must take on all challenges to this and that, and in the process achieve the "unknown passing through the strange," a politico-legal setting that itself contributes to "future shock."

8

Student Revolts, Academic Liberalism, and Constitutional Attitudes

Student Participation

SHOULD the student have a share in controlling university policy and structure equal to or comparable with that exercised by the salaried administrator or tenured professor? The case to be made for the student's side of this currently relevant issue deserves more careful consideration than it is often accorded. The student finds himself participating in a game described by rules that he had no part in making. The institutional order of the university, its traditional procedures, regulations, and methods—these are imposed upon him. The student can, and does, claim a right to an increased participatory role in reshaping and modifying this institutional structure to meet what he considers to be his own ideals.[1]

---

[1] I should point out that the discussion in this chapter largely applies to a model in which the university is conceived as a collectivity. The fact that many persons do conceive the university in this image makes the discussion relevant. More importantly, the larger problems of social order that I want to discuss can only be treated in this university-as-collectivity model. The use of this model does not, however, preclude the discussion of an alternative model, nor does my discussion imply the rejection of the relevance of such an alternative. Insofar as the student faces effective educational alternatives in the form of many institutions competing for his custom, the appropriate analogy becomes the firm selling its services in the open market. In this model of analysis the student who objects to particular rules descriptive of one institution simply selects another one more to his liking. If in fact universities and colleges should be financed exclusively or primarily by tuition payments, the university-as-firm model would be more appropriate than the university-as-collectivity model. The latter increases in relevance as the relative share of tuition payments in university financing is reduced. On some of the effects of this change, and especially as related to the zero-tuition argument in California, see A. A. Alchian, "The Economic and Social Impact of Free Tuition," *New Individualist Review* 5 (Winter, 1968): 42–52.

The predicted academician's response is that the student is to be tutored, not welcomed as a participant in a genuinely democratic community. He is, at best, a relatively short-term resident of a long-lived institution which has developed its own set of traditions and practices and which embodies its own wisdom. To allow the student, who is uninformed, uneducated, and immature, to exercise a voice in the governance of the university would, to the academician, be irresponsible.

This response may fail to convince the student, despite its too-obvious reasonableness in the eyes of the established authorities. Intuitively and inarticulately, the student senses the contradiction in the position of his elders, a contradiction that they themselves often ignore. The senior academician, proudly liberal in his value standards, argues persuasively for the preservation of simple constitutional order and attitude in the narrow world of his own affairs. At the same time, this liberal academician refuses to face the apparent fact that he and his own kind have been instrumental in undermining constitutional order and attitude in the society at large. The student sees through the sham; he properly understands that if modern liberal attitudes toward sociopolitical processes are turned inward to the university setting, the existing structure of the university must be dramatically reformed. The academician who most strongly seeks the maintenance of order in the university community while condoning the disregard for constitutional order expressed by the various agencies of government, including the Supreme Court, may be intelligent, but if he is so his behavior reveals hypocrisy.

The day is past when the Southern scapegoat allowed the academic liberal to make his own private and careful distinction between "just" and "unjust" rules of order. The local statutes that were violated by the restaurant sit-ins of the early 1960's were "Southern" laws, of course, and properly and universally condemned as "unjust." The university regulations that were violated by the campus sleep-ins of 1968 were reasonable and "just." Something has simply gone wrong; someone has the wrong signals. But how is Martin Luther King's moral decision to be distinguished from Mario Savio's or Mark Rudd's? If individual consciences are to be the arbiters in such matters, why are some individuals more respected than others? The pretentious arrogance of those who think that all men must agree on "truth" as defined by their own provincial standards has been exposed. The intolerance that masqueraded as social purpose becomes itself intolerable when the purpose is defined by those whose standards differ. The academic liberal seems hoist by his own petard. Is he reduced to arguments strangely akin to those advanced by the "racist," "hate-mongering" states' righters of the 1950's?

If the academic liberal is forced to think by all this, in retrospect the students' revolts may be seen to have served a major social function. If critical intelligence can begin to replace intolerance among intellectuals, perhaps restoration of effective social order can be expected in due time. Optimism would be misplaced for any short-term perspective, because there are major time lags between ideas and realization. We currently reap the whirlwind of past intellectuals' follies. But at least if thinking begins, a new spirit of critical inquiry may provide some hope for emergence from chaos, provided we can survive the interim without succumbing to the increasingly relevant fascist temptation. Perhaps, and I emphasize the perhaps here, the excesses of student demands in the 1960's will have made the excesses of totalitarian democracy unnecessary. In miniature we may have seen the future, and there may still be time to change it. If this be the course of events, praise be to the student revolutionaries. If the intellectuals refuse to see and to make the proper inferences about their own behavior, our society will get the order that it deserves.

Truth and Academic Liberalism

Any optimism must be tempered, however. The academic liberal is the least sensitive of men. It will be difficult for him to make the required transference of ideas; he will only with struggle take those ideas that seem obvious to him in his private university setting into his thought patterns about the world at large. He will cling to his defenses of the established rules, regulations, and authorities of his university because these, to him, are "true," or "right," not because they were adopted by orderly institutional procedure. He will cry good riddance to those traditions of legal order that the Warren court overthrew even when that court assumed a nonjudicial role. He does so because such traditions were "wrong." To this academic liberal, the student revolutionary of the 1960's was blind to the subtle distinctions between established rules that are "right" and those that are "wrong," between "truth" and "untruth" in judgments on social policy. It simply does not occur to my straw man to raise the question: If the student revolutionary fails to see "truth" in his judgments about the university, is it not possible that the modern social revolutionaries might have failed to see "truth" in their more general judgments about social order? Once he raises such a question, the academic liberal is on the road to wisdom. (As Professor Frank Knight noted, Socrates had to die, not because he recognized how little he knew, but because he also recognized how little others knew.)

If doubts begin to stir about the private vision of "truth" possessed by the academic liberal, he may take the next and most vital step, which is that of questioning the existence of "truth" itself in matters of social policy. Is it possible that reasonable and equally well informed men might disagree finally on particular configurations of the "good society"? Is it possible that the despised and dismissed bigots may have been deserving of more consideration? Once he starts to ask such questions, the academic liberal may recognize that his "truth judgment" approach to politics and to social issues generally is fundamentally illiberal and intolerant. "Truth," in the final analysis, is tested by agreement. And if men disagree, there is no "truth." Acknowledgment of this test prompts an attitude of respect for and tolerance of the views of others, for dissenters, whoever they might be. But this attitude comes close to being the precise opposite of that espoused by the academic liberal in his nonuniversity role— the attitude imitated by the student revolutionary when he repudiated the equal freedom of others to hold views of their own. The point is that the arrogance and intolerance concerning the equal freedoms of others displayed so aggressively by the student revolutionary of the 1960's are simply miniaturization in extreme of characteristics that the postwar academic liberal has exhibited. If we are to be successful in persuading the student to respect the views of others who might disagree with him, to behave with tolerance toward those whose commitments differ from his own, and, finally, to accept the notion that "truth" is measured only in agreement, we must put the modern liberal thought patterns to the same test and demand the same changes. The call for law and order, for respect for established authority, for adherence to rules—all this is empty rhetoric until and unless it is supported by critically intelligent argument by men who themselves command respect. The argument is itself hypocritical if advanced by the academic liberal who disdains the views of others about the constitutional structure of society. Ambivalence in advocacy is rarely convincing.

Constitutionalism

In what respects has the modern or academic liberal's attitude been blameworthy? My attack must be supported, but I face difficulties because of the very generality of the attitude that I criticize. In sum, the view has been one that holds that society, the sociopolitical structure, can be remade at will to serve the explicit objectives dictated by the apparent "truths" of the 1950's, 1960's, and 1970's. To me this represents a terrible perversion of the constitutional attitude initially adopted by the founding fathers and held throughout the first century and one-half of our history. At some stage liberal thought became confused and underwent major transformation. The attainment of specifically defined objectives or goals for the collectivity was allowed to take precedence, in some rank order sense, over the traditional and classically liberal emphasis on the construction and maintenance of a social order within which individuals and groups with divergent goals could live in an atmosphere of mutual respect and cooperation. Once this transformation had taken place, it became necessary to distinguish categorically between the classical and the modern liberal. In continental Europe this confusion has not emerged. A continental liberal remains classical; the academic liberal of America becomes "socialist" in European terminology. Only in the United States has the confusion been manifest, so much so that some clear definitional distinction seems to be required. Many variants have been proposed; none has been widely accepted. On an earlier occasion I suggested the labels *left liberal* and *right liberal*. The word *libertarian* is perhaps more commonly used than any other to refer to the classical position. In this chapter I shall refer to the classically liberal, right liberal, or libertarian position as one embodying a *constitutional attitude*, and to a person who holds this position as a *constitutionalist*. I use these terms here not in particular advocacy of their adoption in all applications, but because they best convey the characteristic features upon which my discussion and emphasis are concentrated.

One further point should be made to avoid terminological confusion. I do not equate "constitutional" and "conservative." The genuine conservative may support the existing social and political constitution because it exists and has been long established. But the obverse need not hold: the genuine "constitutionalist" need not be conservative. He may seek radical reforms in social structure. He differs from the academic liberal not in his radicalism, and not in his willingness to propose change, but in his objectives for change. The constitutionalist seeks to reform the social structure by modifying the general rules of order, and by doing so in a process that preserves orderly measures for making further changes which are now unpredictable but which may be desired in the future. He places "preserving the means for change" high on his scale of valuation relative to "securing the specific objectives of change." He values "process" above "social priorities." By contrast, the academic liberal concentrates his attention, expediently and pragmatically, on specific short-run objectives that he desires the collectivity to achieve. He seeks the "good" directly, and he tends to be relatively unconcerned about the process through which it is sought. To secure the ends, he stands willing, if need be, to subvert or even to destroy the prospects for orderly change in an unknown future.

Once again these differences are summarized in the intolerance exhibited by the modern liberal. Why should we not seek the "good" and the "true," and why not do so directly? Since all men who are not bigots must agree with us, why should we really bother about constitutional process in the making of social reforms? Are not the reforms themselves the relevant and important things? What was wrong with the attitude of the Warren court when it simply declared to be constitutional that which it conceived to be the "good" and "true"? The modern liberal raises such questions only to answer them with his sneers at those who think otherwise. He seldom asks: What happens when disagreement arises, disagreement among those who cannot be readily separated into the right-thinkers on the one hand and the bigots on the other?

In a very fundamental sense, therefore, the constitutionalist views society differently from the academic liberal. The constitutional attitude emerges from a vision of social structure in which individuals and groups hold widely differing objectives of attainment. Collective organization and control are properly directed to prevent conflicts among individuals and groups when privately sought objectives produce clashes and toward the exploitation of joint-production possibilities for commonly shared goods and services. Beyond these limits, the "good society" of the constitutionalist embodies the Jeffersonian ideal of "least government." To such a person, the modern clichés about the loss of national purpose seem meaningless; he considers absurd the attempts to define "national goals."

In sharp contraposition, the liberal vision of social order is one of an organic entity in which individuals exist largely to serve the ends of the collectivity. In communist theology as well as practice this vision is explicitly described and implemented. In the creed of the modern American liberal the collectivism is not so evident, but it remains as the only consistent interpretation of a vision that seems often blurred and, of late, somewhat shopworn.

The student revolutionary of the 1960's adopted a curiously mixed pattern of attitudes. Explicitly and categorically he rejected the implied collectivism of the academic liberal. He recognized that the nation-state is a dead god, that individuals do not and should not be thought to exist to serve the collectivity in the large. In this individualism, which has its base in philosophical anarchism, the student revolutionary seemed to find common ground with the genuine constitutionalist. His behavioral slogan that each man "does his own thing" seemed immediately congenial to that person who holds the constitutional attitude. On the other hand, the revolutionary too often brought with him the intolerance of academic liberalism, and sometimes in extreme forms. He retained a "truth-judgment" approach or, what is even worse in the modern context, a "commitment" approach which often refused to allow time for even rudimentary doubt. In all this the revolutionary failed to see that the two sides of his ideology are mutually inconsistent. Each man's freedom to do his own thing implies the principle of equal freedom upon which constitutional order is based. One man's thing differs from another's, and this principle, in turn, implies that no man can act out of his own commitment so that it prevents others from acting.

Let us consider the dialogue that might have taken place between the student revolutionary of the 1960's and the academic liberal and, second, between both of them and the constitutionalist who stood on the sidelines. In the first of such confrontations, as I have already suggested, the academic liberal might have appealed to values. He might have argued that the revolutionary was "wrong," that he was blind to the "truth." The student's response would have been to the effect that such notions do depend on values, and, since he rejected the values of middle-aged, middle-class America, there was no basis for discussion. The dialogue would have ended before it had begun. The constitutionalist, who observed the frustration in the adversaries, might have had a contribution to make in commencing genuine dialogue in which all might have been able to participate. He might have said to both the student revolutionary and the academic liberal: "Your values differ one from the other and from my own, perhaps, and 'wrongness' or 'rightness' in behavior, 'truth' or 'untruth' in judgments depend on what values one holds. But both of you, and I, should be interested in developing and in maintaining an institutional structure within which all of us, and others, can exercise the freedom to differ in basic values and to behave differently in accord with those values. I criticize the student revolutionary not because he is 'wrong,' but because his behavior tends often to deny similar behavior on the part of others. Is it not possible for us to discuss rules under which individuals and groups with widely divergent value standards can go about doing their own things in harmony and mutual respect?" Perhaps both the student revolutionary and the academic liberal might have been too intolerant to have entered into such an invitation to discussion, but at the least the constitutionalist would have offered a prospect for dialogue.

The University as Collectivity

I do not wish, in this chapter, to present the student-university confrontation of the 1960's as a precise miniaturization of the in-dividual-collectivity confrontation, even if the university-as-collectivity model is accepted. But there seem to be sufficient parallels to make some further discussion of the analogy useful. Consider the university as a community, as a social order. The student revolutionary rejected what he considered to be the misguided objectives and goals of the university. He sought to change them, and in his clamor for reform he sought to substitute demands of his own invention for those in being. The objectives, the goals and purposes of the university, as these existed, seem to have been defined by old-fashioned, outdated authorities, with little relevance to modern reality. The constitutionalist observes and suggests a new vision of the university which provides the base for mutual coordination. He denies the existence of collective goals, objectives, or purposes, specifically and as such. His vision is of the "community of scholars," with each man and each group in this community exercising the freedom to carry out his own or its own objectives as privately conceived, with the university, as such, described by a set of rules designed primarily if not exclusively to insure against conflicts among individuals and groups within the community and to promote mutual respect among them.

If the collectivity does more than this, and if agreement does not spontaneously and mysteriously emerge, the will of the strongest must be imposed on all. Authoritarian definitions of objectives and coercion aimed at implementing these objectives must follow. Authoritarianism is the only effective alternative to constitutional order, whether the social interaction be characteristic of a university, a local community, or a nation. When this simple truth is fully recognized, all parties must acknowledge and accept limitations on their own power to implement their desires in exchange for constitutional protections against having the will of others imposed on them in turn. But even when a genuinely constitutional structure is in being, some decisions must still be made collectively and for application to all members of the community.

Again, let us use the university as our example, while continuing to acknowledge some of the larger implications of the argument. In some constitutionalist ideal we may think of the "community of scholars" as being characterized by an interaction system that allows some spontaneous order to emerge from the private behavior of individuals and voluntary subgroupings with little or no centralized decision making. Properly designed, the university might come reasonably close to such as ideal. Within practical limits, however, there would remain functions to be performed by the collectivity as an entity, decisions to be made that would, once made, be applicable to all members. This amounts to saying that even if the modern university should be stripped of many of its artificially derived powers of control over the free-search processes of its members, there will remain a set of decisions that can only be made for the whole entity. Who shall be admitted to membership? How shall members participate in decision making? What procedures shall be used to allocate scarce budgetary resources? How shall such decisions be made and by whom?

It is here that we return once more to the question posed in the first sentence of this chapter. Shall the student, as a member of the university, be granted a share in decision making, and if so, should this share be equal to or comparable with that granted the salaried administrator or tenured faculty member? Concentrating on this question in its university setting is especially helpful, because answers that seem clear in this focus are not so readily transferable to the larger world of political democracy. The liberal's standard response has already been noted: the student's voice should be listened to with respect, but he is uninformed, uneducated, and immature, and, most importantly, he is a short-term resident of a long-lived institution. One man, one vote, as a decision-making principle, is not applicable to students in the university's democratic processes. Some members are more equal than others in this community.

If this one-man, one-vote principle is *denied* elementary validity in the university setting, however, should it be *granted* elementary validity in political order generally? Again, the student revolutionary who demanded his share of power may have sensed the contradiction in the academic liberal's position. How can the liberal applaud the reapportionment decisions of the Supreme Court, based on an extremely naïve interpretation of the one-man, one-vote principle of democratic process, while denying to the student the relevance of the same principle in university constitutional procedure? The short-term membership of the student should be as equally relevant as the short-term citizenship of the Washington bureaucrat who temporarily resides in Arlington, Virginia. Yet with the near-universal applause of academic liberals, the Supreme Court held that Virginia's argument based on the short-term residence of bureaucrats was wholly inappropriate in allocating legislative seats.

Once again the liberal must face up to issues that he has for too long been allowed to evade. Is he the majoritarian democrat that he seems, or does he support apparent democratic process only as long as his own objectives promise to be advanced? Does the liberal's adherence to the one-man, one-vote principle last only as long as predicted practical implementation of that principle achieves specific short-run collective results? Is he democrat first and collectivist second, or the other way around? I submit that his values are reversed. The modern academic liberal is, first and foremost, collectivist, in that he seeks direct and expedient implementation of policy objectives which he thinks to be possible only through the exercise of centralized governmental powers. He remains relatively uninterested in the processes through which decisions are made, and he is willing to limit his support for democratic procedures if need be. He will be the first to applaud the subversion of orderly constitutional process, as indeed he so amply demonstrated in the 1950's and 1960's. No better example could be provided than the liberal's chameleonlike behavior with respect to presidential powers in the 1960's. He called loudly for an expansion of these powers during the Kennedy reign; he reversed his position dramatically within a few months after Johnson took office. The modern liberal will be the first to abandon the one-man, one-vote crusade when he senses that majorities inimical to his own interests are likely to emerge with force.

By my references to what I have called the "academic liberal," perhaps I have been whipping a horse already dead, despite his occupancy of seats of power in many university communities. How does the constitutionalist respond to the student's demand for a share in university decision making? First of all, and to repeat, the constitutional attitude requires a drastic reduction in the number and scope of centralized decisions that are made. The constitutionalist's first response to many issues is that collective decisions should not be made at all, in the sense of searching for outcomes that are to be applied to all members of the community. His vision is that of the "free university," within limits, and in this vision he again finds much that is common ground with the potential student revolutionary. In this respect the constitutionalist may willingly acquiesce in major dismantling of the existing power structure of the modern university, provided only that one power structure is not simply replaced by another. But how does the constitutionalist respond to student demands to share decision-making power for those decisions that all agree must be taken collectively? On balance, the constitutionalist is likely to be democratic in a much more meaningful sense than is his liberal counterpart. He is democratic, however, only because he sees greater evils emergent from alternative decision systems. While the constitutionalist may hold fast to the Jeffersonian principle of political equality, he recognizes the "as if" nature of the assumptions that must be made in framing constitutions. He is likely, therefore, to agree to assign the student a share in decision making while trying to insure that the decisions that are made are minimized. Perhaps more importantly, the constitutionalist sees little merit in majority rule, per se, and he may well consider that the constitution of the university should lay down varying rules for varying sorts of issues. By definition, once the truth judgment approach is dropped, majority rule implies coercion of minorities, and the constitutionalist desires to minimize coercion.

As I have noted on several occasions, and as would have been obvious even without my notice, I have employed this discussion of the students' reactions against the established university authorities of the 1960's as a vehicle for commentary that has much wider applicability. The university is not a miniature of society at large, but the comparisons are relevant within proper limits. In conclusion, however, I shall shift explicitly from the student-university confrontation and discuss briefly the central issue that seems to be presented in all this. I could rephrase the initial question without reference either to the student or to the university. Should the uninformed and uneducated eighteen- or twenty-one-year-old voter be granted a share in the control over the structure of political society that is equal to that of any other man? Should the illiterate, even if he is mature, be allowed the franchise? These are questions that are now too seldom raised. Can a viable society exist when voters are allowed to decide questions that they cannot remotely understand? Can man be allowed to ask questions that he cannot answer? This is the dilemma that has been posed in progressively serious form since the Enlightenment.

Only in the constitutional attitude is a partially satisfactory answer to be found. If men can learn to live with one another in a social structure where coercion is minimized, in which collective action is rigidly restricted within constitutional limits, political equality and universal suffrage can be constructive features of a free and participatory democracy. If, on the other hand, constitutional process is subverted, if collective action is unbounded, the way is open for the political demagogue to appeal to the lowest common denominator among the rabble. There is no other than the authoritarian way. We have, I think, seen ominous signals in recent years. I am not personally optimistic. It now seems likely that we must undergo the painful and tortuous process of trying, and perhaps belatedly, to learn again what the founding fathers knew only too well. As a people we have forgotten the simple principles of governing in a free society. The urgent question of our time is: Can we relearn these simple principles before destruction makes them irrelevant?

9

Notes on Justice in Contract

AFTER more than half a century of eclipse, social philosophy has reemerged into a position of respectability, within both the sometimes scarred halls of ivy and the pages of highbrow journals. The catalyst in this resurgence was John Rawls's book *A Theory of Justice*, published in 1971. In half a decade we have seen literally scores of critical papers, pro and con, devoted to the Rawlsian argument, several of which have been collected in special issues of journals in philosophy, political science, economics, sociology, law, and perhaps others. At least two books have appeared to counter Rawls, and we cannot yet begin to count the doctoral research projects that in one form or another incorporate Rawlsian criteria as basic reference points.

In this chapter, I shall discuss the Rawlsian conception of justice from my own perspective, which is that of a professional (and academic) economist whose interests have shifted increasingly toward basic issues in social philosophy. I consider myself sympathetic to Rawls's attempt, as I interpret it, while at the same time I remain sharply critical of the image of Rawls that has been so widely promulgated by both his friendly and his unfriendly critics.

Rawls's book has sparked an interest in conceptions of justice undreamed of a decade past. But Rawls's decisive contribution tends to be obscured by an unwarranted concentration of attention on the second of the specific Rawlsian principles, the difference or maximin principle of distribution. I have argued previously that this distributional principle is only one from among a set of possible outcomes that might emerge from a genuine Rawlsian process of evaluation, any one of which would be equally deserving of the attribute of justice. That is, in my interpretation of the Rawlsian framework the attribution of justice is directly derived from process or procedural criteria instead of any nonprocedural or independent assessment of end states, utilitarian or otherwise.[1] This is, of course, the contractarian element in the Rawlsian construction, an element that is wholly unnecessary, and has been held to be so,[2] in those interpretations which themselves incorporate end-state principles. Rawls himself is not without some ambiguity on the point at issue here, and it might be argued that a fully consistent contractarian position should have dictated that its advocate stop short of enunciating specific "principles" that are not, in themselves, embodiments of process.[3] In chapter 14, I shall suggest an explanation of why Rawls was led to suggest the difference principle. At this point I want to discuss in some detail the moral and ethical foundations of contract.

The Contractarian Imperative

Why is it necessary to introduce the notion of "social contract" in discussions of the moral foundations of the state? Only the incredibly naïve among social philosophers could ever have offered a literal contractarian explanation for the historical emergence of governments. If positive explanation is ruled out, however, what is the purpose of introducing an admittedly hypothetical construction?

Ultimately, the social contract offers the only bridge between the consent of those who are governed and the possible or potential legitimacy of the entity that purports to exercise powers of governance. If, however, people have not, in fact, consented to the set of rules—the laws and institutions—in being, what value is there is an imaginary construction which sets up hypothetical consent as a cri-

---

[1] For this reason I find it difficult to accept the applicability of Robert Nozick's persuasive general attack on end-state or patterned criteria of distribution to Rawls's basic arguments, an applicability that seems clearly to be implied in Nozick's treatment. See Robert Nozick, *Anarchy, State, and Utopia.* In this connection I should note that H. Scott Gordon, in his paper reviewing Rawls's and Nozick's books as well as my own, places all three of us in the procedural criteria group. See H. Scott Gordon, "The New Contractarians," *Journal of Political Economy* 84 (June, 1976): 573–590.

[2] See, for example, Sidney Alexander, "Social Evaluations through Notional Choice," *Quarterly Journal of Economics* 88 (November, 1974): 597–624.

[3] This was a central theme of my initial review article, "Rawls on Justice as Fairness," *Public Choice* 13 (Fall, 1972): 123–129.

terion for making evaluative judgments? The answer to this question can best be stated in opportunity-cost terms. What are the alternatives to the hypothetical social contract or quasi-contract? I shall discuss briefly four possibilities, although other variants might be introduced, and of course there are ambiguities in drawing sharp dividing lines among categories of this sort.

Anarchism. In the first approach, which I shall call an anarchist perspective, there is no legitimacy in governance, and it is folly and deception that prompts us to search for an attribute that cannot exist. The state, anywhere and everywhere and regardless of its internal structure, exists for and lives upon the coercion of some persons by other persons. Contractual agreements may emerge voluntarily from interpersonal agreements, but these cannot be used as bases for a normative theory of a nonvoluntary state. This vision of reality has considerable appeal, especially as an ideal, but even here it offers little other than a naïve utopianism under plausible assumptions about the behavior of observable human beings, and it offers no prospect of meaningful improvement by stages. If all state action is equally illegitimate, how can we expect to dismantle the existing structure save by total revolution?

Evolutionism. In the second perspective the whole complex of "laws and institutions" that define the social order, including those of government, is viewed as the outcome of a process of historical evolution. There is no constructive conception of "the state" or "the law" in any overall sense, and indeed, the very possibility of such conceptions is explicitly denied. The institutional results observed at any point in time are generated by the particular adjustments made by people to the various situations they confront. The English common law provides the archetype for this "invisible-hand explanation" of the state. The spontaneous coordination of the competitive market, which is perhaps the basic principle of economic theory and which has been central to this discipline since Adam Smith, is extended to include the emergence of legal-political-governmental structures.

By inference, if not directly, the results of this social evolutionary process are held to be efficient, if not in a static or equilibrium sense at least in the sense of moving gradually toward more efficient forms. In consequence, the existing structure is not readily amenable to improvement by "constructive rationalists." People should, therefore, acquiesce in and accept the existing institutions of society because of their acknowledged inability to generate improvements from any grand design for reform. In this perspective an entitlement conception of justice may emerge, as with Nozick. A less extended variant, exemplified in Hayek, may stop short of attributing "justice" to the status quo.

Marxism. A third, and familiar, perspective is the Marxian one, in which the state, in all of its institutional features, is simplistically interpreted as the embodied power of the dominant economic class. The instruments of government and the law are everywhere viewed as having been designed and as being used for the purpose of oppressing the working classes. Although this "explanation" carries with it strong moral overtones, these need not be present in its purest versions. The state cannot be "reformed"; it is an inherent part of the ongoing class struggle. There is surprisingly little treatment of the state "after the revolution," and some presumed stability in the power structure that is to emerge after the "withering away" of the bourgeois state seems inconsistent with the basic Hegelian framework. (Somewhat interestingly, the Marxian perspective incorporates elements of each of the three other noncontractarian views. Its denial of legitimacy to any activities of the state in being resembles that of the anarchist; its reliance on historical process has much in common with that of the evolutionist; its claim to "scientific truth" is, in itself, transcendental.)

Transcendentalism. In this perspective most often encountered in social philosophy, criteria for the legitimacy of the state, or for "justice" more generally considered, must be derived from values that exist or that may be discovered independently of the individual participants for whom the criteria are exercised. These values may be found in nature, in science, in reason, or from God. In any case, they are deemed to exist by the discernment of the witch doctors and/or the wise of every age and every land. Political-moral philosophy involves a never-ending search for these immutable "truths" that somehow transcend man and his independent and autonomous capacity for judgment. In such a perspective, consent is largely irrelevant.

Despite the dominance of this perspective in both traditional and modern social philosophy and social science (including political economy and welfare economics), I find it less appealing than the other noncontractarian alternatives, and especially that of the anarchist. I find the rejection of the legitimacy of any rule more congenial than the claim of any man to have discovered "truth" in values on his own or the claim that the state itself is God. The discourse among such claimants to wisdom cannot be expected to be other than a continuing, possibly entertaining, but also possibly deadly dispute.

The Contractarian Perspective. The four perspectives sketched out briefly above, and other variants of them, are not the only options that are available. The contractarian perspective or approach finds its value precisely in the deficiencies of its putative substitutes. It is necessarily somewhat more ambiguous in application, less clearly defined than some of its alternatives. Its potential use is inherently difficult, but not impossible. It is subject to abuse. Almost any conceivable activity of the state, either as observed or as imagined, may be explained as a conceptually possible outcome of some sort of "social contract." The problems here should not, however, be allowed to obscure the relative superiority of this perspective over its alternatives. Only some set of contractarian precepts or principles can resolve the problem of obligation of the individual in political society. A person can abide by the "laws and institutions" in existence if he can evaluate them as structural features that might have emerged from a social contract in which he might have participated.

Only the contractarian can effectively discriminate among the activities of the state, among the laws, without recourse to external evaluation. The following summation of the alternative perspectives may be helpful here:

1. To the anarchist all law is illegitimate.

2. To the evolutionist all existing law is legitimate and, by inference, just.

3. To the Marxist all existing law is instrumental to further the interests of the dominant economic class.

4. To the transcendentalist that law is legitimate, and just, which meets the external ethical criteria chosen for him by the witch doctors.

5. To the contractarian that law is legitimate, and just, which might have emerged from a genuine social contract in which he might have participated. That law is illegitimate, and unjust, which finds no such contractual basis.

Justice as Fairness

The notion of "justice as fairness" emerges almost directly from the contractarian perspective, while it carries little or no meaning in alternative perspectives. As a person observes the arms and instruments of the state, the institutions and practices of the law, how can he apply the suggested contractarian criteria? He cannot directly infer from his own relative position anything about the "justice" of the social order. Almost by necessity he is forced to examine the working properties of the whole structure, of the game itself, in the recognition that he is only one among many participants and that the observed results are those that reflect outcomes from a limited number of rounds of play. Relatively little sophistication is required to see, further, that probabilistic elements will enter importantly into the pattern of any set of observable outcomes. The question becomes: Could these results have emerged from a set of rules, a game, that might be deemed "fair"? But this moves the question backward to the one involving the meaning of "fairness" itself.

At this point I want to introduce some elementary economics, since I think that this disciplinary base does provide a better lead-in to an understanding of the contractarian approach and especially to the "fairness' criterion than almost anything else. Consider a very simple example in which there are two traders, A and B, each of whom is initially endowed with stocks of two consumption goods, X and Y (apples and oranges, if you will). We observe these persons to trade, to exchange goods, and we observe the attainment of some end-state result, an equilibrium. Trading stops, and the relative endowments of the two goods will have been modified by the process. How might we evaluate the outcome? There is no way to compare one outcome with another directly. Almost by necessity we are led to suggest that *any* outcome is acceptable as long as the trading process itself involves genuinely voluntary agreement among the persons, neither one of whom defrauds or coerces the other. As economists we say that which emerges from such voluntary trading is "efficient," and we are quite willing to define efficiency in terms of the expressed evaluations of participants in such processes.

It is a relatively small step which would allow us to replace the word "efficient" with "just" in application to the trading example.[4] We could easily say that that result or outcome is "just" which reflects the voluntary agreement of participants. And we move only a bit further to say that an outcome is "just" when the process that produced it is "fair," with voluntary agreement being the central property of "fairness."

Suppose, however, that we cannot directly observe a trading process; we cannot see traders agree one with another. We can observe only what appears to be an arbitrary distribution of endowments, of claims, along with a governmental-legal-institutional structure that sets out rules within which these claims may be enforced and within which further trades may modify the distribution among persons. How can we evaluate this observed complex structure against criteria of either "efficiency" or "justice," since the process through which it has been generated remains inherently unobservable and necessarily hidden in history? It is at this point that something akin to Rawls's "original position" must be introduced. We must ask ourselves whether or not the outcomes that we can observe, or could observe, could have been generated by a set of rules which might have been agreed upon in some conceptualized rule-making or constitutional stage of decision.

Note specifically that we do not ask the historical question of whether or not such a stage of decision can be identified and whether or not such agreement did or did not take place. When the purpose of the contractarian analysis is limited to that of evaluation, this question becomes largely irrelevant. As they may be observed in existence, the various institutions of social order may have evolved independently of design or intent; they may have been imposed by some despotic regime; they may reflect prior adherence to a prevailing set of ethical standards. The precise origins of institutions may be indirectly helpful, but an evaluation of these institutions for po-

---

[4] Adam Smith did use the word *just* in application to voluntary trading. And his system of "natural liberty" was evaluated in terms of justice as well as efficiency. Economists since Smith have perhaps concentrated too much on the efficiency properties of markets and have neglected the application of norms for justice. On this, see my "The Justice of Natural Liberty," *Journal of Legal Studies* 5 (January, 1976): 1–16.

tential reform need not be related directly to their history. The contractarian perspective, when carefully applied, allows us to evaluate institutions in a discriminating fashion regardless of origins.

I should emphasize once again that it is the conceptual agreement among all participants at the constitutional stage or in some original position that is the essential element of fairness. And here the elementary economics or exchange analogy is helpful; any rule is "fair" that is agreed to by all players. This statement is subtly, but significantly, different from the statement that fair rules will be agreed to by all rational players. "Fairness," as an attribute of rules, is defined by agreement; it is not, and cannot be, defined independently of agreement, or at least of conceptual agreement. From this definition it follows, or should follow, that uniqueness is not an expected property of outcomes qualifying under fairness criteria. Once again the simple exchange analogy is useful. Any one of a very large number of final, posttrading distributions of goods may be deemed to be "just." Even behind a genuine veil of ignorance, persons in original positions might unanimously agree to any one of a large set of possible rules for social order, any one of several sets of "principles of justice." There should be no presumption that the Rawlsian test must produce unanimous agreement on a unique set of principles.[5]

An example may be helpful in clarifying this point. In the United States we observe the traffic rule that requires us to drive on the right. In Great Britain we see a rule dictating that we drive on the left. Either one of these rules may have emerged from the unanimous agreement of the relevant participants in some hypothesized constitutional stage of deliberation. That rule upon which agreement emerges, partly by chance, can be classified as "fair" for that set of participants and for others who, in later periods, find themselves confronted with such a rule as a part of their ongoing social order. I shall return to this absence of uniqueness, because it is here that Rawls himself produced ambiguity by extending his basic construction in a manner that has caused the construction itself to be widely misinterpreted.

[5] H. Scott Gordon, in "The New Contractarians," p. 576, incorrectly interprets the veil-of-ignorance, original-position setting to be one which must necessarily produce agreement on a unique set of principles.

Comparative Institutional Evaluation *versus* Idealization of Principles

At this point it is necessary to distinguish two separate ways of using the basic contractarian construction, including the "justice as fairness" norm. In a loose sense this distinction represents the difference between my own efforts and those of Rawls, both of which seem to share essentially equivalent contractarian foundations. In the first we may utilize the contractarian framework to evaluate the existing institutions of social order, in the small or in the large. In *The Calculus of Consent* Gordon Tullock and I looked at the rules for making collective decisions. In his book *The Logic of the Law* Tullock applied essentially the same method to some of the more specific legal institutions. The method here is one of comparative institutional analysis and evaluation. It starts from abstracted models of institutions that are observed to be in existence, and it attempts to evaluate these models against contractarian standards. There is no direct requirement that the practitioner set up idealized principles.[6]

The second way of using the basic contractarian construction is to try first to derive ideal principles, independently of any evaluation of those rules that might be observed to exist. This is the Rawls approach, and the basic question posed concerns what can be predicted to emerge from agreement among reflective men placed behind the veil of ignorance in the original position. This approach is presumably an effective way of organizing one's thoughts about first principles, and it does allow the philosopher to place himself in an imagined setting that requires no appeal to transcendental norms. The question posed is deeper than those presented in the alternative method suggested, but this depth is secured only at the expense of distance from reality. If the philosopher remains unwilling to place existing institutions on some agenda for critical scrutiny, he must make the heroic effort of deriving first principles, from scratch as it

---

[6] The contrasting methods may be illustrated by Adam Smith on the one hand and modern economists on the other. Adam Smith looked at the economic institutions about him and tried to determine whether or not they were consistent with his principle of natural liberty. Modern economists first set up elaborate models of theoretically perfect market systems before even beginning to consider the operation of the institutions that they observe.

were. This now explains to me why John Rawls felt it necessary to go beyond an emphasis on process or procedure, to go beyond his earlier definitions of "justice as fairness." Failure to have done so would have left his construction open-ended and without content precisely because of the nonobservability of any constitutional agreement, precisely because men could never, in fact, be placed behind the veil of ignorance.

Such an extension beyond process was not, however, achieved without major cost. In his attempts to define the specific principles of justice that could be predicted to emerge from conceptual agreement among reflective persons in an original position, Rawls found it necessary to discuss end states, notably in his elaboration of the difference principle of distribution of primary social goods. Since it is logically easy to separate end-state and procedural criteria, it is not at all surprising that Rawls's critics, pro and con, interpreted his effort as one that involved the erection of an unnecessary contractarian superstructure for the end state that he desired to advance for independent reasons. To both his presumed egalitarian "friends" and his presumed antiegalitarian "enemies," Rawls's central emphasis on process is largely obscured.

How might such misinterpretations have been avoided, while still retaining content in some sketch of contractarian principles of justice? In my view, Rawls might have been more successful in getting his message across had he used the fairness criterion to *reject* specific principles of justice (the entitlement principle advanced by Nozick?),[7] even if such principles might have to have been invented or imagined for the purpose of demonstrating the operational content of the contractarian construction. This use would have allowed for the emergence of alternative principles within an acceptable set, any one of which might have been alleged to emerge from conceptual agreement. The difference, or maximin, principle of distribution of pri-

---

[7] It would seem difficult to bring an entitlement theory of justice in distribution of holdings within the contractarian fairness framework. Would reflective persons, behind a veil of ignorance, adopt and agree on rules for a game in which the cards are never reshuffled? In such a game everything would depend on the first-round allocation, and even if the participants remain wholly uncertain about their own position relative to others, it seems unlikely that so much would be left to depend on a single round. At least such a game would tend to become much less interesting than others that involve an occasional reshuffling, even if it is partial.

mary social goods might, in this way, have been presented not as *the* unique principle of justice, the unique rule emergent from agreement, but as *one* possible rule in a set of plausibly acceptable alternatives. The maximization of expected utility, the rule that economists have most often posed in opposition to the difference rule, might have, in this way, been allowed to occupy its claimed place in the Rawlsian spotlight, along with other rules—for example, those embodying an "insurance" motive—that might seem less egalitarian when adjudged in end-state terms.

The Relevance of Rawls

In my view Rawls is not merely a transcendentalist in contractarian cloth. As my discussion in chapter 14 below will suggest, under one interpretation the difference principle emerges as a part of a normative "theory of order," and indeed, it could have been advanced independently of a normative "theory of justice." To the extent that persons and groups are motivated by self-interest, even demonstrably "unfair" games may remain viable if something akin to the difference principle of distribution is implemented. The "bread and circuses" component of acquiescence in governance should never be overlooked. And some of those critics who have interpreted Rawls as having provided the intellectual bases for straightforward socialist schemes of income and wealth redistribution seem to have overlooked the lexically superior principle of equal liberty.

But Rawls's concern is with justice in addition to order, and perhaps his objective might be stated more accurately as that of defining the principles for a "just social order." His central achievement is the derivation of both of his principles from the contractarian process without introducing logically contradictory end-state normative criteria. This is not to suggest that alternative principles might not have been derived under somewhat differing assumptions. Properly interpreted, the Rawlsian principles for a just social order remain "good" because they reflect conceptual agreement among persons in an original position; they are not "good" because they satisfy transcendental norms of "goodness" as defined by Rawls or by anyone else.

Although his central vision of "justice as fairness" was developed in the 1950's, we must recall that *A Theory of Justice* was largely written during the 1960's. Along with the rest of us, John Rawls observed an American society that seemed to be becoming increasingly vulnerable to disruption. As the reception of his book has amply shown, the time was ripe for a thorough examination of our philosophical foundations. To his credit Rawls was unwilling to play at being God, the preoccupation of so many of his colleagues, in philosophy and other intellectual disciplines. And therein lies the relevance of his work. Unless we are to be rescued by a "savior" or "saviors" who will enslave us all, modern men and women must reform their own institutions. Rules can be changed while the game continues to be played, but few players are willing to delegate decisions on such changes to the self-anointed witch doctors. In such case the changes can be implemented only through agreement, and agreement can be reached only when all players test proposals against their own conceptions of fairness.

An American society that was initially grounded in contract may live off its capital for a while longer. Men and women may retain some of the freedoms that history has bequeathed to them. But this capital must depreciate with time, and we stand in real danger that a loss of understanding of our contractarian foundations will place us in a situation comparable to that which faced the Romans when they sought to build the Arch of Constantine. Without some contractarian basis there is no free social order possible. Rawls has contributed greatly to what I have called a "contractarian revival." It would indeed be tragic if his central contribution in this respect should be neglected in some gadarene rush toward end-state norms of measured equality, norms which can only be advanced by an unlimited Leviathan.

10

The Use and Abuse of Contract

In this chapter I propose to examine the limits of the basic contractarian paradigm in helping us to understand and to suggest meaningful improvements in the social order that we observe. I shall defend the contractarian position against modern critics who have mounted attacks from at least two sides of an imaginary spectrum. Social contract theory is pilloried because it is seen as legitimizing everything about the modern state that seems objectionable, while at the same time but from quite different quarters the theory is castigated because it appears to offer a not-too-subtle defense for the ruling classes in the status quo.[1] Each of these criticisms is, within its advocate's interpretation, valid. Both are misdirected when the contractarian paradigm is appropriately articulated.

There are limits to both the explanatory-evaluative potential of contractarianism and its ability to satisfy the normative yearnings for a better world. In part, my aim here is to deflate the excessive claims for social contract theory that have been advanced, directly or indirectly, by some of the theory's critics while upholding the claims that may be properly defended. I shall proceed by first discussing in some detail the explanatory-evaluative use of contractarianism. Following this, I shall discuss the implications for social policy action that may emerge. I shall try to show that it is in the social policy

[1] The first criticism is one of the central themes of the late Alexander Bickel's much-acclaimed book *The Morality of Consent*. Bickel holds up his preferred Whig approach in contrast to his caricature of the contractarian position. The second criticism is advanced perhaps most clearly by Warren Samuels in "The Myths of Liberty and the Realities of the Corporate State: A Review Article," *Journal of Economic Issues* 10 (December, 1976): 923–942.

implications that the most serious distortions of the social contractarian's position may be identified. By defending against the first set of critics, however, my argument may seem to lend support to those who condemn the contractarian limits on normative grounds. The relationship between social contract theory and the alleged defense of the status quo must be squarely faced.

The Economist as Contractarian

Let me commence with my economist's habits, which can be turned to good account here. Economists look at the world and try, or should try, to explain as much of it as they can. They are specialists in exchange; they know, or should know, how the various institutions of exchange work.[2] When they observe a social interaction, they interpret the results in exchange terms, as possibly emergent from voluntary actions. To the extent that results can be fitted into the exchange pattern, economists can infer that *all* parties secure gains, as these gains are measured in terms of the participants' preferences and not those of the observer.

This explanatory task of the economist is, of course, drastically simplified when the exchange process, in itself, may be directly observed. When one person is seen to transfer goods voluntarily to another while the second person is seen to reciprocate with a return transfer, there is relatively little ambiguity in classifying the results as *efficient* and the process as *efficiency-increasing*, terms that necessarily carry with them evaluative meaning. This explanatory-evaluative task for the economist may be extended from the simplest to the most complex institutional structures.

The economist is allowed to say that "markets fail," or, to use the terminology introduced above, to say that an exchange process is not "efficiency-increasing" and the results not "efficient," when he is able to identify, conceptually or in actuality, nonvoluntary changes in personal endowments of goods and services. For example, the welfare

2 This specialization in the institutions of exchange is the domain of the economist; he is not appropriately defined as a specialist in applied maximization, despite much evidence to the contrary in modern economists' practice. For the methodological defense of my position here, see my paper "What Should Economists Do?" *Southern Economic Journal* 30 (January, 1964): 213–222.

economist raises questions when an exchange between A and B inflicts apparent damage on C, who is not a party to the contract between A and B. He is also likely to evaluate negatively the results of an exchange between E and F when he observes that G and H have apparently been prevented from entering the potential exchange as either alternative buyers or alternative sellers.

In this familiar explanatory-evaluative role the economist is remaining within the *contractarian paradigm,* although this term is rarely applied in this context. Before shifting discussion from the economist to the social scientist generally, however, it is useful to clarify the economist's evaluative task. What lies beyond diagnostic evaluation? Suppose that a feature in the environment is defined to be "inefficient." From this it follows that a shift toward "efficiency" should be socially desirable. But it is precisely at this point that many economists become inconsistent with their own contractarian model. They fail to keep within the bounds of voluntary exchange. To say that a situation is "inefficient" is to say indirectly that there must exist means to move toward "efficiency" by voluntary agreement. It is not to say that all moves toward "efficiency" in results are independently desirable, including those moves which might have to be imposed against the desires of participants. Any economist worth his salt can diagnose a tariff as generating inefficient results in terms of the standard criteria; he *cannot* use this diagnosis as the basis for recommending that the tariff simply be repealed.

The observing economist can suggest ways and means through which improvements may be made by agreement among all parties, and the test of his hypothesis lies only in agreement itself.[3] In the tariff example, agreement may require that those owners and workers in industries previously protected be compensated, that their existing entitlements be "purchased" by those in the community who stand to secure net benefits by the removal of the tariff barrier. If the tariff does, indeed, generate inefficient results, the gains will be more than sufficient to compensate those who are harmed.

In terms of the economists' standard criteria, observed ineffi-

[3] This basic normative position for the economist was discussed in some detail in my paper "Positive Economics, Welfare Economics, and Political Economy," *Journal of Law and Economics* 2 (October, 1959): 124–138; the paper was reprinted in my *Fiscal Theory and Political Economy,* pp. 105–124.

ciency may or may not be consistent with agreed-on constitutional rules. Some inefficiency must be predicted to emerge from the sequential operation of any less-than-unanimity decision rules, and the costs of securing unanimity may exceed those reflected by such economic inefficiency. To an extent, at least, some economic restrictions such as tariffs may fall within this category. On the other hand, the economic inefficiencies observed may exceed those limits imposed by the costs of less-than-unanimity decision rules, reflecting in this case a situation that could not have emerged from the agreement among informed participants at the constitutional stage.[4]

It is the latter situation that places in clear relief the most difficult question that the contract theorist confronts. Suppose that an entitlement in the status quo is acknowledged to be demonstrably contrary to that pattern of entitlements that might have emerged from voluntary contract, from agreement among parties at some stage of constitutional negotiations. Is this entitlement to be respected in the sense that its holder (or owner) is to be considered as a necessarily willing participant in any change? Is the status quo distribution to be respected as the starting point or basis from which contracts may be renegotiated for the purpose of implementing change? In my view we must answer these questions affirmatively, not because the entitlements deserve "respect" in some normatively evaluative sense, but because there exists no alternative means of deriving acceptable judgments about change.

Can Prescription Follow Diagnosis?

Implicit in several of the modern criticisms there is what might be called a pseudocontractarian position involving a quite different stance. This position suggests that something akin to a contractarian logic is to be applied in evaluating the existing pattern of entitlements, but that there exists no contractual constraint on imposing changes in the status quo. It is precisely this use of hypothetical contract as the basis for nonvoluntary impositions of changes in political-

---

[4] The economist can readily diagnose cases of inefficiency in the first sense noted. He faces a much more difficult task in trying to determine whether or not the "economic constitution," which includes the costs of decision making as well as the costs of the results, is or is not "efficient."

legal structure that Bickel so sharply criticizes. In this interpretation the whole contractarian argument becomes little more than rhetoric for construction of the observer's own version of a "social welfare function."[5]

The normative constraints within which the contractarian must operate seemingly become much more severe when we shift away from the familiar economic examples—tariffs and restrictions on entry into trades and professions—toward examples of political and legal entitlements. I shall introduce only one example that has been recently important in American constitutional law, the issue of apportionment of legislatures. Using the notion of social contract in its evaluative role, can an observed disproportion in representation among districts be rejected out of hand? That is, would a legislative assembly containing members from rural districts smaller in population than those represented by urban members necessarily be inconsistent with contractarian precepts? Could such a structure have emerged from a constitutional agreement in which potential residence was unknown? The answers here depend on the predicted working properties of alternative structures of representation. If predictions were made to the effect that rural citizens tend to be more stable in some meaningful sense than their urbanized counterparts, the apparent divergencies in political power may be rationalized, even on strict contractarian grounds.

By comparison, however, consider a situation in which legislative districts vary widely in population, but in which such variations exhibit no relationship to meaningful criteria for stability or anything else, and in which the observed pattern seems clearly to have been produced from explicit discriminatory motives. In this case the observer can reject the status quo apportionment on contractarian principles. But from this it does not follow that reapportionment is thereby justified in the absence of consensus or agreement. Just as in the more familiar economic examples, the shift from diagnostic evaluation to action independently of agreement involves a leap beyond contractarian limits. Diagnoses based on hypothetical contract can be useful in making initial evaluations of existing institutions, evalua-

[5] This is the interpretation, or misinterpretation, that Sidney Alexander placed on Rawls's work in "Social Evaluations through Notional Choice," *Quarterly Journal of Economics* 88 (November, 1974): 615.

tions that can become inputs in attaining consensus upon suggestions or proposals for change. But hypothetical contract provides no justification for the imposition of change nonvoluntarily. In this respect hypothetical contract has no advantage over the more familiar transcendental norms—economic efficiency, natural law, reason, truth, God's will, and so on. The contractarian construction used in evaluative diagnosis finds its advantage only when attempts are made to reach agreement on change.

But why should persons who possess advantages in the distribution of entitlements in the status quo ever agree on any change? Why should voters in the small-number districts ever agree to proposals for equitable reapportionment? Once again we may refer to the tariff example for comparison. We suggested above that for the latter, compensations might be required to secure the agreement of those owners and workers who have been protected behind an existing tariff barrier. Legal-political institutions that may be judged to be "inefficient" on contractarian principles are different from economic institutions only because they seem more difficult to analyze in value-equivalent terms. In principle there is no difference between suggesting that those protected by an existing "inefficient" tariff be compensated in order to secure their agreement on some change in trade policy, and suggesting that those who have been assigned more political power by historical gerrymandering of legislative seats be compensated in order to secure their agreement on some change toward a more "efficient" and equitable apportionment.

I am not suggesting that the compensations required to secure the approval of presently advantaged groups on changes from "inefficient" to "efficient" institutional arrangements will be easy to work out, whether the institutions be economic or political. I am suggesting that in the absence of general agreement or consensus the contractarian has no more license to impose his preferred changes than has any other "reformer." This restriction implies that the contractarian who genuinely seeks improvement on his own terms must necessarily enter the sometimes grubby world of debate, discussion, compromise, bargains, long-range deals, logrolling, package arrangements, and side payments. This apparently pedestrian effort, which may fail even in what may appear to be potentially the most promising opportunities for improvement, is necessarily less appealing aesthetically than the manipulation of imposed idealist solutions with or without the power to impose them on the community.

Because I write as an economist and because I use economists' terminology, it is necessary that I clarify the meaning of *compensation* in the discussion, lest my argument be seriously misinterpreted. The compensation payment required to secure agreement is measured only by the result itself, only by the observed agreement on the part of those who, for any reason, initially stand in opposition to proposals for changes that might emerge from a contractarian diagnosis. Consider the apportionment example once again. If soundly based contractarian argument succeeds in convincing holders of differentially greater political power in the status quo that the existing situation is unjust, they may possibly agree to a constitutional change even in apparent contradiction with their own economic interest. In this context the convincing argument itself is the compensation; it meets the test of achieving agreement. It is precisely in this sense that basic contractarian argument on principles of justice, exemplified by the work of John Rawls, may be highly productive. To the extent that argument, debate, and discussion can generate consensus on change, on reform, the need to resort to more overt means of compensation is reduced or eliminated. But regardless of means, the aim of compensation is to secure agreement and in so doing to further the prospects for achieving genuinely voluntary reform.[6]

If the normative use of the contractarian paradigm is restricted as I have suggested, the second major criticism becomes applicable. If contractarian evaluation is not to be employed for the derivation of standards that may be imposed on all participants in the social order, changes from the status quo secure normative approval only to the extent that they emerge from voluntary action. That is to say, normatively sanctioned movements must themselves be "contractual" in the broadest meaning of this term. (The contractual elements may, of course, be applied at several levels of institutional structure.)

---

[6] I can place my argument here more directly in a Rawlsian context. We may interpret *A Theory of Justice* as an essay in persuasion, as an attempt to convince readers that they should agree on, and by implication implement, Rawls's "principles of justice" where these principles are not met by existing institutions. It would be, in my view, a misinterpretation to suggest that Rawls's effort was aimed at offering a putative normative basis for the imposition of his "principles" by whoever might possess the power to modify existing institutions, independently of agreement.

This restriction suggests to some critics that the whole contractarian argument necessarily lends support to the relative distribution of entitlements in the existing status quo.

Contract and the Status Quo

I have suggested that the first argument against the contractarian approach is misdirected and that it is aimed at a "pseudocontractarianism" which cannot be defended. The second argument is more critical, since it is directed against the limited applicability of contractarian precepts that I have attempted to defend above. Bickel has attacked pseudocontractarianism because it justifies too much; Samuels has attacked "Wicksellian" contractarianism because it justifies too little. The status quo distribution of entitlements must be the starting point for the limited application of the normative contractarianism that I have outlined above. It is superficially plausible to suggest that this position must be an implicit defense of the status quo.

There are several effective counterarguments that may be made. First of all, it is essential to distinguish between *external* and *internal* evaluation and action. The contractarian rejects the role of external observer, the omniscient being who stands outside the network of personal interaction that a social community represents and whose values are not directly related to those of the participants, save as the latter may enter into the observer's own utility or preference function. The contractarian who remains himself a participant, and who acknowledges such a role, cannot simply "jump outside himself" and take on the trappings of a god. For the person who chooses to act in such a capacity, everything is possible, and he may approve or reject any given structure of holdings at will. Discussions among would-be gods are likely to be uninteresting to the contractarian who seeks to improve the world in which he lives.

Even if the possibility of external evaluation is rejected, however, and even if the observer acknowledges that he is among the observed in a complex social order, there seems nothing to prevent the observer from assigning his own private and personal value weights on alternative distributions of rights or entitlements among all participants.[7] And in such an evaluation process, the particular distribution existent in the status quo may be ranked well below many preferred alternatives. It is the operational usefulness instead of the intellectual possibility of such an evaluation that must be called into question here. The participant-observer may deplore the imputation of entitlements that exists, but this reaction amounts to little more than ranting unless and until it begins to inform those who have power to modify the existing order. If the participant-observer does possess such power, he will presumably exercise it; he will impose involuntary changes in the positions of those who have no power to prevent them. We could, however, scarcely refer to a status quo distribution of rights or entitlements in any equilibrium sense until all such moves have been completed. That is, meaningful description of a status quo distribution of rights among members of a community must presume that all unilaterally motivated changes that are within the powers of the persons concerned to implement have been made. We may then ask: What is the meaning and purpose of a *cri de coeur* in such a setting, a protest that is centered on the notion, passionately held, that something other than the status quo would be "better"?

Such protests may, of course, be explicitly "revolutionary," in the sense that their purpose is to incite people to form new coalitions that may exploit the coercive power implicit in joint action to impose the changes desired. To a large extent, normative discussion of social policy falls within this category. Most reform advocates consider themselves to be engaged in a persuasion effort which, if successful, will produce a coalition that will command sufficient political power to enforce its will. And the reform advocates of this stripe express no moral inhibitions about imposing their preferred outcomes on all of their fellows, independently of expressed agreement or consent. In part, this demonstrated willingness to impose nonvoluntary changes on the existing pattern of entitlements in social order finds its own moral support in some "truth judgment" conception of politics generally. To the extent that the existence of "truth" in politics is accepted, the intellectual problem is one of discovery and definition.

---

[7] For purposes of simplifying the argument at this point, we may assume that the evaluation is not based on contractarian criteria, as earlier discussed.

Once "truth" is found, there is no moral argument to be raised against its implementation. Consent is meaningless in this context. Opposition can be variously characterized as stemming from ignorance, folly, or the exercise of selfish interest. In any case, the views of those who actively oppose the truth-carrying zealots are not treated as worthy of respect. And any requirement to compromise with such views arises only because the reformists might otherwise lack the power to impose "truth" unilaterally.[8]

The contractarian acknowledges from the outset that he holds no such universal keys to social wisdom. There is no "truth" in politics that is at all akin to that in science. Politics is beyond truth; it is concerned with a process of social interaction involving individuals. Once the participants are defined by the entitlements they claim in the existing order, each person's attitudes count for as much as any other person's.

At some personal level the contractarian may, along with his fellow noncontractarian observer-participant, deplore elements of apparent "injustice" in an existing distribution of entitlements. But he is morally prevented from imposing changes in this distribution, even should he, or a political coalition armed with his advice, possess the power to do so. Who is to say that A's claims should be reduced so that B's claims might be increased? The contractarian cannot assume the moral arrogance that would enable him to answer such questions. And more importantly, he denies the legitimacy of any such arrogance on the part of any person or group of persons in the community.

Indirectly, however, this position may seem to provide moral sanction for the distribution of entitlements, *any* distribution, that may come to exist in the historically determined status quo. If no one is allowed to say that A's claims should be increased at the expense of B's, then are we not saying that both A's claims and B's claims, as they now exist, are somehow "just," or, at the least, "legitimate"? As I have suggested earlier, the contractarian must acknowledge the status quo as the starting point or basis for any agreement upon change. Does such an acknowledgment of existential reality amount to an entitlement theory of justice? Surely the contractarian need not go

8 See my review of *Rational Decision*, Nomos Ser. No. 7, ed. Carl J. Friedrich, in *The Annals* 359 (May, 1965): 189–190.

further than, or even nearly so far as, Robert Nozick in attributing "justice" to the status quo distribution.[9] Using his own version of hypothetical contract, the observer may identify and classify existing institutions as "unjust." But this identification and classification process can be appropriately used only to provide inputs in a discussion that might lead to agreement upon change. To classify an institution as "unjust" does not allow the observer to make a major moral leap beyond this classification and say that such an institution should be eliminated or reformed in the absence of consent.[10]

It should be evident that the contractarian paradigm is more natural to the economist than to his fellow social scientists and philosophers, and it is not surprising that modern contractarian discourse has been conducted within a logical, analytical structure that is like that employed by economists. Contractarian precepts can be conceived as ultimately productive of genuine social reforms as long as application is limited to economic institutions. "Inefficiency" seems to be more readily identified through the analysis of welfare economics, and both the direction and the quantitative dimensions of the compromises that might be worked out seem capable of estimation. It is not nearly so easy to see the advantages of a contractarian approach to social reform of legal and political institutions. "Efficiency" in the operation of such institutions seems to lose the more precise meaning that is present when evaluating the performance of economic institutions.

The difference in precision is more apparent than real. Even in the simplest economic examples a position is defined to be "efficient" or "optimal" when gains from trade have been fully exhausted. There is no objectively identifiable "efficient" allocation apart from

---

9 Robert Nozick, *Anarchy, State, and Utopia.*

10 In this context "justice" may be likened to "truth" in scientific inquiry. A scientist may advance an argument to the effect that a proposition is "true." His argument is entered into the scientific discourse, which may succeed in establishing a consensus among his fellow scientists. But the "truth" of the proposition emerges only in this agreement and not from some original objective reality. The scientist who originally advances the proposition has no grounds for imposing his hypothesis about its "truth" on his fellow scientists independently of the process of discussion leading to agreement. This is what Frank Knight meant when he stated that social scientists and social philosophers should adopt the morals instead of the methods of the physical scientists.

the observations of traders' unwillingness to engage in further exchanges. Economic institutions lend themselves to contractarian evaluation no better than do political institutions. But economists, who are specialists in exchange, do possess some comparative advantage both in understanding the contractarian logic and in appreciating its potential for application to social reality. Another way of stating this is to say that economists tend to concentrate their attention on a particular form of social interaction, on situations in which participants have divergent interests that are partially in conflict, but in which there exist potential gains to all. In the terminology of game theory, the emphasis is on positive-sum settings.

To the extent that real-world institutional reform can embody mutual gains, only the social contract theorist is intellectually and emotionally equipped to provide the initial critical groundwork for some ultimate organization of consensus. The noncontractarian tends to be too impatient. He will rarely seek out the consensus paths toward reform, even if such paths exist. And his apparatus does not allow him to make either a moral or an empirical distinction between positive-sum and zero or even negative-sum prospects. On the other hand, the social contract theorist must acknowledge his own inability to say much about alternatives that fall within the range of pure conflict, the regime of zero-sum social games. If "exchange," conceived here in its broadest possible meaning of cooperation and agreement, is not possible, all solutions are equal. The transcendentalist, of any one of several variants, may be able to discuss purely distributional shifts more adequately than the contractarian if only because his thought patterns force him to treat all social and political changes within a pure conflict paradigm.

A Public Philosophy

In conclusion, I want to stress the importance of contractarianism as a part of a public philosophy. Even if the processes through which political and institutional changes are made do not require generalized consent or agreement among all persons and groups in the community; even if majority coalitions in legislative assemblies are observed to be decisive on many issues; even if the sometimes arbitrary dictates of the executive agencies and the judiciary can modify the distribution of entitlements within wide limits, the public attitudes toward these decision-making institutions are critically important. On the one hand these institutionalized departures from contractual processes at the postconstitutional level can be viewed as embodying the continuing struggle of opposing interests, each one of which seeks to capture the arms and agencies of the state to promote and to further its own private ends, be these "noble" or "selfish." On the other hand, these institutional forms of postconstitutional decision making can be viewed as second-best alternatives to more inclusive decision rules made necessary by the presence of political transactions costs, but still reflecting consensus at the constitutional level. In the latter view, the results are still evaluated by the degree of consensus produced instead of the "victory" of one group over others.

In the latter contractarian view, the state in all its forms is interpreted as a necessary part of a complex exchange process that generates mutuality of gain. In the former view, the state becomes a mechanism or means through which some groups in the community secure "profits" at the expense of other groups. Social philosophers should recognize that their own conceptions of the state can have critically important effects on the attitudes of the citizenry.

PART III
THE ENFORCEMENT DILEMMA

11

Ethical Rules, Expected Values, and Large Numbers

WHAT influences an individual's choice among ethical rules? I shall demonstrate that the size of the group within which he consciously interacts is a critical determinant. Behavior for individual choice, even at this fundamental level of ethical rules, may differ sharply between small groups and large groups. This hypothesis is corroborated by well-known and commonly observed experience. To my knowledge, however, ethical theorists have neglected the apparent importance of group size.[1]

In the remainder of this introductory section I relate my discussion to the standard questions in ethical theory. In so doing I am guided solely by the necessities of the argument that I want to develop. My lack of competence to discuss ethical theory per se will be fully apparent. In the next section I shall discuss the individual's choice among ethical rules in terms of an ordering of potential social states or situations. One particular ordering will be advanced as plausible, and its appropriateness will be defended. The individual's choice among ethical rules will be shown to depend on this ordering along with his probability calculus concerning the ethical choices made by "others" in the relevant group. The section "The Relevance of Numbers" examines the importance of group size for this probability calculus, and simple examples are introduced to show how the individual's decision can be modified solely by a change in numbers.

---

[1] M. G. Singer's argument comes close at one point to incorporating size as such, but in a context different from that of this chapter. See his *Generalization in Ethics*, p. 137.

The dilemma of the individual who finds himself a member of a critically large group is treated in some detail. The section "Free Riders and Perfect Competition" develops comparisons with individual choice behavior in economic theory, where the relevance of group size has been recognized even if not sufficiently clarified. The final section briefly explores some possible implications of the critical-size hypothesis for reforms in social institutions.

To avoid preliminary misunderstanding, let me state what this chapter is not. It is not an essay in "ethics," by which I mean a discussion of what individuals should or should not do. Aside from that, as will be evident to informed readers, it is not designed to contribute to Kantian criticism, either in the traditional sense of discussing what Kant really meant or in the modern version of discussing the generalization principle. I shall be concerned exclusively with an individual's choice among ethical rules and with the possibilities of *predicting* that choice. Any analysis of choice must involve some consideration of the alternatives, and it is here that I accept, without argument, the relevance of something akin to the Kantian distinction between the *moral law* and the *subjective* or *private maxim*. My concern is with a question similar to one stated by Beck: "it is a question of what are the conditions, in a being like man, that make it possible for him to take an interest in the law and have the law as his incentive."[2] I am not directly interested in the individual's ability to make an appropriate distinction between that action dictated by the moral law and that dictated by the private maxim, either universally or in specific instances. I simply accept that the generalization or universality principle can be applied in a sufficient number of cases to make my argument, which is restricted to those cases, worth developing.[3] The analysis requires only that the individual be assumed to confront a choice among ethical rules and that something loosely similar to the Kantian dichotomy should describe the alternatives that he faces.

In this setting I want to examine the possibilities of predicting

2 Lewis White Beck, *A Commentary on Kant's Critique of Practical Reason*, p. 219.

3 My reading of the literature is admittedly spotty, but within these limits I find my own position to be reasonably close to that stated by Warner Wick in his review paper "Generalization and the Basis of Ethics," *Ethics* 72 (July, 1962): 288–298.

this choice. Note that the choice to be analyzed is that between separate *rules* for behavior, not that between separate *acts* in particular circumstances. Much of my discussion can be applied directly to the latter choice, but for reasons to be noted, there are advantages to limiting specific analyses to the choice between rules, which, once chosen, will serve to predetermine acts within the limits implied.

The individual is presumed to be facing the following question: What ethical rule shall I adopt as a guide to my behavior in subsequent actions? There are two alternatives before him. He can adopt a rule which we shall call the moral law, or he can adopt a rule which, loosely, we shall call the private maxim. By selecting the first, the individual commits himself to act in subsequent situations on the basis of something like the generalization principle. That is, he will not act in ways other than those which allow his particular action to be universalized, regardless of the specific consequences. By selecting the second rule instead, he commits himself in advance to no particular principle of behavior. He retains full freedom to act on the basis of expedient considerations in each particular situation that arises. Note that in terms of observed or revealed behavior in particular acts, there need be no difference in the results of these two ethical rules. The person who rejects the moral law as an ethical rule that effectively constrains his choices among acts may, nonetheless, fully accept the behavior dictated by this law in particular circumstances. For this reason the choice with which I am centrally concerned should not be interpreted as one between "moral" and "immoral" rules.

The Ordering of Social States

As soon as the notion of generalization or universalization is introduced, individual behavior embodies social content. The choosing, acting party interacts with other parties, whose behavior in turn becomes a part of the necessary environment within which his own choices take place. In this respect much of the Kantian criticism seems to me to have been overly individualistic. The individual's decision whether he should adopt the moral law or the expediency criterion as an ethical rule surely depends upon his own predictions about the behavior of others and upon his evaluations of comparative states of society incorporating that behavior. The rules predicted to be chosen by others will be important in determining the descriptive characteristics of alternative social states or situations.

We want to examine now the individual's evaluation of separate social states or situations, and we can best do so in terms of an ordering that he places on alternative consequences or outcomes. These outcomes can be described in terms of two sets of ethical rules: his own and those of others. Listed below in ascending rank is an ordering of six social states.

1. *The worst possible world.* The individual himself adopts the moral law, but almost none of his fellows do so. He should expect to be grossly exploited. This is clearly an undesirable state of affairs for anyone other than a masochist.

2. *Mondo cane.* This second state is only slightly better than the first. Here the individual predicts that almost none of his fellow citizens will follow the moral law as an ethical rule. However, in this combination he, too, follows the criterion of expediency. He can, by following the dominant behavior pattern, prevent differential exploitation.

3. *Commitment in a mixed world.* This is a state in which the individual predicts that roughly one-half of his fellows will follow some version of the moral law and in which he also adopts this law as an ethical rule. Along with the other committed persons in the group, he will expect to be forced, on occasion, to behave contrary to the dictates of expediency.

4. *Expediency in a partially committed world.* This state differs from the third only in the individual's own choice of an ethical rule. Here he adopts the rule of following his own private maxims in determining particular acts. Clearly, he will expect to experience, on some occasions, differentially favorable consequences from this retained freedom.

5. *The generalized world.* This state may, within limits, be called the idealized Kantian world. The individual who is making the ordering, along with substantially all of his fellows, adopts the moral law as a general rule for behavior. Mutual self-respect, honesty, duty— these make for a highly desirable social interaction process.

6. *Expediency in a duty-bound world.* In this final state the indi-

vidual himself retains the rule that allows him to act from his own private maxims, whereas substantially everyone else in the group follows some version of the moral law. Clearly, this state is the most desirable for the individual. He retains complete freedom to follow the dictates of expediency in particular actions as his own subjective attitudes may suggest, while he also enjoys a wider freedom to act, if he so chooses, strictly in terms of the categorical imperative.

I suggest that the ordering presented above is a reasonable one for most individuals. It may be objected that this ordering of social states itself reflects the evaluations of an immoral person because it does not impute to the adoption of the moral law itself a positive component or value. An individual, it might be argued, "should" and, if moral, "will" prefer a world in which he himself acts in accordance with the moral law because of some intrinsic worth of morality itself. I do not propose to quarrel with those who might take this position, even were I equipped to do so, but the possible objection along these lines is not germane to my analysis, and it is precisely to cover myself in this respect that I have concentrated on the choice of ethical rules rather than on the choice of acts. The individual may, for reasons indicated, prefer to act in accordance with the moral law even though he does not choose to adopt this law as his overriding ethical rule. However, if he places any value at all on a widened area of choice, he will tend to rank the states in which he retains such choice, all other things being equal, higher than the states in which this choice is explicitly narrowed.

The suggested ordering was presented in a simple numeral listing, from 1 through 6. Some numerical scale will be helpful in discussing the individual's choice of rules, but this scale is wholly arbitrary as long as the numbers stand in the same order one to another. For simplicity only I shall use the numbers in the simple listing to indicate the relative evaluations that the individual might place on the several possible social states. Alternatively, any number of zeros could be added to each number, or, perhaps more realistically, there may be multiples placed between each subset of two in the listing. In the latter case the ordering might run, in ascending rank, 1, 2, 30, 40, 500, 600, indicating wide differentials between the world of moral law as an ethical rule and the world of expediency. The point to be emphasized is, however, the essential arbitrariness of the particular numbers assigned. It is in part to emphasize this, as well as for simplicity, that the simple numerical listing will be used here.

We can summarize the individual's ordering that has been suggested in a simple two-by-three matrix (Fig. 3) in which the rows indicate the alternative rules that he may choose, while the columns indicate the possible behavior patterns that he predicts for others in the interacting group. It is evident that there can be as many columns as desired, depending on the detail with which the individual might want to specify his predictions about the choices of rules by others.

The information summarized in the matrix is not sufficient to enable us to predict how the individual will actually choose between the two ethical rules that he confronts. There is no indication at this point of his estimates of the probabilities of the choice patterns of others. Until we introduce such estimates, expected values for his own choice alternatives cannot be derived. We need to know what probability the individual assigns to each of the three possible behavior patterns of his fellows.

Let us suppose that he assigns a probability of 0.6 to the first pattern, 0.3 to the second, and 0.1 to the third. The matrix is then rewritten in the abbreviated form shown in Table 1, with the predicted or assigned probabilities in parentheses. Given the values in the ordering, along with the probabilities assigned in Table 1, we can compute expected values for each alternative confronting the individual who must decide. As the right-hand column indicates, the expected value from following the moral law as a rule is less than that from adopting the rule of expedient behavior. Under the conditions depicted, the individual can be predicted to reject the moral law as an ethical rule and to adopt instead a rule that will allow him to act in each case on his own subjective maxims.

| | | OTHERS | |
	ALMOST NONE FOLLOW MORAL LAW AS RULE	ABOUT ONE-HALF FOLLOW MORAL LAW AS RULE	ALMOST ALL FOLLOW MORAL LAW AS RULE
FOLLOW PRIVATE MAXIMS AS RULE	2	4	6
FOLLOW MORAL LAW AS RULE	1	3	5

INDIVIDUALS

Fig. 3

TABLE 1

Individual	Others			Expected Value
	None	One-half	All	
Private maxim	2(0.6)	4(0.3)	6(0.1)	3
Moral law	1(0.6)	3(0.3)	5(0.1)	2

The expected values depend, of course, on the probabilities that the individual assigns to the various patterns of behavior for others than himself. Careful examination of the numerical example reveals, however, that a change in these probabilities will not modify the choice of a rule that is dictated. Suppose, for illustration of this point, that the probabilities are changed from (0.6, 0.3, 0.1) to (0.0, 0.4, 0.6). Clearly, under this new situation the expected value under either rule is increased; the individual simply lives in a "better" world. But note that given the same rank ordering and same valuations, the expected value from adopting the moral law as a rule, which is now 4.2, remains less than the expected value from the alternative-rule choice, which becomes 5.2. Hence, we conclude that in this model, regardless of the pattern of rule choice that the individual predicts on the part of his fellows, he will not be led to adopt the moral law as a binding ethical rule for his own behavior as long as his evaluation of comparative social states remains that indicated in the matrix illustrations.

Ethical theorists may object to the use of any numerical scale to indicate the evaluations that the individual places on social states, and because I am an economist I may stand accused of introducing expected utility by the side door. I am, of course, tempted to call "that which the individual maximizes in his choice behavior" something like "utility," and the approach here stems from the expected utility analysis that is familiar in modern economics. I must emphasize, however, that the numerical scale does nothing except provide a helpful tool for analyzing individual choice among ethical rules, and any connection between this scale and "utility" in any connotation of "happiness" or "pleasure" can be quite explicitly rejected. Individuals choose what they choose, whether this be apples or ethical rules, and we can, in both cases, discuss their choices in terms of some ranking of "better" and "worse" results. If we could not do so, we should be unable to discuss choice at all. This facilitation of discussion is the only function of introducing the arbitrarily precise numerical ordering of social states. If this were the end of it, much of the matrix illustration would, of course, be almost wholly unnecessary baggage. As I shall demonstrate in the following section, however, the construction does enable us to reach significant conclusions.

The Relevance of Numbers

In a sense, the example presented above is deceptive because one assumption that is essential for the results has been deliberately left unmentioned. Recall that changes in the probabilities assigned to different rule choices on the part of others do not change the ranking of the expected values of the two alternatives for the individual who is trying to decide which rule to adopt for himself. But this is true only within the limits of the particular example, and it should have been noted that the reference individual was assumed to assign the *same* probability distribution to others, *regardless of his own choice of an ethical rule.* In terms specifically of the matrix of Table 1, the same probability distribution was assumed applicable for each row. This assumption will be appropriate only to those situations in which the individual predicts that his own choice of a rule in no way modifies or influences the similar choices of others.

Consider, now, a sharply different setting in which only this one element is modified. The probability distribution in the first row of the matrix, which applies when he rejects the moral law as a rule, is assumed unchanged from that of Table 1. For the second row, which holds when he chooses to adopt the moral law as a rule governing future acts, let us introduce a different probability distribution—that which was previously used as the modification of our illustration. The matrix will then look as shown in Table 2. Note that in Table 2

TABLE 2

Individual	Others			
	None	One-Half	All	Expected Value
Private maxim	2(0.6)	4(0.3)	6(0.1)	3
Moral law	1(0.0)	3(0.4)	5(0.6)	4.2

the expected value for the choice represented in "follow the moral law" now exceeds that for the alternative "follow private maxims." There is no change in the individual's ordering of the social states or even in his presumed numerical evaluations.

The question is one of determining the conditions under which an individual's rational calculus will lead him to assign probabilities of one sort or another. When will he assign probabilities of the sort shown in Table 2 instead of those of Table 1? The central hypothesis of this paper is that the size of the interacting group is one of the important determinants in this assignment. An individual who consciously interacts with only a small number of other persons in ethical relationships will tend to assign probabilities similar to those illustrated in Table 2, while the same individual, if he consciously interacts with a critically large number of other persons, will assign probabilities similar to those of Table 1. The precise numerical values are not, of course, important here. The only requirement is that there be some positive relationship between the individual's own choice of an ethical rule and the choices that he predicts for others.

The general validity of this hypothesis for the small-number model may be shown by reference to a simple three-person example. There are three persons in an isolated setting, say, a desert island, and each person faces the choice among ethical rules when considering how to behave with his fellows. Clearly, any one of the three will tend to recognize that his own choice of a rule, and subsequent adherence to it, will to some considerable extent influence the similar choices to be made and followed by the other two members. Since we may assume that each of the three prefers to live in a setting of mutual self-respect, as shown by our ordering, the most likely outcome will surely be one in which each and every person adopts, and follows, something that is akin to the Kantian categorical imperative.[4] His standard for behavior will be some version of the generalization principle.

This result will tend to emerge in a small group quite independently of the individual's particular evaluations of the several

---

[4] In the extreme, the analysis may be extended to the one-person group. In such cases the behavioral rule chosen or the action taken will necessarily be the one-person analogue to the generalization principle. It is essentially on these grounds that the Aristotelian defense of private property is based.

possible social states as long as the suggested rank order holds. The differences in evaluation between the idealized Kantian world and that peopled by subjective maximizers may be great or small. The critical requirement is located only in the diagonally weighted probability assignments of the matrix. The upper right-hand cells must tend toward zero in expected value because of the unlikely event of the indicated combinations of rules emerging in the social interaction process. In small groups the individual simply cannot expect uniquely to enjoy a widened range of choice.

The small-group model can be contrasted with that which includes a large number of persons, for which the matrix illustration of Table 1 applies. Here, the individual considers his own choice of an ethical rule to exert no influence on the choices of rules made by others; in effect, the choices of others are treated as a part of the natural environment, so to speak, and not dependent on the individual's own decision. In this limiting case the individual must make probability assignments that are described in their critical characteristics by Table 1. An interchange between the rows in the matrix will not change the probability distribution of the choices of rules by others.

It is perhaps worth emphasizing that my argument is not the relatively familiar one that presents the plight of the potentially honest man who finds himself among thieves. In a group of critically large size, the individual will tend to adopt the rule of following the expediency criterion even if he thinks that *all* of his fellow citizens are saints, provided only that the suggested ordering holds. Numerically, this is clearly shown in the illustrations, but repetition of the point seems warranted. The conditions of individual choice are such that there will be a rationally based rejection of the rule, "follow the moral law," quite independently of predictions about the ethical rules that may be chosen by others in the interacting group.

If the analysis is applicable for any one individual in the critically large group, it must, of course, be applicable to all. Because of this interdependence, each member (and hence all members) will find himself in a genuine dilemma. He may value the social state depicted by the combinations on the right-hand side of the matrix much higher than those on the left. But despite this valuation he will find that he ends up, necessarily, in the upper left-hand cell. Rationally, he cannot adopt the moral law as a principle for his own behavior. Neither can his fellows. Therefore, the predictable consequences of ethical choices are those characteristic of a world in which all persons reject the moral law as a controlling rule and, instead, follow their own private maxims. Each and every person may, of course, consider that he would be "better off," in terms of his own evaluation, in a different world where the moral law is widely accepted as an overriding ethical rule. But privately and voluntarily there is simply no means through which the single individual can choose to make this alternative state of the world more nearly realizable.[5]

The dilemma is a real one, and it is similar to, although not identical with, that which is commonly discussed in game theory as "the prisoners' dilemma." In the latter dilemma, each of two prisoners is led to confess by the conditions of the situation in which he is placed, despite the fact that both prisoners would be in a more desired position if they would both refrain from confessing. The difference between the prisoners' dilemma and the large-group ethical dilemma discussed here lies in the fact that as ordinarily presented, the former remains a small-group phenomenon. The results emerge because of the absence of communication between the prisoners and because of their mutual distrust. The large-number dilemma is a more serious one because no additional communication or repetition of choices can effectively modify the results.

There is nothing in the analysis that suggests the actual size that a particular group must attain before the individual choice calculus undergoes the relatively dramatic change that has been noted. It seems evident that the dividing line between the critically small group and the critically large group will vary with many circumstances, and no attempt will be made here to list them. Similarly, it is also clear that individual differences will make for important differences in ethical choices. Under identical external circumstances, some members of a group of a given size will tend to choose rules as if they are

5 The large-number dilemma is apparently familiar to ethical theorists through numerous examples, but the relevance of large numbers per se has not been appreciated. For examples of situations in which the dilemma appears, see Singer, *Generalization*, pp. 69–70, 86–87.

interacting in a critically small setting, while other members may choose rules as if the group is critically large.[6] The hypothesis does not require that these distinctions be made. All that is necessary for the hypothesis to hold is that for any given individual who may be observed to follow what may loosely be called the rule of moral law in his small-group interactions, there is some increase in group size that will cause him to modify his ethical rule and become a private maximizer.

When stated in this fashion, the numerous corroborations of the hypothesis in everyday experience are familiar. Volunteer fire departments arise in villages, not in metropolitan centers. Crime rates increase consistently with city size. Africans behave differently in tribal culture than in industrialized urban settings. There is honor among thieves. The Mafia has its own standards. Time-tested honor systems in universities and colleges collapse when enrollments exceed critical size limits. Litter is more likely to be found on heavily traveled routes than on residential streets. Even the old adage, Never trust a stranger, reflects a recognition of this elemental truth, along with, of course, additional ethical predictions. Successful politicians organize grassroots support at the precinct level.

Only some of these examples are explicitly ethical, but the phenomenon is not limited to the choice of ethical rules or acts. The large-number dilemma pervades many areas of social interaction.

Free Riders and Perfect Competition

The proposition that this paper extends to ethical theory has been widely recognized in economics, although even there the vital distinction between behavior with respect to individual choice in small-group and in large-group situations has not always been fully appreciated. Two separate applications will be summarized here. The

---

[6] In an interesting study of individual voting behavior in American municipalities, Edward C. Banfield and James Q. Wilson have noted significant differences in patterns of choice among different ethnic groupings. They attribute these differences in part to the divergent "public consciousness" of these groups. See their "Public-Regardingness as a Value Premise in Voting Behavior," *American Political Science Review* 58 (December, 1964): 876–887.

first of these, commonly called "the free-rider problem," is a direct analogue to the ethical theory extension, and my work on this problem provided the specific stimulus for this chapter. The second application is, in one sense, the inverse analogue; it is the whole notion of "perfect competition," a notion that has been basic to economic theory for almost a century.

The free-rider problem arises in the theory of public finance or, more properly, in the theory of the supply of public goods. This analysis attempts to derive an explanation for the supply of public goods, as contrasted with private goods, from the choice behavior of individuals. The question is: Why is political or governmental organization required at all? Why does the market or exchange process "fail," in some meaningful sense, when goods and services exist that must necessarily be shared in common by large numbers of persons? An examination of the conditions for equilibrium attained under private or independent trading adjustment reveals that the results are clearly nonoptimal. If so, what is there to prevent further pressures designed to remove the remaining mutual gains from trade? The answer to these questions is found in the tendency of each person who is a potential beneficiary from the commonly shared public good to choose, rationally, to remain a "free rider." If the potential benefits are genuinely nondivisible among separate persons, each one will find it to his own private advantage to refrain from making voluntary contributions toward the costs of provision. This tendency remains true despite the possibility that the total benefits to be derived from supplying the good, over all persons, may greatly exceed the total costs. And it may apply for each and every member of the group simultaneously without changing the results. Each person may consider that he would be better off in a situation where he, along with each of his fellow citizens, contributes a share in the common cost than in a situation where no one contributes anything. Yet each person may refuse, rationally, to contribute to this cost on an individualistic and voluntary basis. The equilibrium position is evidently nonoptimal, which may be recognized by all participants, but unless the rules are somehow changed, the large-number dilemma holds. This result emerges, of course, only when the size of the group is critically large. Only in such large groups will the individual consider his own action to exert substantially no effect on the actions of others.[7]

The very use of the term *free rider*, however, suggests that the significance of the large-group dilemma may not have been fully appreciated. This term suggests some deliberate effort on the part of the choosing individual to secure benefits at the expense of his fellows. In the only situation in which the problem really emerges, however, the choosing individual enjoys no sensation of riding free, of "letting George do it." There is no personal interaction present at all. The individual is simply reacting to an environment in which he finds himself, to "nature," so to speak, not in any way against his fellow citizens.

Once the large-number dilemma is understood, the failure of the market process to produce optimal results when public goods are present is explained. Further, as the argument has been developed, an explanation is provided for the tendency of individuals to turn to changes in the rules, specifically to the introduction of political, governmental processes as substitutes for market processes. Such changes in the institutions or rules can, of course, impose upon all members of the group common standards of conduct. From the analysis developed along these lines it becomes conceptually possible to demonstrate why, under certain circumstances, individuals will, on purely rational grounds, agree to allow themselves to be coerced.

The similarities between this analysis of individual choice behavior in contributing to the cost of public goods and that applied

---

[7] The first explicit recognition of the problem here is found in Knut Wicksell's classic work *Finanztheoretische Untersuchungen*. Relevant portions of this work are published in translation as "A New Principle of Just Taxation," in *Classics in the Theory of Public Finance*, ed. R. A. Musgrave and A. T. Peacock, pp. 72–118. The classic modern treatments of the theory of public goods all recognize the existence of the free-rider problem. See Paul A. Samuelson, "The Pure Theory of Public Expenditure," *Review of Economics and Statistics* 36 (November, 1954): 387–389; his "Diagrammatic Exposition of a Theory of Public Expenditure," *Review of Economics and Statistics* 37 (November, 1955); 350–356; and R. A. Musgrave, *The Theory of Public Finance*. The discussion in this chapter owes much to an unpublished paper by Otto A. Davis and Andrew Whinston, "Some Foundations of Public Expenditure Theory," mimeographed (Carnegie Institute of Technology, 1961). Also, many aspects of the problem, especially in relation to large organizations, have been discussed by Mancur Olson. In an early draft of the original version of this chapter I was influenced by Olson's mimeographed manuscript "The General Theory of Public Goods," 1963, which later became *The Logic of Collective Action*.

to the choice of an ethical rule are obvious. The second application of essentially the same proposition has an even longer history in economic theory, although its similarity is perhaps less evident because of its inverse relevance. It concerns the behavior of the individual or the firm under conditions of perfect competition. This state of affairs is, in fact, normally defined strictly by the presence of the large-number dilemma. Perfect competition is said to exist when a single buyer or a single seller exerts so small an influence on the total market demand or supply of a product that he acts as if his own behavior exerts no influence on the price that is established in the market. Each seller and each buyer is a price taker.

Among the sellers of a single commodity, as a group, each single unit finds itself in a position precisely analogous to that of the "free rider." Each of the sellers would prefer to be in a position where all sellers restrict supply (with the net result being an increase in market price), but no single unit acting alone will find it profitable to restrict production. Given the situation, each must simply react to the external environment.

The large-number dilemma in this competitive context is different from that confronted in the ethical-choice or public-goods examples. Its applicability is the inverse of these other instances of the same proposition. Broadly speaking, the direction of desired change in the first examples is toward reducing group size, or at least modifying the rules so that something similar to small-group results emerges. In the organization of markets, however, explicit attempts are made to place buyers and sellers in the large-number dilemma. The economic system works efficiently only to the extent that the large-number dilemma prevails over wide areas, and institutional reforms are aimed directly at extending group size. Legal restrictions are imposed on attempts to consolidate, and enforcible rules over whole groups are forbidden. The essential difference between the ethical-choice and public-goods models and the perfect-competition models stems from the fact that in the first cases the groups are presumed inclusive of all members in the interacting social group. In market process, by contrast, only the particular sellers of one product, as a subgroup, find themselves in the large-number dilemma. And any change in the rules that will provide them with relief will automatically result in their exploitation of still other groups in the larger social system. Broader considerations involving the "social" constitution for the whole system may dictate that institutions of the economy be organized to foster the deliberate placement of single buyers and sellers in the large-number dilemma. This is simply another means of stating that the public at large may rationally choose to enforce the rules for perfect competition to the extent that this enforcement is possible.

Frank Knight often stressed that "in perfect competition there is no competition." This statement summarizes the essence of the large-number dilemma. The single seller in a perfectly competitive market; the single individual who considers his own voluntary contribution to a commonly shared public good; the single individual who tries to decide on an ethical rule in a large group—in each case rational choice dictates that he make the best of the environmental situation that he confronts. He can, by the nature of the conditions that he finds himself in, experience no sense of personal influence on the behavior of others directly or indirectly.

Implications

The large-number hypothesis in the theory of public goods supplies a possible logical explanation for the emergence of political, governmental institutions as replacements for institutions of market exchange in the provision of goods and services that exhibit the requisite "publicness." Before specific reforms can be suggested, however, additional questions must be answered. First, what value do individuals place on the voluntaristic elements of market processes, elements that must necessarily be sacrificed, at least to some degree, under political organization? What is the appropriate trading ratio between freedom of individual choice and economic efficiency? Even if this question were provisionally answered, another and equally difficult one would arise: How can the analyst, as an external observer, distinguish or classify those goods and services that exhibit "publicness"? Merely to raise these questions indicates that the pure theory of public goods remains in its infancy; the theorist remains a long way from that position which would allow him to provide normative advice to statesmen concerning the specifics of institutional reform.

This estimate of the current state of theory may seem pessimistic, but modern developments have placed economists in the position where they now ask the proper questions. With this questioning has surely come a more comprehensive understanding of political as well as economic processes. Such an understanding can yield suggestions for reforms that may not be initially apparent. Public finance theorists have, by and large, accepted the difference in classification between "private goods," which may be efficiently supplied through market institutions, and "public goods," which cannot be so supplied, as being determined by forces not subject to social control. Closer examination reveals, however, that this important dividing line may itself be variable. To the extent that it is variable, under certain circumstances it may be possible to secure both the greater freedom of choice that market organization allows and the potential enhancement of efficiency that modified rules can introduce. Careful analysis of the structure of legal and property rights may reveal prospects for converting apparent cases of free-rider behavior into situations in which individual behavior can produce substantially optimal results.

This chapter is not the place to develop this particular line of argument; my purpose here is to contribute something to the analysis of ethical choice. The brief review of the implications of similar theorizing about the public-goods problem is specifically helpful only to the extent that the analogy with ethical choice is relevant. If the sweep of history is considered to make inevitable and irrevocable the interaction of larger and larger numbers of persons in an ethical context, the analysis must imply that a smaller and smaller proportion of individuals will come to base their own actions on some version of the generalization or universalization principle. The scope for individualistic, voluntarist ethics must, of necessity, be progressively narrowed through time. As individuals increasingly find themselves caught in the large-number dilemma with respect to ethical choices, a possible logical explanation is provided for resort to political and governmental processes which can, effectively, change the rules and impose standards of conduct common to all individuals. In this respect the analysis yields helpful insights concerning the "legislation of morals" in terms of straightforward predictions if not of propriety. Common standards of conduct imposed and enforced by authority of the collectivity can, in the limiting case, result in "improvement" for all members of the community by their own standards.

The limiting case is precisely that, however, and the overwhelming probability would be that collectively enforced standards of conduct would be those desired for "others" by "some." Here, as in the public-goods case, the question that must be asked is: What is the appropriate trading ratio between the greater freedom of choice allowed the individual under a voluntaristic ethics and the greater social "efficiency" that might possibly emerge under legislated and enforced common standards of behavior? The theorist can provide no answers here, and analysis suggests only that the price paid for freedom increases with the size of the relevant interacting group.

As in the public-goods case, avenues of reform other than collectivization should be explored. Must the effective size of interacting groups become ever larger, in the context of ethical choice? What are the possible means of factoring down complex social interaction systems into small-group patterns? Imaginative and exciting modifications in traditional property rights arrangements are currently emerging to "internalize the externalities" in private market processes for certain types of interactions.[8] Can an analogous change in institutions be predicted to emerge in the realm of ethics? Perhaps those whose professional competence and interest lie primarily in ethics should begin to reexamine the biblical admonition to "love thy *neighbor*." In the large-number group, who is my "neighbor"? The lawyer's question was evaded, not answered, in Jesus' parabolic response.

[8] Cf. Spencer MacCallum, "The Social Nature of Ownership," *Modern Age* 9 (Winter, 1964–1965): 49–61.

12

The Samaritan's Dilemma

THIS chapter is an essay in prescriptive diagnosis. It represents my attempt to show that many different social problems can be analyzed as separate symptoms of the same disease. The diagnosis, as such, may be accepted without agreeing that the disease amounts to much or that, indeed, it is disease at all. Prescription for improvement or cure is suggested only if the disease is acknowledged to be serious. Even if the diagnosis and prescription are accepted, however, prospects for better social health may not be bright because, as the analysis demonstrates, the source of difficulty may lie in modern man's own utility function. We may simply be too compassionate for our own well-being or for that of an orderly and productive free society.

Formal Structure

Consider a very simple two-by-two payoff matrix confronting two players, A and B. Player A chooses between rows; player B chooses between columns. The payoffs are utility indicators, and they are arranged in ordinal sequence; there is no need to introduce cardinal utility at this point. As indicated in Fig. 4, for player A the second row dominates the first, in the strict game-theory sense. In a simple game setting, he will choose row 2 regardless of what player B does or is predicted to do. Furthermore, and this is important for the main points of this paper, player A will select row 2 even if he fails to recognize that he is in a game at all. Row 2 is simply his pragmatic or independent-behavior response to the choice situation that he confronts, whether or not he recognizes that B exists as a choice-making entity who opposes him in a gamelike situation.

B

Fig. 4

Note, however, that player B does not find himself in a comparable position to A. The way that B chooses does depend on A's action, observed or predicted. If A should choose row 1, B will choose column 1. But if A chooses row 2, player B will always select column 2. If B knows A's payoff matrix, he will predict that A will choose row 2. Hence, the "solution" of this simple game would seem to be cell IV of the matrix. If we look carefully at this outcome, however, we see that player A is worse off than he would be in cell III. His payoff is maximized in cell III, but he cannot, in and of himself, accomplish a shift into cell III. Nonetheless, since player B's choices depend strictly on those of A, player A should be in the driver's seat in one way or the other. Player A surely could, by some appropriate changes in behavior or strategy, insure an outcome in cell III. To secure this outcome, however, A must first recognize that he is in a game with B. That is, he must realize that his own choice behavior does, in fact, influence the choice behavior of B. Second, player A must begin to behave "strategically"; that is, he must make his own choices on the basis of predictions about the effects of these choices on B's behavior. If A knows precisely what B's utility payoffs are, he can insure that an outcome in cell III is realized. He can do so by playing the game in terms of the false payoffs that would be indicated by switching his own utility indicators between cells II and IV.

This strategy may be quite difficult for A, however, when we allow for the problems of communication and credibility between the players. Player A cannot simply announce to B what his strategy is and then expect player B to believe him. We are interested here only in a sequential game, and A's strategy is revealed only through his behavior on particular plays of the game itself. In order to convince B that he is playing strategically, A must actually act as if the false payoffs are real. Only in this way can he establish credibility.

But this strategy raises difficulties for A precisely because of the dominance features of his true payoff matrix. If strategic behavior dictates that he actually act as if the false instead of the true payoffs exist, player A must suffer utility loss. He must, in order to make the strategy work, choose row 1 rather than row 2 when player B is observed or predicted to select column 2. This choice will "hurt" A. Admittedly, the utility losses may be short-term ones only, and there may be offsetting long-term utility gains in a sequential game, but once the trade-off between short-term utility and long-term utility is acknowledged to be present, we must also acknowledge that A's subjective discount rate will determine his behavior. If this rate is sufficiently high, A may choose to behave nonstrategically, even in the full recognition of the game situation that he confronts.

I shall return to this point when I introduce examples, but first let us consider a second game, which involves merely the transposition of the payoff numbers for player A as between cells I and III. This game is illustrated in Fig. 5. In this setting dominance no longer characterizes A's choice; his behavior initially becomes dependent on that of B, either observed or predicted. Here we shall expect that either a cell I or a cell IV outcome will be secured, depending strictly on who gets there first, so to speak. For purposes that will, I hope, become clear later, let us assume that a continuing sequential solution in cell I is in being. Player A faces no dilemma of the sort discussed earlier. He need not introduce strategic behavior.

Suppose, however, that player B becomes cognizant of A's utility payoff matrix and that B begins to behave strategically. Suppose that B, independently, shifts to a column 2 strategy, in the knowledge

B

	1	2
1	I 4, 2	II 1, 1
2	III 2, 3	IV 3, 4

A (label on left side)

Fig. 5

that A will quickly adopt a row 2 course of action. B will, of course, suffer in the process, but let us suppose that he willingly takes the short-term utility losses that are required here. Clearly, A will have been placed in a position less desirable than the initial one by B's strategic behavior. Player A will be forced into the cell IV outcome. In this event, B can be said to have exploited A successfully.

If we look at this situation from A's vantage point, the required strategic offsets to B's behavior are the same as those indicated for the first game discussed. To prevent being exploited by B, player A must refuse to be influenced by B's shift to column 2. Once again, A must act as if his utility payoffs from cells II and IV are reversed. Once again, however, A may find this strategy difficult to carry out because he must suffer utility losses in the process. B's introduction of strategic behavior in this game places A in an acute position of suffering unless he acquiesces in a shift into cell IV.

The Specific Hypothesis

I have quite deliberately presented these two simple two-player interactions without identification or example, although the title of the chapter already may have tipped my hand. I have left off labeling the players because I want to forestall, to the maximum extent possible, the instant emotional identification that my examples seem to arouse. But I cannot go beyond this point without examples, so I shall now attach specific labels. I shall call the first situation the *active samaritan's dilemma* and the second situation the *passive samaritan's dilemma*. Let me emphasize, however, that I am attempting to develop a hypothesis that is generalizable to much of the behavior that we observe in the modern world. The samaritan example is used for descriptive clarity, in part because I could think of no better one. You may have suggestions here. The hypothesis does apply to certain aspects of the current policy discussion of welfare reform, but this subject is only one among many applications, and by no means the most important one.

Stated in the most general terms possible, the hypothesis is that modern man has become incapable of making the choices that are required to prevent his exploitation by predators of his own species, whether the predation be conscious or unconscious. The weakness may be imbedded in man's utility function. The term *dilemma* seems appropriate because the problem may not be one that reflects irrational behavior on any of the standard interpretations. Origins of the dilemma are, in part, economic, and they are found in the increasing affluence of choice makers. Analysis of the dilemma lends substance to the cliché that modern man has "gone soft." His income-wealth position, along with his preference ordering, allows him to secure options that were previously unavailable. What we may call "strategic courage" may be a markedly inferior economic good, and what we may call "pragmatic compassion" may be markedly superior.

If my general hypothesis is accepted, the direction of reform and improvements lies first in an explicit recognition of the dilemma by those who are caught up in it. Before "play" can even begin, the players must recognize that a game exists. Once this sort of recognition is passed, the players involved must, individually and collectively, accept the possible necessity of acting *strategically* instead of pragmatically. The very meaning of a game implies that the behavior of one player can control, to some extent, the behavior of his opponent. Optimal behavior for one player is dependent on the predicted reciprocal or response behavior on the part of the others in the game.

One objective of strategy is precisely that of influencing the behavior of others to produce the preferred outcome or solution. The implied strategy may and normally will violate norms for simple utility maximization in an assumed nongame or state-of-nature setting.

In the first game discussed, which I have called the active samaritan's dilemma, strategic behavior may be dictated for the samaritan even if the opposing player does not, himself, recognize the existence of the game, as such. That is, the player who is in the role of the potential samaritan may find it desirable to behave strategically even if his opponent, whom I have labeled the potential parasite, behaves pragmatically. In the second game, however, strategic behavior on the part of the potential samaritan may be dictated only when a specific gaming situation is forced upon him by his opponent.

In a very broad sense, the argument suggests the appropriateness of adopting rules for personal choice as opposed to retaining individual flexibility of action. The ethic that is closely related to, if not exactly derivable from, the samaritan's dilemma is one of individual responsibility. Initially, the dilemma is discussed in an individualistic choice setting, but there are important social and group implications that emerge from widespread adherence to the behavioral norms. More significantly, the analysis lends itself readily to extension to situations in which separate individual choices are clearly interdependent.

The Players Identified

To facilitate specific discussion, let me identify player A as a "potential samaritan" and player B as a "potential parasite." Furthermore, let us suppose that the potential samaritan faces two possible courses of action. He may do nothing concerning the potential parasite; that is, he may behave noncharitably (row 1). Alternatively, he may behave charitably. For purposes of discussion here, let us suppose that his charity involves the transfer of thirty dollars per month to the potential parasite (row 2). To the other person in the interaction there are also two courses of action open. He may work (column 1), in which case we may assume he earns an income, say, one-fourth as large as that earned by the more capable samaritan (or more talented or more lucky), or the potential parasite may refuse work (column 2).

As indicated earlier in the discussion of the nonidentified game, an outcome in cell IV might be predicted to emerge as the continuing solution of the sequential game unless the samaritan recognizes the strategic prospects open to him and begins to behave accordingly. But this change may be difficult for him. Vague threats or promises to cut off the charity if the recipient parasite does not work will remain empty unless there is demonstrated willingness to carry them out. But to carry them out, the samaritan will actually suffer disutility, which may be severe. He may find himself seriously injured by the necessity of watching the parasite starve himself while refusing work. The samaritan's task becomes more difficult to the extent that the parasite also recognizes the game situation and himself responds strategically. If the samaritan's strategic plan is to be at all effective, which requires first of all that credibility be established, he must accept the prospect of personal injury.

A family example may be helpful. A mother may find it too emotionally painful to spank a misbehaving child ("This hurts me more than it does you"). Yet spanking may be necessary to instill in the child the fear of punishment that will inhibit future misbehavior. If the temporal interdependence of choice is fully recognized, adjustments in behavior may, of course, be noted. A samaritan's payoff matrix that incorporates present values may not look like that shown in Fig. 4. Unfortunately, however, the samaritan's dilemma cannot be resolved fully by appeal to a temporal extension of the rationality postulate. Failure of the samaritan's telescopic faculty may explain much of what we seem to observe, and a correction in this faculty may be important. But such a correction, in itself, cannot remove the dilemma in all cases. Even when she fully discounts the effects of her current action on future choice settings, the mother may still find it too painful to spank the misbehaving child. Behavior that will influence the potential parasite to act in preferred ways must involve short-term utility losses to the samaritan. And if his subjective discount rate is high, present-value payoffs may still indicate that the charitable or acquiescent course of action is the dominating one.

Is there any objective sense in which we may say that the samaritan's discount rate is "too high"? This rate is purely subjective, and it is derived solely from the person's intertemporal utility function. It seems improper to label any rate as "too high" without resort to some externally based "social welfare function."

We might, for example, say that a person's portfolio adjustment reflects irrationality if he is observed to be borrowing at, say, 10 percent while simultaneously lending at 5 percent, transactions costs neglected. Rational behavior implies that marginal rates of return on all alternatives be equalized. It is not clear, however, just how a discount rate appropriate for portfolio adjustment might be brought into equality with that which is implicit in a person's intertemporal behavioral trade-offs, nor is it self-evident that a rationality postulate implies such equalization. Will the mother vary the severity of child discipline as the real rate of return of investment varies? If she does not, the hypothesis of equalization is refuted. This refutation would, in turn, allow for the possibility that observed behavior of persons in samaritanlike settings reflects discount rates greatly in excess of those to which these same persons adjust their portfolios. Unfortunately, there seems to be no direct means to corroborate or to refute this proposition.

When the illusory nature of the short-term utility losses dictated by strategic behavior is fully recognized, the rationality of applying almost any positive discount rate may be questioned. For the samaritan, utility losses are directly related to the potential parasite's disbelief in his strategic plan. To the extent that the parasite believes that the samaritan has, in fact, adopted a strategic behavioral plan and that he will, in fact, abide by this plan once adopted, there need be *no* utility loss to the samaritan at all. The situation is one in which the samaritan must convince the potential parasite of his willingness to suffer utility loss in order to insure that the expected value of this loss is effectively minimized.

An understanding of the dilemma confronted by those whom I have called active samaritans points directly toward means through which credibility can be increased and/or utility loss reduced. In the setting described, there should be genuine advantages to be gained by the samaritan from locking himself into a strategic behavior pattern in advance of any observed response on the part of his cohort. An advance commitment of the type described by Schelling may be central to the more sophisticated rationality that is dictated here.[1] This advance commitment may be accomplished in several ways. The samaritan can, in the first place, delegate the power of decision in particular choice situations to an agent, one who is instructed to act in accordance with the strategic norms that are selected in advance. The agency device serves two purposes simultaneously. First, the potential parasite is more likely to believe that the agent will behave in accordance with instructions. Second, by delegating the action to the agent, the samaritan need not subject himself to the anguish of situational response which may account for a large share of the anticipated utility loss.

We may return to our family example. The mother may delegate spanking to the nanny, with definite and clear instructions for spanking upon specific instances of misbehavior. This delegation increases the child's awareness of the consequences of misbehavior. At the same time, it removes from the mother the actual suffering which personal infliction of punishment might involve. The nonspanking, misbehaving option (cell IV) is effectively eliminated from the mother's choice set as well as the child's.

In general terms, the analysis points toward the choice of utility-maximizing rules for personal behavior as opposed to the retention of single-period or single-situation choice options. Having once adopted a rule, the samaritan *should not* be responsive to the particulars of situations that might arise. He should not act pragmatically and on a case-by-case basis. The argument specifically confutes the rationality of situational ethics in samaritanlike settings.

Practical examples are readily available. Standards for determining welfare eligibility, either for governmental or private programs, should not be left to the discretion of social workers who get personally involved with potential recipients. This institutional arrangement would force social workers into an acutely painful form of the

[1] Cf. Thomas C. Schelling, *The Strategy of Conflict*. Also see his later paper "Game Theory and the Study of Ethical Systems," *Journal of Conflict Resolution* 12 (March, 1968): 34–44, especially p. 40. This paper raises somewhat indirectly the central issues discussed here.

dilemma discussed. University administrators should not enter into direct dialogues with "concerned" students and faculty members. By so doing, the administrators invite difficulties which might be avoided by detached adherence to preselected rules.

The Passive Samaritan

Much of the analysis can be extended directly to the problem confronted by the passive samaritan in the second game discussed. In the case of the active samaritan, pragmatic or nonstrategic behavior by both parties produces results that are not desired by the samaritan. He must first recognize the game that he plays and then behave strategically. By contrast, the passive samaritan finds himself in an optimally preferred position as long as *both* players continue to behave nonstrategically. In the illustrative matrix of Fig. 5, the only change from Fig. 4 is the transposition of the samaritan's utility payoff indicators between cell I and cell III.

As long as the potential parasite fails to recognize the game setting, he will view column 1 as his only alternative. The outcome in cell I will be stable over a sequence of choices. The dilemma of the passive samaritan emerges only when the potential parasite wakes up to his strategic prospects while the samaritan is left sleeping at the switch. If the parasite begins to adopt a column 2 course of action, the samaritan who responds pragmatically will modify his own behavior to avoid the threatened utility loss of cell II. As a result, the outcome will settle in cell IV. Once in this situation, the passive samaritan's position becomes fully analogous to that confronting the active samaritan. He must recognize that he is in the game, and he must consider behaving strategically instead of reactively. The analysis points similarly toward the advance selection of rules for behavior, rules that are chosen independently and in advance of particular choice situations.

Real-world examples of this model are perhaps even more familiar than examples of the first one, both in international relations and in domestic affairs. Ecuador and Peru seized tuna boats on the presumption that the United States would not respond strategically. North Korea captured the *Pueblo*. Terrorists kidnap diplomats in many countries. Prisoners go on hunger strikes.

Applications

In a strict sense, the analysis to this point has been limited to interactions between two players with an anticipated sequence of choices. However, as the several examples possibly suggest, the problem discussed has much wider applicability. To the extent that comparable choice settings are faced by different players and to the extent that behavior is interdependent, the implications can be readily extended.

Consider, first, a setting in which a samaritan is confronted with only one choice against a single opponent. Simple utility maximization will be indicated only if a comparable choice with some other opponent is not anticipated or, if such a choice is anticipated, there are no behavioral interdependencies. On the other hand, if the samaritan expects to confront a whole set of possible parasites, one at a time, and if he predicts that his own choice behavior in confronting any one will influence the behavior of others, the motivation for considering the prospects for strategic behavior is as strong or stronger than in the simpler sequential choices with a single opponent. Most instructors are familiar with cases in which modification of the grade of a single complaining student offers the short-run utility maximizing course of action. Experienced instructors will recognize, however, that this behavior will increase the number of student complaints generally, and that long-run utility maximization may require rigid adherence to some sort of rule against grade changes.

As long as the interdependence is among the strategies employed against differing opponents of a single player in comparable samaritanlike settings, we may remain within an individualistic decision model. More relevant implications emerge, however, when interdependencies among the behavior patterns of different samaritans are recognized as pervasive. Each samaritan may find himself confronted with the necessity of making a once-and-for-all choice concerning his treatment of a single potential parasite. The uniqueness of this choice insures that there are no direct future consequences; simple utility maximizing behavior dictates that the samaritan take the soft option. If other persons are expected to confront similar choices with respect to other potential parasites, and if the treatment afforded in one setting modifies the expectations of payoff from similar ones, the dilemma becomes a public or social one instead of a private one. In this case, self-interest on the part of an individual samaritan might never imply strategic behavior of the sort discussed. The rules describing such behavior become fully analogous to "public goods" in that the person producing them secures only a small portion of the benefits. His action confers external economies on remaining samaritans in the community, on all those who might anticipate being placed in comparable situations.

Airplane hijacking provides a single dramatic example. A single captain is unexpectedly confronted with a choice, and simple utility maximization dictates accession to the demands of the hijacker. Nonetheless, the benefits to the whole community of airline captains (and other members of the community) from a refusal to surrender may far exceed the more concentrated possible losses. Strategic courage exercised by a single captain or crew member may generate spillover benefits to all others who might face hijacking threats. This spillover will occur if the predictions of potential hijackers are modified and if their behavior is adjusted accordingly. This direction of effect can be denied only if all elements of rationality are assumed to be absent from potential hijackers' choices.

The Ethic of Responsibility

Avoidance of the samaritan's dilemma in its public form can be secured by voluntary adherence to individual rules of conduct or by explicit cooperative action to impose such rules. Voluntary acceptance of what we may call "responsible" standards requires that acting parties behave in ways different from those indicated by direct and apparent self-interest. Some pressure toward following such rules will exist if persons fully recognize the interdependence among behavior patterns, that is, if they acknowledge the generalized game setting in which they find themselves. An individual ethic of responsibility is akin to the Kantian generalization principle, although here it is necessarily limited to the group of potential samaritans in the community.

Individual adherence to such an ethic has in no way disappeared from the modern scene. Its widely observed appearance may, however, be explained as an anachronistic carryover from earlier periods instead of a reflection of voluntarily chosen current commitment. At least two influences have been at work to undermine motivations for responsible behavior in the sense defined here. An individual's motivation for behaving to influence the behavior of others in the direction of generating preferred outcomes for the all-inclusive community varies inversely with the size of the group. The expected influence of any one person's behavior on that of others diminishes sharply as numbers are increased. Beyond some critical size limit, the individual who finds himself in a samaritanlike setting must rationally treat the behavior of others, parasites and samaritans alike, as beyond his power of influence. When this point is reached, the pattern of behavior in others is accepted as a parameter for his own choice; others' actions become a part of the "state of nature" that the individual confronts. The game setting disappears in his subjective calculus, and there are no rationally derived reasons for behaving with the strategic courage that the community interest may require.

The effective size of community has become larger over time, and this size factor has been reinforced by a complementary influence. Western societies have been increasingly "democratized" in the sense that a larger and larger proportion of the potential membership has been effectively enfranchised in the formation of the social environment. The power of an "establishment," a possibly small and well-defined group of leaders, to set patterns of behavior that might then serve as norms for others has been reduced, often dramatically. A familiar descriptive cliché classifies the modern age as one without heroes. Without heroes to emulate, each man "does his own thing."

Implications in Collective Action

The quasi-revolutionary shift in modern behavioral standards that widespread adherence to the responsibility ethic would represent does not seem likely to occur. Indeed, all signs point in the opposing direction, and we shall probably witness a continuing erosion in strategic courage at all levels of decision.[2] There may be no escape from the generalized samaritan's dilemma, in its public form, except

---

[2] Implicit in this whole analysis is my own attitude that "improvement" lies in reversing the direction of change, in escaping, wholly or partially, from the samaritan's dilemma. This value judgment may, of course, be rejected. Even if the analysis

through the collective adoption and enforcement of rules that will govern individual situational responses. As they are applied, such rules must be coercive, and they must act to limit individual freedom of action. This restrictiveness need not, however, imply that individuals may not freely agree to their adoption at some constitutional stage of deliberation. Indeed, if the public form of the dilemma is a genuine one, it will be in the potential interest of most members of the community to adopt some such rules.[3] The implied limitations on individual freedom of response which such rules must embody are no different, conceptually, from those limitations that are embodied in the necessity to pay taxes for the financing of jointly consumed public goods and services.

If the collectivity acts to impose uniform behavioral rules on all potential samaritans, and if these rules are observed to be enforced, the response patterns of potential parasites will be modified. As a result, the whole community of potential samaritans will enjoy the benefits. Examples may be found in university administration or in airplane hijacking. In the turmoil of the 1960's separate university administrators in, say, a statewide or nationwide system might have welcomed the imposition of uniform rules for dealing with militant students, rules which effectively would have bound their own choice making under pressure. Similarly, separate airline companies may welcome the imposition of governmental regulations regarding countermeasures against potential hijackers despite the fact that no company would find it profitable to introduce such measures independently.

It should be evident both from the analysis and from the examples that the samaritan's dilemma as it appears often involves a mixture of its several forms. There may be an expected sequence of choices with the same potential parasite such that the samaritan is placed in a dilemma of the sort discussed in the first section, "Formal

---

is fully accepted and the vulnerability to exploitation is acknowledged, the benefits from behavior that reflects increased "compassion" generally may be judged larger than the costs that would be involved in any attempt to encourage more discrimination in personal choices.

[3] For a general discussion of the distinction between the constitutional stage and the operational stage of choice making, see James M. Buchanan and Gordon Tullock, *The Calculus of Consent.*

Structure," of this chapter. At the same time, however, the samaritan may expect to confront a series of decisions with respect to different potential parasites. Furthermore, he may also recognize that some effects of his own behavior will impose potential costs or benefits on other potential samaritans. Once again, the university turmoil of the 1960's provides a good example. Administrative officials, faced with a single disruptive group, knew that they must make decisions over a sequence of events. To the extent that they expected to be confronted by the same group, they were in the personal or private version of the dilemma discussed in the section "Formal Structure." They should have recognized, however, that their own behavior with respect to the single group would also affect the behavior of other groups which they might confront in subsequent periods. Finally, who can doubt but that the choice behavior of administrators on one campus exerted significant effects on disruptive activity on other campuses?

Because the dilemma appears mixed in several forms, there are interdependencies in corrective adjustments. The adoption of individual rules for behavior aimed at removing the personal dilemma does much toward resolving the group or social dilemma that may exist simultaneously. Strategic utility maximization may reduce the necessity of reliance on an explicit ethic of responsibility. Conversely, general acceptance of this ethic makes personal calculations of optimal strategies less necessary and resort to collective action less important. On the other hand, collective selection and enforcement of uniform codes of conduct reduce the pressure on the individual to select either an economically or an ethically optimal course of action. The dilemma is most pervasive in a situation in which individuals do not maximize utility in the strategic sense, where they do not adhere to an ethic of responsibility, and where no collective action is taken toward laying down jointly preferred codes of conduct. Perhaps this situation describes modern society all too well.

Prospects and Potential

Increasing economic affluence is only one among many explanations for the pervasive importance of the phenomenon that I have called the samaritan's dilemma in twentieth-century Western society.

As incomes have increased, and as the stock of wealth has grown, men have increasingly found themselves able to take the soft options.[4] Mothers can afford candy to bribe misbehaving children. Welfare rolls can be increased dramatically without national bankruptcy.

The economic explanation may, however, be dwarfed in significance by other historical developments. The influence of organized religion in earlier periods inhibited personal behavior that was aimed solely at the gratification of instant desires, whether they were charitable or selfish. There is content in the Puritan ethic, and when this content is interpreted favorably it resembles the ethic of responsibility suggested above. As it was institutionally represented, Christian love was "love of God," which was effectively translated into a set of precepts for personal behavior.

It is difficult to be optimistic about the prospects for escaping the samaritan's dilemma. There are few if any signs of a return to the behavioral standards of a half-century past. If anything, short-term utility maximization seems on the ascendancy, and even for the individual, long-term utility maximization seems less characteristic of behavior now than in periods that are past.[5] Individuals who find themselves in positions comparable to those of the samaritans in the models of this paper seem unwilling to behave strategically or to adopt rules of conduct that will eventually achieve the differing outcomes.

There is little to be observed in the behavior of collective units to counter the individualistic pattern of selecting the soft options.

[4] In earlier and impoverished epochs survival may have depended on man's willingness and ability to make strategic choices, and evolutionary selectivity may have instilled behavioral characteristics in man that remain irrational in modern environments. As these characteristics disappear from observed behavior patterns, the necessity for conscious recognition of the dilemma increases. Benjamin Klein has suggested that the sheer animal instinct for protecting property, which has been emphasized by Robert Ardrey and others, may serve as an important "social" purpose in inhibiting courses of action that seem to be preferred in a short-term or nonstrategic context. In more general terms, Schelling discusses at some length the role of instincts in imposing constraints on behavior. See Schelling, "Game Theory and Ethical Systems," pp. 36–39.

[5] Interestingly in this connection, it is precisely short-term utility maximization, as opposed to long-term utility maximization, that E. C. Banfield singles out to be characteristic of the lower classes. In this context, and if my predictions are correct, what we are witnessing is a transition into lower-class habits on a massive and pervasive scale. See E. C. Banfield, *The Unheavenly City*.

There might be grounds for guarded optimism if we should observe collectivities laying down rules for personal behavior in those situations for which individual norms have not appeared, but what we see is just the opposite. Collectivities, in their separate arms and instruments, are expanding the soft options. They seem everywhere to be loosening upon prescribed rules for behavior, and in this way they encourage similar reactions on the part of individuals. When the conventional wisdom of government is exemplified in the slogan "kindness for the criminals," we can hardly expect individuals to become enforcers. The correspondence between the individual and collective responses might be predicted. Governments do little more than reflect the desires of their citizens, and the taking of soft options on the part of individuals should be expected to be accompanied by an easing up on legal restrictions on individual behavior.

The phenomenon analyzed here takes on its most frightening aspects in its most general biological setting. A species that increasingly behaves, individually and collectively, so that it encourages more and more of its own members to live parasitically and/or deliberately to exploit its producers faces eventual self-destruction. Unless an equilibrium is established which imposes self-selected limits on samaritanlike behavior, the rush toward species destruction may accelerate instead of diminish. The limit that is defined by existing utility functions may lie beyond that which is required for maintaining viable social order. By some leap of biological faith we may believe that behavior will be constrained to insure species survival. I can conceive of no such leap of faith that might allow us to predict that our innate behavior patterns must preserve a social and civil order that is at all similar to the one we have historically experienced.

I conclude with a paradox. If you find yourself in basic agreement with me, my hypothesis is at least partially falsified. Agreement would signal that you are fully aware of the dilemma that I have discussed, and your awareness could be taken as a reflection of general awareness in the academic community.

On the other hand, and I suspect this is the case, if you find yourself in basic disagreement with me, my hypothesis is at least partially corroborated. Disagreement would signal your failure to recognize the dilemma, along with your implied willingness to submit to further exploitation than we yet have witnessed.

13

Political Constraints on Contractual Redistribution

MODERN contract theories of distribution represent significant advances over the value-laden statements of preference that were passed off as serious intellectual constructions by the utilitarians. The modern theories attempt to explain observed institutions on the basis of conceptual contractual agreement among members of defined political communities. These theories may be classified in three distinct sets: preconstitutional, constitutional, and postconstitutional.

In the first set, a preconstitutional state of anarchy is postulated, and hypotheses are then derived concerning the types of property rights that might emerge. Given a property rights structure and assumptions concerning individual behavior, conjectures can be made concerning the distribution of property.[1] In the second set, the contractual process occurs at the constitutional level where the position of individuals (families) is not fully identifiable; here, the alternatives for choice are institutional arrangements that are presumed to remain in being over a succession of time periods. In the third set, the contractual process occurs postconstitutionally, within a defined institutional framework, and the alternatives for choice are explicit transfers of income and wealth among individuals and groups in the community. In the second or constitutional category we place John Rawls's difference principle and also the related insurance principle.[2]

---

[1] See James M. Buchanan, *The Limits of Liberty: Between Anarchy and Leviathan*, and Winston C. Bush and L. S. Mayer, "Some Implications of Anarchy for the Distribution of Property," *Journal of Economic Theory* 8 (August, 1974): 401–412.

[2] See John Rawls, *A Theory of Justice*, and James M. Buchanan and Gordon Tullock, *The Calculus of Consent*.

In the third set, we place the so-called Pareto-optimal redistribution models, based on utility interdependence.[3] As a somewhat in-between model, we note the self-protection theory recently advanced by Brennan.[4]

We restrict our discussion to contractually derived institutions that might emerge at the constitutional stage. We postulate that individuals are wholly uncertain about their prospective income-wealth positions in the periods for which the institutional structure to be chosen is to be applicable. Individuals make their own decisions, each behind a Rawlsian "veil of ignorance." For our purposes this postulate is a positive assumption about the actual states of persons making constitutional choice; it is not a normative statement concerning how persons should conceive themselves in making choices.

We want to address ourselves specifically to the questions raised by the recognition, at the time of constitutional contract, that actual in-period transfers of income and/or wealth must be implemented within an institutional setting peopled by individuals whose income-wealth positions are known. In other words, our questions concern the potential viability of the "terms of constitutional contract," the difficulties that might arise in enforcing these terms in a practically working political process, and, importantly, the possible feedback that these latter considerations may exert on the constitutional decision itself. These are issues which have not, to our knowledge, been examined in the burgeoning modern literature on contractual distribution.

We define a potentially viable constitutional contract as one in which a majority of the individuals in the postconstitutional stage benefit when the terms of the contract are executed. Although the majority rule is arbitrary, it does not substantially affect the results. This rule also conforms to the orthodox idealizations of the institutions of democracies.

Let us assume, first, that individuals in a constitutional stage reach agreement on an institutional structure that will generate in-period transfers from the relatively rich to the relatively poor, as measured

[3] See Harold Hochman and James Rodgers, "Pareto Optimal Redistribution," *American Economic Review* 59 (September, 1969): 542–547.

[4] Geoffrey Brennan, "Pareto Desirable Redistribution: The Non-Altruistic Dimension," *Public Choice* 14 (Spring, 1973): 43–68.

against the no-transfer distribution that would emerge from pure-market payments to resource owners under the constitutionally defined property rights in existence.[5] Initially, we assume that there is only one period in the postconstitutional sequence. Assume more specifically that the contractual agreement dictates that posttransfer incomes of the lowest-income recipients shall be maximized in accordance with some Rawlsian difference principle. Table 3 presents two separate no-transfer and posttransfer distributions for a community of five persons. (Note that measurable and adverse incentive effects are incorporated in these examples.)

As Table 3 suggests, the enforceability of redistribution schemes will depend significantly on the pattern of pretransfer market distribution. In distribution 1 the assumed contractual rule for income transfers would clearly be viable. A majority of the community's members would benefit from it; indeed, by definition, no other rule could be better for them. By sharp contrast, in distribution 2 implementation of the constitutional rule for redistribution will require that a majority of the community's members suffer transfer losses. In the absence of direct utility interdependence, implementation of the

TABLE 3

Individual	1	2
	No-Transfer Income Distributions	
A_1	$10,000	$10,000
A_2	10,000	10,000
A_3	1,000	10,000
A_4	1,000	1,000
A_5	1,000	1,000
	Posttransfer Income Distributions	
A_1	$ 5,000	$ 6,333
A_2	5,000	6,333
A_3	4,000	6,333
A_4	4,000	6,000
A_5	4,000	6,000

[5] For purposes of this discussion we are restricting the analysis to the "distributive branch" of government budgets, in the Musgrave terminology. Cf. R. A. Musgrave, *The Theory of Public Finance*.

previously agreed-on constitutional rule for redistribution will be difficult to secure.

We may now consider the obverse of the above example. Suppose that there is no agreement on transfer policy reached in the constitutional state, which is equivalent to saying that the market-determined shares are to be left unchanged. In this case, note that the results may be viable only if distribution 2 emerges. If distribution 1 emerges, postconstitutional transfers will tend to emerge, regardless of the absence of constitutional agreement.

The single-period arithmetical example is extremely simple, but it demonstrates one central point. The enforceability and maintenance of any constitutionally determined institution for income-wealth distribution will depend on the actual pattern of pretransfer distribution. The individual's prediction about this pattern will, therefore, influence his choice among alternative constitutional rules on income-wealth transfers. Other things being equal, he will be more egalitarian in his constitutional choice the larger the proportion of relatively poor members he predicts to be in the pretransfer pattern of distribution. Note particularly that this result depends only on the relative numbers of poor and rich and not at all on the relative income levels of the two groups.

We can now relax the single-period assumption and examine the applicability of the chosen constitutional rule over a sequence of periods. We assume, as before, that the individual at the time of constitutional choice is wholly uncertain about his own position in the market distribution that will emerge in the first period of the postconstitutional sequence. We need to specify, however, the relationship of the distributional position of an individual in each of the several postconstitutional periods. If his position is the same in all periods, the multiperiod model is no different from the single-period one. At the opposite extreme, assume that individual positions in the separate distributions are wholly unrelated. The individual who finds himself in a favorable income position in the first period remains wholly uncertain about his position in the other periods. Consider the model in which distribution 1 is predicted to emerge in each of the several periods of the sequence. As suggested, the Rawlsian redistributional rule is viable in the one-period setting. It will continue to be viable in the multiperiod setting under these assumptions only if

individuals maintain the same set of attitudes or tastes for redistribution policy that they held at the time of the initial constitutional
contract. If individuals observe that their own positions are unrelated
over separate periods and that they shift among different income
levels, this experience may itself modify attitudes. Individual members of a political majority in a single period may find themselves
unwilling fully to implement the redistribution that is dictated by
the Rawlsian constitutional precept. In more general and relevant
terms, this is the effect of observed upward social mobility on attitudes toward redistributional alternatives. Individuals may be unwilling to transfer maximinal incomes (dictated by Rawlsian precepts)
from the relatively rich to themselves if they expect that policy, once
introduced, will become permanent.

The introduction of a multiperiod sequence reduces somewhat
the expected political viability of the extreme distributional rule
postulated under the predictions that distribution 1 will prevail in
all periods. But the basic conclusion that a less extreme version of
this scheme might well be selected and be expected to be viable holds.

Consider now the prediction that distribution 2 will characterize
market results over the whole sequence of postconstitutional periods.
As indicated, the redistributional alternative would not be expected
to be maintained in the one-period model, and a no-transfer policy
might be the only agreed-on rule. In the multiperiod model, however, something between these extremes might emerge. Individuals
who are in the relatively rich majority coalition, but who are wholly
uncertain about their own positions in subsequent income periods,
will have some incentive to build in transfer mechanisms on the expectation that, once established, these policies will tend to be accepted
in subsequent periods.[6] To accomplish this institutional result they
may accept net transfer losses during the period when income shares
are known. In anticipation of this, there may be constitutional agreement on a redistributive scheme, even in the expectation that distribution 2 will characterize each income period, an agreement that will
be expected to be implemented by the majority coalition in the community.

[6] The argument here is related to that developed by Peter Hammond in his
paper "Charity, Altruism or Cooperative Egoism" in *Altruism, Morality, and Economic Theory*, ed. E. S. Phelps.

The general point made with respect to the single-period model remains valid, however. More redistribution will be constitutionally agreed upon if distribution 1 is predicted than if distribution 2 is predicted. The principle may be more generally stated. If *all* members of a community agree on a redistributional scheme at the constitutional level, those persons who find their income positions settled even for a single period will find their postconstitutional preferences for redistribution inversely related to income position. In the multiperiod model, lifting of the "veil of ignorance" for even a single period will modify the costs and benefits of any previously agreed-on redistribution scheme.

In real-world circumstances something between the two extreme models of income expectations surely prevails. An individual's income-wealth position in any one period is related to that which he expects to hold in subsequent periods, although there may well exist considerable uncertainty. In this setting, results that fall somewhere between the single-period and the multiperiod models can be derived.

The examples have remained unreal because of the assumption of two distinct income classes. Somewhat more realism may be introduced by adding a middle class of income recipients in an example that becomes slightly more descriptive of existing distributional patterns. Consider a nine-member community, with no-transfer or market

TABLE 4

Individual	Predicted No-Transfer Distribution	Idealized Rawlsian Rule
A_1	$10,000	7,000
A_2	8,000	6,500
A_3	6,000	5,500
A_4	5,500	5,200
A_5	5,000	4,600
A_6	4,500	4,400
A_7	4,000	4,000
A_8	1,500	4,000
A_9	1,000	4,000
Mean Income	$ 5,167	
Median	5,000	

incomes arrayed as depicted in Table 4, column 2. Assume that this pattern of market distribution is predicted to emerge in each post-constitutional period, but that the individual remains wholly uncertain about which position he will come to occupy as the actual pattern emerges.

Initially, assume that there will be only one postconstitutional period or, what amounts to the same thing, that an individual's position in the distribution will remain unchanged once it is settled in period 1. From Table 4 it is clear that if there are no incentive effects, a policy of full equalization will be politically workable. Since the mean income is above the median, at least a majority of the persons in the group will find themselves improved as a result of the constitutionally selected redistribution policy. If incentive effects are allowed to enter the model, however, this conclusion need not follow. The set of transfers that would be required to maximize the position of the least advantaged person in the predicted distributional array need not be consistent with the political structure.

Suppose, for example, that ignoring incentive effects, a policy of full posttransfer equalization is adopted in the constitutional assembly. As individuals earn incomes in the market, however, they will be motivated in part by the knowledge of this equalization policy. As a result, total community income falls to such a level that the income realized by each person amounts to, say, only $3,500, as opposed to an average income of $5,167 when no transfers are anticipated.

The position of the least advantaged may be improved on if some allowance of inequality is reintroduced. If a benevolent despot is in control, the position of the least advantaged may, say, be increased to an income level of $4,000, with a posttransfer income array like that indicated in column 3, Table 4. Note, however, that this posttransfer distribution would not be supported in a strictly democratic political process. Six of the nine members of the community find their own posttransfer incomes to be lower than those which they secure in the no-transfer setting.

The example suggests that the minimal political constraint on the implementation of any redistributional rule would be the requirement that at least one-half of the community's members find their own income positions improved over the no-transfer setting. Further consideration of the limits that political process may place on redistribution rules may suggest more restrictive constraints. Some evidence suggests that the observed beneficiaries of income transfers in democratic structures are middle-income instead of low-income recipients, and public-choice arguments have been advanced to explain this observation.[7] As a plausible constraint reflecting something of this discussion, models might be examined which require that the median members of the community receive absolute transfers at least as large as those of persons falling lower on the income scale.

Our purpose here is not to examine alternative constraints in detail. We make the more general point that political constraints must be recognized to exist when the problem of implementing constitutionally approved rules on income-wealth redistribution are discussed. In any real-world setting, of course, the discussion of institutional rules affecting income-wealth distribution must take place in recognition of existing legal definitions of property rights, of existing political decision-making mechanisms, and of predicted patterns of income distribution as well as predicted positions of persons within these predicted distributions.

---

[7] See George J. Stigler, "Director's Law of Public Income Redistribution," *Journal of Law and Economics* 13 (April, 1970): 1–10; and Gordon Tullock, *The Social Dilemma.*

14

A Hobbesian Interpretation of the
Rawlsian Difference Principle

In this chapter I offer an interpretation of Professor John Rawls's principle of distributive justice that has not, to my knowledge, been previously developed, despite the lengthening bibliography of criticism and analysis inspired by Rawls's *A Theory of Justice*. Critics of this principle have concentrated attention almost exclusively on the extreme aversion to risk that is implied, and indeed, the term *maximin principle* has been widely substituted for Rawls's own preferred term *difference principle*. In an earlier review article,[1] I expressed misgivings about this principle similar to those of other critics. My own emphasis was, however, on what I considered to be Rawls's unsatisfactory reconciliation of the two parts of his analysis: "(1) the interpretation of the initial situation and of the problem of choice posed there, and (2) the set of principles which . . . would be agreed on."[2] I argued that Rawls's fundamental contribution lay in his elaboration of the contractarian approach or method, essentially (1) above, and I suggested that both Rawls and his critics should abandon their utilitarianlike search for uniqueness in the outcomes of idealized agreement. As later discussion will indicate, this remains my own position, but under the interpretation advanced here, Rawls's insistence that both parts of his analysis remain essential and complementary can be readily understood. Rawls does not, however, properly describe the assumptions that are required to make his model internally consistent. These assumptions can appropriately be classified

[1] "Rawls on Justice as Fairness," *Public Choice* 13 (Fall, 1972): 123–128.
[2] John Rawls, *A Theory of Justice*, p. 15.

as Hobbesian in tone.[3] Some of these assumptions have been drawn more fully by Robert Cooter,[4] but neither he nor Rawls seems to have fully recognized the implications. When these assumptions are carefully presented, the whole Rawlsian construction takes on quite different characteristics from those normally attributed to it.

The interpretation in this chapter allows the analysis of Rawls to be related closely with the analysis of Hobbesian anarchy that has been recently developed.[5] In particular, it allows me to relate Rawls's usage of the original position to my own use of the equilibrium position in Hobbesian anarchy as the basis for a hypothetical social contract. The interpretation also places Rawls's construction in a somewhat more positivistic setting than has appeared to be the case.

A Crusoe-Friday Model

It will be helpful to present the analysis initially in a highly simplified two-person model in which the dimensionality of agreement is limited to a minimum. This model is familiar to economists, and it allows most of the relevant points to be developed. The more complex dimensions of agreement required in full-fledged, even if hypothetical, social contract can be readily appended to this basic "economic" model. I should emphasize, however, that the analysis is intended, as is that of Rawls, to be applicable to conceptual agreement on the basic structural arrangements of society.

Consider Crusoe and Friday alone on the island. They live in Hobbesian anarchy; no law exists, and each person acts on his own to produce and to defend stocks of a single all-purpose consumable commodity, fish. Let us assume that in this setting the net income of each person amounts to only one or two units per day. Under our interpretation, this is the "original position" from which any idealized contractual agreement emerges.[6] This is not made fully explicit by

---

[3] Rawls does say explicitly that his original position corresponds to the state of nature in traditional contract theory (*Theory of Justice*, p 12). But he does not go beyond this.

[4] Robert Cooter, "What is the Public Interest?" mimeographed (Harvard University, 1974).

[5] See Gordon Tullock, ed., *Explorations in the Theory of Anarchy*, and my own book, *The Limits of Liberty: Between Anarchy and Leviathan*.

[6] Strictly speaking, the "original position" need not be the equilibrium of

Rawls, and his discussion does not fully describe the characteristics of the position which would be maintained in the absence of agreement.[7]

Note that I have not assumed that Crusoe and Friday are "natural equals" in the sense that their net incomes in the state of nature are equivalent. This may or may not be the case, and the model should allow for either equal or unequal incomes. I postulate only that a "natural distribution" will come to be established, implying that each person has the strength and ability to maintain whatever position comes to be defined in this equilibrium.[8] In this rude setting both Crusoe and Friday should recognize the advantages of cooperation, of joint action, of contractual agreement. The critical questions involve the degree of information about the results of cooperative action that the parties may possess in the initial position and the basic technology which cooperative action embodies. As the analysis will demonstrate, the Rawlsian framework as here interpreted must contain rather full information about alternatives for production and distribution available under cooperation, while remaining within the restriction that individualized positions cannot be fully identified. Also, the interpretation is more readily understood if we assume that cooperative action necessarily introduces a dramatic shift in the technology of producing income or product. The jointness aspects of the basic structure of social arrangements become predominant. By way of a simplified economic illustration, we might say that the Rawlsian model allows Crusoe and Friday to commence fishing with a boat once agreement is reached, whereas in anarchy this degree of cooperation is not pos-

---

Hobbesian anarchy. As the discussion below will indicate, the initial position conceptually may be different. However, the knowledge that this Hobbesian equilibrium will be the social state in the absence of agreement must inform the choices of parties, whatever the characteristics of the initial position. Hence, for clarity in discussion it is best to treat the Hobbesian equilibrium as the initial position.

[7] However, see Rawls, *Theory of Justice*, p. 103, where he states that in the absence of agreement "no one could have a satisfactory life." In a 1974 response to critics, Rawls said, ". . . being in the original position is always to be contrasted with being in society" (John Rawls, "Reply to Alexander and Musgrave," *Quarterly Journal of Economics* 88 [November, 1974]: 638). See also Cooter, "What is Public Interest?" pp. 27–28.

[8] For a formal analysis of the equilibrium natural distribution in Hobbesian anarchy, see the paper by Winston Bush, "Individual Welfare in Anarchy," in Tullock, *Explorations in the Theory of Anarchy*.

sible, and each man has to fish without a boat. The cooperative arrangement involves participation in the provision and use of a genuinely public good. In this framework it becomes impossible to impute separate income shares to the two parties, Crusoe and Friday, since the whole production is clearly a joint product.

Crusoe and Friday agree to act jointly, to become partners in social arrangements; gross production increases dramatically, but there is no means of imputing separate shares. Furthermore, in the original position and before agreement is reached, although both persons can predict with accuracy the vector of production and distributive shares, neither person can predict what his role in joint production will be. Once joint action is taken, there is one quantity of the good that could be produced under a simultaneous agreement to share equally in income or product. This result represents one point on a "production-distribution" possibility frontier. And this equal-sharing regime involves a higher net income for each party than the income attainable in anarchy.[9] There may exist, however, different and larger quantities which could be produced under regimes of unequal sharing. The increase in total output is presumably possible because of the response to income incentives. Agreement could be reached on one of these unequal-share imputations only if the income total of the least advantaged is thereby increased over the income total attainable under equal sharing. This is the much-discussed "difference principle," and we must try to see precisely why the results indicated by this principle will emerge in the setting postulated.

Each of the two persons can, by withdrawing his cooperation, plunge the system back into Hobbesian anarchy. And this is predicted to be possible by both parties at the time of the initial agreement. The "marginal product" of each man is extremely large, and payment in terms of "marginal productivity" would far more than exhaust the total product. For illustration, think of the situation in which Crusoe secures an income of one unit and Friday secures an income of two units in genuine Hobbesian equilibrium. Cooperation promises to

[9] This is not a logical consequence of joint action. It is possible that the increase in total product consequent on joint production can be realized only in regimes of unequal shares. In terms of Fig. 6, below, there may be no point C on the forty-five degree line that is Pareto-superior to A. This result would, however, seem sufficiently bizarre to rule out its serious consideration.

yield a total income of twelve units, provided that these are shared equally between the two parties, with each person getting a net income of six units. The "marginal product" of each man is nine units, since this represents the difference in total product between the cooperative outcome and the Hobbesian outcome. Each person can, therefore, enforce the equal-sharing version of the cooperative outcome.

At this point the veil of ignorance, stressed by Rawls, becomes relevant. In the original position, in Hobbesian anarchy, the persons do not know their respective abilities within the cooperative technology, nor do they know how each will respond to income incentives in participating in joint production. They know only that each of them can, by unilateral action, shift the whole system back into anarchy by the simple expedient of withdrawing cooperation. Conceptually, therefore, it is plausible that an initial stage of agreement will be some common acceptance of the symmetrical-sharing outcome. Having reached provisional agreement on this stage, however, the actors may, on further consideration, find that the income positions of *both* persons can be improved by the specific introduction of distributional inequality. Work incentives may be such that unequal sharing will increase total product. This step in the agreement may, but need not, involve the identification of the recipient of the high income. Even if the two persons are identical in their work-effort responses to rewards, an unequal-sharing outcome may still be Pareto-superior to an equal-sharing outcome.[10] Or, perhaps more plausibly, there may arise some mutual recognition of the potential responses to work incentives which allows the person who will secure the high-income share to be identified. In either case, to the extent that envy is absent, there should be contractual unanimity on a shift from Hobbesian anarchy to a set of social arrangements that will maximize the income of the least advantaged.

This scenario places a somewhat different light on the concept of

---

[10] Consider a situation in which the two persons are basically similar but in which efficiency requires that one of the two take the role of residual claimant who monitors the performance of the other. On problems of organization raised by the recognition that monitoring must take place, see A. A. Alchian and Harold Demsetz, "Production, Information Costs, and Economic Organization," *American Economic Review* 62 (December, 1972): 777–795.

justice inherent in the predicted final outcome. In the original position, acting behind the veil of ignorance, individuals agree on the
difference principle of income distribution because they mutually
recognize the threat potential possessed by the relatively disadvantaged in any sharing outcome that fails to meet the requirement of
Pareto-superiority over the equal-sharing solution.[11] The latter position or solution becomes, in effect, a necessary way station, at least in
terms of the agreement, between Hobbesian anarchy and the final
position. The existence of many possible unequal-sharing outcomes
that are Pareto-superior to the original position but which may not be
Pareto-superior to the equal-sharing position under social cooperation
becomes irrelevant. Behind the veil of ignorance, neither person
would accept any one of these former unequal-sharing arrangements.

Note that this argument does not, at any point, rely on aversion
to risk, and indeed, in this argument it seems wrong to substitute
"maximin principle" for "difference principle." The parties in the
original position are not considering alternative production and distribution arrangements in the sense conceived by most of Rawls's
critics. They are considering alternative social structures, all of which
require the cooperation of all parties for continued viability. The arrangement chosen must satisfy minimal requirements of justice if it
is expected to be maintained. For this reason the arrangement that
qualifies may, but need not, maximize *expected* utility for the participants. The arrangement dictated by the expected utility criterion
might not be maintainable as a system of social cooperation, as a joint
contractual venture, for the simple reason that the least advantaged,
whoever they might be, would not stand for it, and this attitude might
well be predicted at the time of the initial agreement.[12]

We may illustrate the analysis arithmetically in our simplified
Crusoe-Friday model. Four situations may be specified: (1) Hobbesian anarchy, (2) equal sharing under joint production, (3) unequal sharing advantageous to the least advantaged under joint pro-

---

[11] At one point in his argument Rawls comes very close to making this the basis
for his whole construction. See Rawls, *Theory of Justice*, p. 15. See also Rawls,
"Reply to Alexander and Musgrave," pp. 647ff.

[12] See Rawls, *Theory of Justice*, pp. 175ff, and also Rawls, "Reply to Alexander
and Musgrave," pp. 652–653.

duction, a Rawlsian solution, and (4) the utilitarian solution in which total product or income is maximized. These situations may be shown in Table 5.

In this illustration, expected income (10.5) is higher under solution 4 than under solution 3 (9), on the equiprobability assumption which seems plausible enough in this setting. But rational choice makers in the initial position, in solution 1, will eschew the selection of those institutions required for solution 4 because of their shared prediction that these institutions will not be viable. The person who finds himself on the short end in solution 4, with an income of only five units, will be predicted to act to force the system back to that of equal shares, where his income moves up to six units. He can enforce this threat since his continued cooperation is required in what is essentially a joint venture.

Geometrical Analysis

We can remain within the two-person model and present these results geometrically, using a construction that is an emendation of that introduced by Rawls.[13] This analysis allows us to clarify the distinction between the Rawlsian solution, as here interpreted, and the utilitarian solution. In Fig. 6 the incomes of the two persons are measured on the two axes. The initial situation is the equilibrium natural distinction in Hobbesian anarchy, shown at point A in Fig. 6, where Friday secures the higher income of two units. The equal-

TABLE 5

Solution	Technology	Total Product	Shares of Crusoe:Friday
1. Hobbesian anarchy (the original position)	independent production	3	1:2
2. Equal sharing	joint production	12	6:6
3. Unequal sharing, Rawlsian	joint production	18	11:7
4. Unequal sharing, utilitarian	joint production	21	16:5

[13] See Rawls, *Theory of Justice*, pp. 76, 77.

sharing outcome when joint action is undertaken, upon contractual agreement to engage in a cooperative venture, is shown at C.[14] Note that as illustrated, this shift represents a dramatic increase in total product, and, hence, in the income of each party. This position becomes, in the process of agreement, a way station toward agreement on a more complex arrangement which might involve unequal shares. Both parties can improve their income positions by moves toward the upper right from C. The Rawlsian solution is shown at R or R', both of which might be considered equally likely if there is genuine ignorance of the roles in the original position. The shift from C to R (or R') is a Pareto-superior move, and hence one upon which agreement should be forthcoming at the time of the initial agreement. Considered as a discrete and lumpy set of alternatives, any point along either curve to the upper right of C can qualify on Rawlsian precepts. But if the whole set of possibilities is examined, the single point for step-wise agreement would seem to be that shown at R (or R').

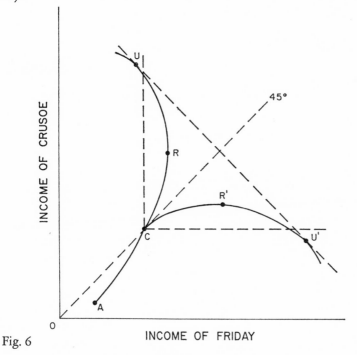

Fig. 6   INCOME OF FRIDAY

[14] See footnote 9 above in this chapter.

The total income of the two-person community is maximized at U (or U'), the utilitarian outcome. And under an equiprobability assumption (with the outcome at U equally likely with that at U'), expected utility for each person is maximized by the selection of the institutional regime that will generate this result. Note, however, that in U (or U') the low-income partner in the cooperative enterprise secures *less* than he would in the much less productive equal-sharing regime. In the original position each party must surely ask himself something about the workability and enforceability of any contractual agreement that might be reached. In particular, he must ask whether or not the least advantaged person, himself or the other, will readily acquiesce in a regime that will generate an outcome such as that shown at U (or U'). Will a person not predict that, finding himself in the low-income role at U (or U'), he would threaten to plunge the whole system of social cooperation back into anarchy unless he secures at least that which he can guarantee in the equal-shares regime? Hence, rejection of the utilitarian regime in the initial position emerges from the rational choices of participants who recognize the extreme vulnerability of such a regime to the threat potential held by the low-income party, whoever that might be.

From Two to Many Persons

As we shift from a two-person to a many-person setting, the limitations of the difference principle of distribution become somewhat more evident. In the two-person example discussed above, the dependence of the cooperative gains on the continuing acquiescence of each of the two parties is reasonable, especially when the technological shift from noncooperative to cooperative behavior is assumed to produce relatively large increases in total product. Consider, however, a society of n persons. As before, the original or initial position is one of Hobbesian anarchy, in which the life of each person is "poor, nasty, brutish, and short." There is no requirement that the net incomes of each person be substantially equal in this setting; all that is required is that each person secure a sustainable income that is dramatically lower than that which he might expect to secure under a regime of social cooperation. Why should the rational choice of a distributional rule be represented by agreement on a position analogous to R or R' in the two-person case depicted in Fig. 6?

To generate this result it is necessary to assume that *any* person who might find himself in the role of least advantaged can, by withdrawing his cooperation, plunge *all* of the other persons back into Hobbesian anarchy, back to the setting in which all incomes are dramatically reduced. That is to say, the whole structure of the society, as a society generating real income for its members, must be vulnerable to almost total disruption by the defection of any one member. In a sense, this is the extreme converse of the idealized competitive equilibrium. In the latter, the withdrawal of effort by any one person has, in the limit, no effect on the welfare, the income levels, of other persons. The total product of the group falls by precisely the amount of the marginal contribution which the person who withdraws previously added to total product. The income receipts of persons remaining in the game are not modified by marginal changes in the number of players. In the limiting case at the other extreme considered here, the withdrawal of any one member of the team essentially reduces the whole product of cooperative endeavor to zero.[15] In in-between cases, where there are increasing returns to numbers, the withdrawal of a person will reduce the amount available to others (there will be externalities), and these effects may be small or large depending on the shape of the total returns function. The marginal product of each man may exceed the average product, in which case the threat potential of any one person will vary depending on the size of the divergence.

A model of increasing returns may be plausible if there are extreme advantages of joint action—if the structural arrangements of society require the cooperation of all members for their productivity

---

[15] Consider the utilitarian solution, a non-Rawlsian production and distribution that may be the core of the game in that *no* coalition can secure gains by defecting from the cooperative arrangements. However, *any* coalition, including one-person coalitions, may impose major damages on *all* others in the group by defection. In this case the stability properties often attributed to the core may be almost wholly absent. A distribution satisfying Rawlsian norms may also meet the requirements for the core, but it possesses the additional feature that the threat of defection, even if wholly successful, probably cannot secure an improvement in the position of *any* coalition.

in generating net incomes or product. An assumption to this effect may be an inference of Rawls's analysis, as here interpreted. But additional argument may be adduced in favor of its relevance for the objectives that John Rawls set for himself. Consider the question: Under what conditions can a social group, a community, insure against its vulnerability to disruption by a tiny minority, or even by a single person? The immediate answer is that it can do so by adopting, establishing, and enforcing laws, legal rights, which limit, sometimes severely, the ability of noncooperative persons to disrupt the functioning of the basic structural order of the society. In a system without laws, without punishment for violation, without a police force, it is not at all implausible to suggest that a single dissident can indeed wreak havoc on all of his fellows.

In this context Rawls may be implying that he is simply not interested in a society with policemen.[16] In a meaningful, if overly restricted sense, such a society cannot meet reasonable criteria for justice. In that sense Rawls may be trying to lay down distributional rules or principles that will insure against defection in the absence of law and law enforcement. The Rawlsian world that satisfies the norms of justice can remain an anarchy, an ideal one that is ordered by the willing acquiescence of all persons, including those who are least advantaged. Interpreted in this light, we can place the whole Rawlsian construction in more obvious relevance to the events of the modern world.

This relevance is, of course, enhanced when we extend the difference principle from the level of the single person to that of groups. This possible extension is related to the implicit assumptions made about the potential enforceability of law in the community. For example, in the original position a person may rationally choose on the basis of an assumption that potentially dissident isolated persons, or even very small organized groups, will not be able to disrupt the orderly functioning of society or will not be able to reduce its productivity dramatically, in which case there would be no Hobbesian argument for applying the difference principle within these limits. On the other hand, rational choice in an original position might well

<hr/>

[16] See, for example, Rawls, *Theory of Justice*, p. 261. However, when he discusses the free-rider problem in connection with the provision of public goods, Rawls seems to accept the necessity of an enforcing agent. See ibid., p. 266ff.

incorporate the assumption that a potentially dissident large minority, or a majority of persons finding themselves in disadvantaged positions relative to those of a small minority of high-income persons, would abandon the support without which legal order could not survive. Indeed, in such a setting the majority may simply enforce a distribution akin to that suggested by the difference principle, quite independently of what should be chosen in the original position.

There is, of course, no need to adopt this large-group model for applying the difference principle. The point to be stressed is that there is a specific relationship between the presumption made about the enforceability of law and the range over which the distributional principle adopted is to be extended. Realistically, dissidence of a relatively large minority may promise social chaos, in which case care must be taken lest a group of this size should emerge in postconstitutional sequence with income less than it might expect to secure under an equal-sharing regime.

Informational Requirements and Outcomes
under Alternative Contractual Settings

The informational requirements for rational choice in the original position are severe in the interpretation placed on the Rawlsian analysis here. Individuals must be fully informed about the alternative positions available to the society under cooperative action, positions described by a vector of total production and distributive shares. They cannot, however, know anything at all about their own roles or situations relative to those of others in the community. As Robert Cooter suggests, an individual must know everything in general and nothing in particular.[17] If these requirements are accepted, and if the norms of justice are interpreted as elements of a social order in the absence of enforcement institutions, rational agreement on the difference principle of income distribution becomes logically predictable.

We may, however, accept the original position as the meaningful basis for contractual agreement and seek to derive norms for social order without resort to such restrictive requirements for information. It is reasonable to suggest that in the equilibrium of Hobbesian anar-

---

[17] Cooter, "What is Public Interest?" p. 25.

chy, persons are largely ignorant about the gross productivity of cooperative endeavor. Their initial step toward improvement in their status may lie in their recognition that mutual gains will be forthcoming from a simple definition of rights, a drawing of boundaries on allowable behavior concerning both persons and things. Having acknowledged this potentiality for mutual gains, however, the persons may also recognize the necessity for some enforcement of whatever rights are agreed. Each man will know that without some means of enforcement, each person will have a free-rider incentive to violate the agreed-on terms, to defect from the social contract. This knowledge will prompt, as a part of the rationally chosen initial agreement, some contractual structure of enforcement that will insure that costs are imposed on those who violate its terms.[18]

Once these steps are taken, the structural arrangements of society are complete, and persons can produce income and product independently or jointly as efficiency considerations dictate. They may, however, also recognize distributional considerations at the time of the original agreement. They may seek to insure that broad bounds or limits be placed on the degree of distributional disparities which might emerge under the operation of the social institutions chosen. These limits may be drawn without knowledge of the production and distribution feasibility set.

This arrangement of distribution may be illustrated, again for the two-person model, in Fig. 7. Crusoe and Friday commence in Hobbesian anarchy, the same original position as that described in Fig. 6. In this different framework for analysis, however, the two parties cannot predict the locus of possibilities as in the Rawlsian setting of Fig. 6. Instead, the parties know only that substantial gains can be secured from an agreed-on structure of rights. But they also seek to insure that final outcomes fall within certain distributional limits. For purposes of discussion, let us say that the two persons agree that one shall not receive a net income more than two times that of the other. The allowable range of income distribution is then bounded by the rays T and P in Fig. 7.

Suppose now that a position such as M is attained under the set of institutions chosen in the original position. There is no way of

---

[18] This summarizes the analysis of the hypothetical contractual process that is developed in detail in my book, *Limits of Liberty*.

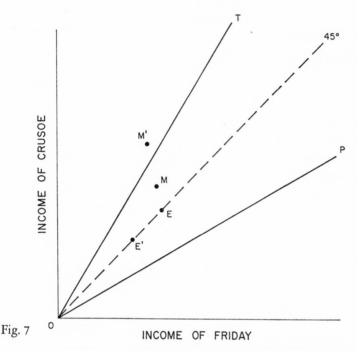

Fig. 7

INCOME OF FRIDAY

knowing how this position stands with respect to the Rawlsian criterion for distributive justice. If, in fact, point E should be an alternative possibility, M would not qualify as just under Rawlsian precepts. If, however, E' should be the equal-shares outcome that lies on the feasibility locus, then point M would in fact meet the requirements of the difference principle. Note also that the distributional boundaries emergent from an agreement of this sort may involve either more or less ultimate income inequality than that implicit in a Rawlsian contract. For example, if the distribution M' should emerge, it might qualify as acceptable under Rawlsian precepts if E' is the equal-shares prospect, but M' would not qualify under the insurance criterion offered here as an alternative set of terms in the original contract.

The Fragility of Social Order

The consideration of an alternative contractual framework in the preceding section was, in one sense, a digression from the main argument of this paper, the Hobbesian interpretation of the difference principle. Economists in particular have been unwilling to look behind their benign assumptions, so to speak, and to examine the vulnerability of the socioeconomic-political structure to disruption. Economists, intellectuals, and politicians alike have tended to concentrate their attention on flaws in the social process that seem amenable to easy correction, on the implicit and almost unrecognized assumption that remaining elements in society are indubitably fixed. It is, for example, relatively straightforward for economists to call attention to the external diseconomies generated by industrial discharges into our streams or internal combustion engine discharges into the air and for politicians to enact legislation imposing regulation or, on occasion, penalty taxes. It must surely be recognized, however, that the reduction in real income, meaningfully measured, produced by the increase in crime probably exceeds manyfold the damage caused by, say, water pollution. The quality of life in major American cities since World War II has been affected much more by crime in the streets than by smog. And where are the economists who bring into their simplistic welfare analytics the potential for social damage wrought by industry-wide strikes, notably in public utility and public service enterprises?

Honest assessment of life about us should suggest that there has been an erosion in the structure of legal order, in the acknowledged rights of persons, and that, indeed, modern society has come to be more and more vulnerable to disruption and the threat of disruption. Increasing interdependence is acknowledged, but the increasing vulnerability that this interdependence brings with it has not yet been properly incorporated into our thinking.

It is at this point that the contribution of Rawls, as here interpreted, can be extremely valuable. In this view Rawls is not, as many of his critics have charged, providing a philosophical, ideological basis for egalitarian income-wealth transfers superimposed on a market order.[19] Rawls warns repeatedly that this is not what he is about and that he is trying to derive principles for the establishment of the basic structure of society itself. The assumption natural to the think-

[19] This critical assessment of Rawls's work is shared both by those who welcome the implied argument for egalitarian transfers and by those who oppose it. For one of the most severely negative reactions, see Robert Nisbet, "The Pursuit of Equality," *The Public Interest* 35 (Spring, 1974): 103–120.

ing of economists, to the effect that a market-determined distribution would emerge *de novo* and that this distribution would always be available for use as a benchmark from which transfer policy might be discussed, is inappropriate in the Rawlsian analysis. This point is clarified under the interpretation advanced in this chapter in which the benchmark, the position that is the effective alternative in the absence of agreement, is defined as the equilibrium in Hobbesian anarchy. Instead of presenting a sophisticated rationalization for egalitarian transfers in a sociopolitical order which in its basic structure is implicitly assumed to be invariant, Rawls may be viewed as attempting to call attention to the increasing vulnerability of this structure to disruption.

I should emphasize that this interpretation represents an attempt to bring Rawls's efforts more closely in line with my own. We share a set of quasi-Kantian, contractarian presuppositions as opposed to a Benthamite utilitarian conception. In the latter respect, the various attempts that have been made to treat Rawls's whole effort as little more than the derivation of a "social welfare function" reflect misunderstanding of his basic construction.[20] To a contractarian there exists no means of evaluating alternative positions of society external to the conceptual agreement among participants in that society. In the utilitarian calculus, no matter how sophisticated its mathematics, the original position is a redundancy. To the contractarian the original position provides the basis from which the social structure must be derived, the starting point for analysis. The veil of ignorance becomes the device which allows agreement to become possible, since behind this veil individuals cannot predict their own narrowly defined self-interest. As Rawls clearly suggests, his construction does *not* depend on persons acting on the basis of motives other than self-interest. The original position forces them, in effect, to choose on the basis of precepts of fairness because these precepts, in that setting, are consistent with self-interest.

My earlier criticism of Rawls's book was based on the notion that the presentation and elaboration of the idealized contractarian process was his important contribution and that his complementary argument

[20] For an example of this nature, see Sidney Alexander, "Social Evaluation through Notional Choice," *Quarterly Journal of Economics* 88 (November, 1974): 597–624.

concerning just what precepts for justice might emerge from this process was both narrow and distracting. In the alternative interpretation that I have tried to develop here, the tie-in between the two parts of Rawls's construction becomes logically consistent. The specification of the particular norms of justice emerges from a recognition of the difficulties in and even the necessity for enforcement.

Empirical questions become important in assessing the significance of Rawls's construction for possible institutional reforms. How interdependent have persons become in complex social order? How vulnerable is the system to disruption? These questions are tied together by the efficacy of legal institutions. One cannot begin to answer them without making predictions about the willingness and ability of decision makers to enforce nominally defined rights and to punish violators of these rights. If attitudes in the society of the 1970's are such that they make individuals in positions of authority unwilling to punish defection, continued drift toward the chaos of anarchy must be predicted.

How might this drift be arrested? My own efforts have been directed toward the prospects that general attitudes might be shifted so that all persons and groups come to recognize the mutual advantages to be secured from a renewed consensual agreement on rights and from effective enforcement of these rights. Rawls may be, in one sense, more pessimistic about the prospects for social stability. Enforcement may not be possible unless the prevailing distribution meets norms of justice, and notably those summarized in the difference principle. Whereas I might look upon the breakdown of legal enforcement institutions in terms of a loss of political will, Rawls might look on the same set of facts as a demonstration that the precepts of a just society are not present.

As noted earlier, this interpretation of Rawls's analysis and construction is more positive than may seem warranted. Parts of his argument may be read to suggest that individuals *should not* abide by the distribution of rights assigned in the existing legal order unless this distribution conforms to the norms for justice. And persons in the original position *should not* agree on a set of social arrangements that are predicted to place strains on individual norms of adherence and support. This more normative setting is consistent with Rawls's ambiguity and ambivalence on enforcement and punishment, but it leaves open the definition of the norms themselves. The difference principle can be identified as emerging from contractual agreement in the initial position only if the participants make the positive prediction that least-advantaged persons and/or groups will, in fact, withdraw their cooperation in certain situations and that the threat of this withdrawal will be effective.

PART IV
ECONOMIC APPLICATIONS

15

The Relevance of Pareto Optimality

In his basic paper "On Welfare Theory and Pareto Regions"[1] Ragnar Frisch properly emphasized the necessity for specifying carefully the constraints that confine the Pareto region, that region within which the Pareto criterion for classifying positions is to be employed. As he demonstrated, the region will depend upon the nature of the constraints introduced, and the set of points or positions that may be classified as "optimal" will vary with these constraints. I propose here to discuss the nature of the appropriate constraints in a somewhat different manner and from a different philosophy than that of Frisch. His view, which is that "social value judgments" must be introduced in order to determine the form of constraints, leaves the relevance of the whole Paretian construction up in the air since, by implication, any change in the set of "social value judgments" employed will change the definition of optimality. By contrast, I shall try to demonstrate that meaningful criteria may be used to delineate the "appropriate" Pareto region, and the notion of Pareto optimality may, in this way, be rescued from the almost meaningless state to which any use of "social welfare functions" or "social value judgments" seems to reduce it.

In the discussion that follows, I shall show that the Pareto criterion is of little value when employed solely to classify "results" defined with respect to the orthodox economic variables, inputs and outputs of goods and services possessed by different persons in the social group. I shall instead argue that the criterion must be extended

[1] See Ragnar Frisch, "On Welfare Theory and Pareto Regions," *International Economic Papers* 9 (1959): 39–92.

to classify social rules which constrain the private individual behavior that produces such results. When the discussion of "optimal" rules is introduced, it may be shown that such rules produce results that themselves may be "nonoptimal." This apparent paradox will be illustrated in three separate cases, each of which has relevance for policy issues.

The Rules of the Game

Frisch separated the conditions or constraints confining Pareto regions into two groups, which he labeled *obligatory conditions* and *facultative conditions*. The first group includes those conditions that are exogenous to the group, taking the form of technical and physical limitations to production. These conditions are, of course, familiar, and they serve as part of the environment for any problem of choice, whether it is confronted by the individual or by the group. Indeed, without these conditions no choice problem should ever arise. I shall not be concerned directly with this set of physical constraints. The second group of constraints includes those that the group chooses to impose upon itself. They constitute, so to speak, the "rules of the game" within which individuals of the group make decisions and organize activity. The discussion will be devoted largely to this set of conditions or constraints. It is this set that has been largely neglected by welfare economists who have used the Pareto criterion, with the result that much of the analysis has been empty of content.

In discussing this second set of conditions, I shall depart from Frisch's terminology and from his analysis. Henceforward I shall refer to these conditions or constraints as *rules*, considered as standards of conduct applicable to all the members of the social group. Frisch defined facultative conditions in terms of what I call result variables, inputs and outputs of goods and services assigned to individuals. He then separated the *selection* problem from the *realization* problem. By the former he meant the classification of positions within the broad region defined by both the obligatory and the facultative constraints. In the realization problem he asked whether or not there exists a "régime" or "régimes" which will produce these Pareto-optimal positions. Frisch's approach, in this respect, seems both cumbersome and misleading. It tends to direct attention away from the basic issues of choice that members of the group confront. In a free society (the only society for which Pareto construction seems at all relevant) the group chooses or decides collectively upon the rules that are to be mutually imposed upon the behavior of its members. As Professor Rutledge Vining has stressed, the game analogue is quite close here. Members of the group may, of course, choose among different rules and sets of rules on the basis of predictions concerning the results expected from the operation of these rules, but explicitly the group makes a choice only among rules. Thus, the issues facing the group are solely those of realization, to use Frisch's terminology. The selection problems do not arise explicitly.

At any particular moment of time there must exist a set of rules, either legally imposed and enforced by some collectively organized agency or conventionally honored, and these rules serve to constrain the behavior of the members of the group as they act in their capacities as private individuals. The first point to be made is that given *any* such set of rules, *any* position reached by the group is Pareto-optimal provided only that individual members of the group are both fully informed and fully rational.

The set of rules serves to define a "Pareto region," which is described as the set of all possible positions or points attainable under both these social rules and the physical constraints that are present. Each of these positions may be defined, formally, as a vector in the "welfare space" so limited, components of this vector being inputs and outputs of goods and services assigned to each person in the group. Any change in the rules governing private behavior will change the structure of the region. Once a region is defined, however, the Pareto criterion may be employed to classify all points or positions into two sets, those that are "optimal" and those that are "nonoptimal." In a region so strictly confined, however, *any* position finally attained will be in the Pareto-optimal set of positions, except for ignorance and irrationality in the behavior of some or all individuals in the group. No paradox is involved here when it is recognized that each individual, if rational and fully informed, will maximize his expected utility within the constraints imposed on his behavior by the existing social rules. If each individual does this, there is no change, within the existing rules, that can make anyone better off. The Pareto criterion in this situation has relevance only insofar as it provides some assistance in dispelling areas of ignorance or in removing certain barriers to rational behavior. This application of the criterion is not without usefulness; the observer may be able to assist persons by demonstrating the presence of "gains" that can be made, even within the rules.

It seems clear, however, that welfare economists have not intended that the Pareto criterion be used only in so limited a fashion. In the models that have been generally employed, individuals are assumed to be both rational and fully informed. In such models, therefore, all positions attained are, by definition, Pareto-optimal, and hence the Pareto criterion loses relevance. But the Pareto scheme has been directed explicitly toward assistance in the formation of *policy*, that is, toward changes in the existing set of rules that constrain the private actions of individuals. Once this is admitted, however, the question that immediately arises concerns the extent to which rules changes are to be allowed.

Most of the actual discussion among welfare economists has concerned a rather well-defined "region," but almost no attention has been given to the requirement that to be relevant at all this region must be defined by "constitutional" limits placed on changes in social or organizational rules of the game. If, by contrast, the situation is assumed wholly open in this respect, with only obligatory constraints applying, the Pareto criterion becomes almost as meaningless as it does in the strictly confined case in which no rules changes are allowed at all. Should we allow a change in the rules so that if he is able, one man could make all his fellow citizens his slaves? Positions could still be classified as "optimal" and "nonoptimal," but obviously the content of the classification scheme becomes relatively empty.

Meaningful use of the Pareto criterion for classifying positions or states must therefore be limited to "regions" that allow for *some* but not *any and all* changes in an existing set of social rules. In the section "The Unanimity Criterion," below, I shall argue that the requirement of consensus or unanimity among members of the group on such "constitutional" changes does provide the appropriate limits to their relevant Pareto region. Before that, however, I shall in the next section present a simple illustration of the analysis.

Illustration

Let us assume a very simple two-person, two-goods world. The two individuals differ in their capacity to produce the two goods, although each person can, to some extent, produce some of each good. Production possibilities confronting each individual are shown in Fig. 8, and for simplicity only, production possibility curves are assumed to be linear.

We may first examine the strictly confined case discussed in the previous section. Assume that there exist rules which wholly prohibit trade between the two persons. Within this set of rules each individual will act to maximize his expected utility. Individual A, who is highly skilled in the production of good Y relative to X, will reach a position of individual equilibrium at $x_a y_a$; similarly, individual B will reach a position of individual equilibrium at $x_b y_b$. The final position of the "group," which may be defined by the quantities $x_a y_a$, $x_b y_b$, is Pareto-optimal, within the relevant Pareto region. The region in this case is that set of points or positions that might be attained by the movement of the two individuals within the production possibility

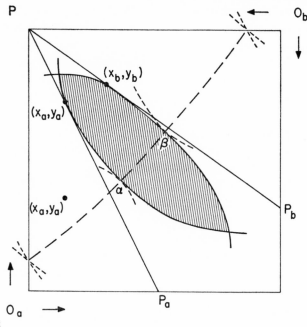

Fig. 8

frontiers, PP_a and PP_b, without trade. Thus, for example, the position defined as $x_a y_a'$, $x_b y_b$ is within the region defined, and it is classified as a nonoptimal position. Any such position, however, can be departed from upon a realization of the individual of his own opportunities. If A, in this case, is rational and informed, he will not, of course, remain at the nonoptimal position.

Let us now examine the second case. Assume that existing social rules allow the two individuals to cooperate through specialization and exchange, but that mutually respected rules enforce sanctions against deliberate exploitation through fraud, robbery, subjugation, and murder. These restrictions convert our model into one that is familiar to economists. Individual A will specialize in the production of good Y; individual B will specialize in the production of good X. Individual shares in total production are shown at P. After trade, a position of "equilibrium" is attained along the contract locus $\alpha\beta$. The Pareto region in this case becomes the whole set of positions that were potentially attainable in the first case, without trade, plus that set of points shown by the lightly shaded area in Fig. 8. (Only the second group of these point sets may be represented in Fig. 8 by single points, since only with trade is the whole "box" used.) Within this well-defined Pareto region the set of points falling along the locus $\alpha\beta$ is the Pareto-optimal set. Note that as the form of the imposed constraints is changed, the Pareto region is expanded and the set of optimal positions is changed. In this case note that the whole of the Pareto region in the first, strictly confined case is contained within the Pareto region appropriate to the second case, in which trade is allowed to take place. There is no intersection, however, between the Pareto-optimal set of positions in the first case and the Pareto-optimal set of positions in the second case.

We may now consider the third case, that in which *no* restrictions are placed on the behavior of individuals. No "rules of the game" are respected by members of the group. Trade can, obviously, take place, but also one individual can defraud the other, rob the other of his possessions, and even make the other his slave if he is able to exert sufficient physical force. In this extreme model only the external obligatory constraints confine the Pareto region. All positions that may be represented as points within the area of the Edgeworth box of Fig. 8 are contained in this region, as are, of course, those that are within the region relevant to the strictly confined case. This unconditional Pareto region of the third case, which we may call the unconstrained, includes within it the appropriate regions of the first and second cases. The Pareto-optimal set of positions in this third case is defined as those points falling along the locus $O_a\alpha\beta O_b$. Note here that should A be the strong man in the two-man group, he could make B his slave and move to a position in the vicinity of O_b, provided that we neglect, for purposes of this model, the pure subsistence requirements of B. The position on the locus in the vicinity of O_b would be defined as Pareto-optimal, despite B's complete exploitation. Note that there does exist an intersection between the Pareto-optimal sets in the second and third cases. Those positions that are Pareto-optimal under the more loosely defined Pareto region and which fall within the more closely defined region must also be Pareto-optimal in the second region.[2]

The Unanimity Criterion

The illustrative model presented above suggests that welfare economists have normally assumed, implicitly, that the second case describes the situation when they have applied the Pareto classification scheme. The first, or strictly confined, case, in which the Pareto criterion is useful only in dispelling ignorance or irrationality, is not the implicit model upon which the new welfare economics has been constructed. Nor is the third case, in which only the physical or obligatory constraints serve to inhibit the private behavior of individuals, the relevant one. Almost all discussions relating to the Edgeworth box limit the set of Pareto-optimal positions to those defined by some contract locus. This limitation to a "contract" locus amounts to the placing of additional constraints on human behavior, constraints that can only be interpreted in the form of mutually accepted rules and regulations.

What are the characteristics of these additional constraints which are purely facultative, to employ Frisch's term? As the analysis above demonstrates, these constraints cannot be wholly described by any existing set of social rules within which private behavior takes place.

---

[2] This proposition, in general terms, is one of the important relationships that Frisch stresses.

To be at all relevant for discussions of policy, the Pareto criterion must be applied to the classification of positions that may be attained through *changes* in the existing set of social or organizational rules. But the analysis has also demonstrated that the criterion loses much of its meaning if all changes in rules are permissable. How is an effective limit to be placed on the admissibility of rules changes, on modifications in the "constitution"?

One answer to this question is provided by the Wicksellian unanimity criterion. Given any existing set of social rules, changes in these rules are permissible to the extent that all members of the group agree. By *permissible* I mean only that the effective Pareto region is assumed to be limited by the extent of such unanimously approved changes. Welfare economists have not explicitly accepted this unanimity principle for limiting constitutional changes, but the principle is implied in much of the analysis.

An analogy with voluntary games is helpful here. In discussions of changes in the rules through which a game is defined, it is normally assumed that each individual player retains the alternative of withdrawing from play. This constraint serves to limit the set of possible rules changes. Within this "constitutional rule" a region of optimal and nonoptimal positions becomes possible, and this region may be described and the Pareto criterion employed in making the relevant classification. Coerced games, those in which the individual is forced to play quite independently of his possible preference for withdrawing, have not been fully discussed. The genuine "prisoners' dilemma" can be considered as a coerced game, but the mere fact that game theorists have treated it as an exceptional or peculiar case illustrates the overwhelming emphasis that has been placed on voluntary games.

The unanimity criterion for changes in the set of rules that govern individual behavior allows a unique, and generally applicable, Pareto region to be defined. This approach requires, of course, that a start be made from an existing set of rules. Meaningful analysis must, however, always start from some base or reference position. This approach does not sanctify the status quo or elevate it to any position of special respect. It rests, instead, on the elemental proposition that changes must be made on some existing situation and meaningful limitations must be placed on the sort of changes that are to be allowed. Unless the unanimity principle is applied to constitutional changes, we are left with the necessity of introducing "social welfare functions," of which there are as many as there are individuals in the group.

Accepting the Wicksellian approach, the Pareto criterion can be applied at two levels. First, within the existing set of rules the classification may be helpful in dispelling ignorance and irrationality, as noted previously. Second, the criterion may be used to classify positions unattainable under existing rules but which, conceptually, may be attained through the adoption of rules which themselves can be agreed upon by all members of the group. It should be noted that this application and use of the Pareto criterion is not subject to the charge made by Frisch that it amounts to saying that "free competition is the best of all possible régimes in the class of régimes which consists of the régime of free competition."[3] The unanimity principle for constitutional change will allow departures from free competition, free trade, when the necessary side conditions are not satisfied. The existence of interactions among individual utility functions or among individual production functions may reflect the existence of "mutual gains from trade" that may be secured through changes in the rules, either through the collectivization of activities or through the restriction of certain types of human behavior.[4] The introduction of the unanimity principle does emphasize an element of the competitive or market process that has, however, been seriously neglected. As Professor Frank Knight has suggested, much of the support for the market form of organization arises from the simple fact that it is the only form of organization upon which men seem able to agree.

The Notion of "Optimal" Rules

Through the use of the single constitutional constraint suggested, a determinate Pareto region is defined, given the obligatory constraints. Changes that do not fall within this limited set, that is, changes upon which all members of the group do not agree, may, of course, be made. This possibility suggests that changes in the organi-

---

[3] See Frisch, "On Welfare Theory," p. 67.

[4] For a more complete discussion, see James M. Buchanan, "Positive Economics, Welfare Economics, and Political Economy," *Journal of Law and Economics* 2 (October, 1959): 124–138.

zational rules themselves may be classified in two sets—those that are Pareto-superior and those that are not. As we shall demonstrate, the Pareto classification may prove more relevant in such a classification of changes in rules than in the discussion of results or outcomes.

If all members of the group were *always* to benefit from changes in the rules, it seems obvious that such changes would be carried out. And any failure to make such generally beneficial changes must reflect, at a different level from that previously discussed, the presence of ignorance concerning the results of the changes proposed. Even at the level of rules changes, therefore, the Pareto criterion can be helpful only insofar as it assists in dispelling ignorance and irrationality. But the ignorance about the working out of social rules is clearly a more pervasive phenomenon than that concerning the availability of individually attainable alternatives. Changes in social rules involve the necessity of making predictions of a considerably more sophisticated nature than those involved in changes in individual habits or modes of conduct. For example, it is probably much easier for me to predict the consequences of changing my own working hours than to predict the consequences that might result from a general change in the working hours of the whole community. The Pareto criterion, as employed by the political economist, can serve a useful function in demonstrating the mutuality of gain to be expected from proposed rules changes.

Few problems arise, however, in the simple cases postulated here—that is, those cases that produce results that are *always* beneficial to all members of the relevant social group. For an illustration, return to the first case discussed in connection with Fig. 8. Existing social rules prohibiting all trade between the two individuals would obviously be modified to allow trade which would, in the model, produce results that would, in each case, be mutually preferable to both parties or, at the limit, preferred by one and indifferent to the other.

Many situations are not so simple. A change in any existing rule need not produce results that will, in every case, be beneficial to all members of the group. But note that this situation need not imply that the unanimity principle for constitutional changes is inapplicable. The members of the group may be observed to agree on changes in the rules that produce results that, when classified by the orthodox

Pareto criterion, are clearly "nonoptimal"; in other words, "optimal rules," *defined as those that cannot be changed by general agreement,* may generate results that may be classified as nonoptimal. Note that this definition of optimal rules is identical with the standard definition for the optimality of a position or point.

The Enforcement of Competition

I propose now to examine three separate situations, in each one of which the operation of organizational rules accepted by general consensus, and thus optimal, may be predicted to produce results which, if independently classified within the region proposed above, seem clearly nonoptimal. That is, there may exist no means of securing agreement among all members of the group on any change in the rule, despite the fact that observed results may be classified as nonoptimal by the orthodox use of the Pareto criterion. Three separate situations are discussed, because the reason for the apparent paradox is different in each one. Numerous illustrations may be introduced in each situation, but I shall confine the discussion largely to three important issues of policy.

The most familiar situation is that presented when the results produced by the operations of a constraining rule are, to some degree, indeterminate. Predictions must be made about the pattern of some probability distribution of results, with some elements in this pattern being mutually beneficial to all parties while others are harmful to some members of the group, beneficial and harmful being defined here relative to the situation produced under some alternative state of affairs. In this situation any rule must produce results that on occasion are nonoptimal and that, if independently considered, could be improved upon in such a way that all members of the group would secure mutual gains. As Ronald Coase has pointed out, each time a driver is forced to stop at a road sign or signal in an isolated place with no traffic, Pareto optimality is violated. Clearly, the driver could be made better off and no one else made worse off should the sign or signal be removed for that particular moment. Nevertheless, we observe such traffic signals in profusion, and few persons would choose to see them abolished. The implication is that somehow predictions are made to the effect that the costs to the group stemming out of all cases of nonoptimal results are more than offset by the benefits occurring in those perhaps few cases when the signals do insure optimal results. A comparison of costs and benefits, or, more broadly considered, a comparison of alternative institutional arrangements or social rules over a whole sequence of possible results, is necessary.

Are there economic analogues to the situation with the traffic signal? Communities are observed to adopt rules that prohibit certain business practices with the aim of preserving or enforcing competition. Among such rules are those that prevent separate firms in an industry from entering into wholly voluntary agreements on prices, market shares, and mergers. For members of the specific industrial subgroup such rules are equivalent to prohibitions on trade or exchange. For this subgroup changes that remove this constraint would clearly be mutually beneficial to all parties. But the Pareto construction is rarely, if ever, applied at this level. Presumably, for some larger social group, which includes the firms in question, the restrictive rules may be optimal. If such rules are to be judged optimal, however, the logical basis for their support requires examination. Why should the inclusive social group impose upon its own members rules that prohibit the reaching of wholly voluntary agreements? Any such rule must be predicted to produce nonoptimal results on occasion.[5]

The standard response here is that the predicted presence of external (spillover, neighborhood) effects can dictate the imposition of such constraints on private behavior. Firms within an industrial subgroup may, if allowed freedom of action, reach agreements that will damage members of the more inclusive group who are not party to these agreements, consumers, or potential rivals. This familiar explanation begs more questions than it answers, however, for it is evident that such prohibitive rules are not imposed in all cases where voluntary agreements among members of a subgroup exert some ef-

---

[5] For an interesting group of papers that suggests the development of economists' attitudes in this direction, see M. A. Adelman, "The Antimerger Act, 1950–60," *American Economic Review* 51 (May, 1961): 236–244; Almarin Phillips, "Policy Implications of the Theory of Interfirm Organization," *American Economic Review* 51 (May, 1961): 245–254; and Donald Dewey, "Mergers and Cartels: Some Reservations about Policy," *American Economic Review* 51 (May, 1961): 255–262. Dewey, especially, explores the possible conflict between the restriction on freedom of contract and the orthodox criteria for economic efficiency.

fects on the utility of those external to the agreements. The marriage contract may be cited as one that would surely be prohibited under such a rigid application of the externality principle. What is required here is obviously some comparison, some balancing off, between the operation of a rule that prohibits voluntary agreements that exert external effects and the situation that would prevail in the absence of such a rule.

Such a comparison is more difficult than it might appear. How can third parties be injured by voluntary contractual arrangements among others? Provided freedom of contract is present, and provided that the costs of organizing voluntary agreements can be neglected, there is no damage that may be inflicted on third parties. Hence, there is no justification of the rule prohibiting "trade," regardless of the presence of externalities. No rules prohibiting mergers, for example, could be supported in this case. If firms in a specific industry should find it advantageous to merge, and if the threatened result should portend injury to consumers, then surely the organizational arrangement that would emerge under the conditions postulated would be that of a consumers' cooperative, large enough to secure the full efficiencies of scale but without monopoly exploitation. If the organization of agreement is costless, the capital value of the assets of the firms in question will always be as great to consumers as to the existing owners. A "bargaining range" will exist, and trade will tend to take place.

The optimality or efficiency of any rule prohibiting voluntary agreements can only be demonstrated in those cases in which some external effects are present and in which there is some asymmetry in the costs of organizing different voluntary arrangements.[6] Of course,

---

[6] The importance of organizational costs in determining the institutional structure has been seriously neglected by economists. There are indications, however, that the problems in this area are beginning to be recognized and that significant modifications to economic theory, and to welfare economics especially, may result. For an early recognition of the importance of these factors, see Ronald Coase, "The Nature of the Firm," *Economica* 4 (1937): 386–405, reprinted in American Economic Association, *Readings in Price Theory*, pp. 331–351. For essentially the same line of reasoning applied to the Pigovian welfare calculus, see Ronald Coase, "The Problem of Social Cost," *Journal of Law and Economics* 3 (1961): 1–45. In this connection also see Buchanan, "Positive Economics," pp. 130–131; James M. Buchanan and Gordon Tullock, *The Calculus of Consent*; and Otto Davis and Andrew Whinston,

the reaching of voluntary agreements is not costless, and the costs of reaching agreement are not identical for all possible arrangements. When this fact is recognized, the comparison of alternative rules that govern human behavior takes on different aspects. Rules that serve to restrict the reaching of wholly voluntary agreements among members of the group can be justified if predictions suggest that certain types of voluntary arrangements are relatively costly. In the particular example here, that of industrial combinations, the required asymmetry does seem to be present. Firms that are party to an agreement or to a potential agreement are fewer in number than consumers and potential consumers of almost any final product or service. The costs of reaching agreement increase significantly as the size of the group required to agree is expanded.[7] It therefore follows that the firms, faced with the lower costs of agreeing or combining, may enter into agreements that will significantly damage consumers without these consumers being able to enter into the appropriate offsetting agreements. Under such conditions as these it becomes rational for the members of the larger and more inclusive social group to adopt a general rule or set of rules that may prohibit, or severely restrict, voluntary agreements within an industrial group. The benefits to be secured from the operation of this rule may be expected to outweigh the costs when a whole sequence of events is considered.

The important conclusion for purposes of our analysis here is that in any particular application, observed results from the operation of such a rule may seem to be clearly nonoptimal. Firms may be observed to be too small to take full advantage of efficiencies of scale. Pareto optimality in the standard sense involved in the measurement of results is violated. Yet the rule prohibiting firms from merging into units of optimal size may itself be "optimal" in the sense that even with full compensations there may be no way of securing consensus on any change. Thus, the mere demonstration of some violation of Pareto optimality in the orthodox classification of *results* may not be sufficient to suggest that some change in *policy* is dictated.

"Externalities, Welfare and the Theory of Games," *Journal of Political Economy* 70 (June, 1962): 241–262.

[7] This relationship is central to the analysis contained in Buchanan and Tullock, *Calculus of Consent*, which is essentially an analysis of the choice among political decision-making rules.

Such a demonstration will, of course, always remain a necessary condition before any change in policy is to be considered.

Rules *versus* Authorities

The familiar debate over rules versus authorities in monetary policy may be introduced as an illustration of a second type of situation in which optimal rules, those from which no changes may be made by unanimous consent, may operate to produce nonoptimal results. When attention is concentrated on particular events, as these may be described by the relevant variables, a strong case can always be made for the superiority of an administrative authority or authorities over any rule or set of rules prescribing action in advance. A monetary authority, endowed with wisdom and prudence, can take full advantage of the information peculiar to the particular event. Such an authority, empowered to act independently of specific constraining rules, should be able to insure a closer attainment of the Pareto frontier than would the operation of any automatic or quasi-automatic general rule for policy action.

The specific decisions or actions that an authority will take cannot, however, be predicted in advance, at least to the same degree that the operations of an automatic rule can be predicted. When the beneficial effects expected to result from predictability per se are significant, some general rule may be more acceptable than the loosely confined authority, even with the expectation that particular results from the operation of the rule will be less than optimal in many cases. The foreknowledge that the rule will be followed can modify behavior to make the rule, over an expected sequence of events, more desirable than the authority. If, in adjusting their behavior to a predictable rule for monetary action, private individuals and firms eliminate much of the need for such action, the rule may be preferred over even the most efficient authority, which must, by definition, remain more unpredictable in its own actions than the constraining rule. In each and every particular event, considered in isolation, the authority could, conceptually at least, produce more desirable results for *all* members of the social group. But these results are produced within a framework governing private decisions that is different under the presence and absence of the rule. It may become largely irrelevant, therefore, to compare the efficacy of the authority and some alternative rule in terms of the specific results that would be produced under a single framework.[8]

There are numerous noneconomic examples of this situation in which the alternative institutional arrangements exert important differing effects on the pattern of human behavior. Perhaps the most familiar discussion is found in the debates over capital punishment. Those who argue in support of capital punishment do so largely on the grounds that a "rule" requiring punishment will deter potential criminals, whereas those who argue for the abolition of executions do so on the grounds that in each particular case little is to be gained by the execution of the condemned prisoner.

The Pareto classification of "results" into optimal and nonoptimal sets is less relevant in this situation than in the first type that was discussed in the preceding section. There, the rule, to be optimal, must be predicted to produce both optimal and nonoptimal results, with the former events outweighing the latter on balance. In this second situation, by contrast, particular results could, conceptually, be nonoptimal in each particular case while the rule producing these results remains an optimal one.

Collective Decision Making

An example of a third situation where nonoptimal results are produced from the operation of rules that may embody general consensus is provided in the institutions for collective decision making. A constitutional rule may, for example, dictate that group decisions on specific matters shall be made upon agreement among some designated proportion of the total population or its representative assembly. Simple majority agreement is a familiar device in democratic societies, although the range of institutional arrangements for collective decision making is extremely wide. The slightest observation

[8] Even if, over the course of historical experience, a hypothetical rule for monetary policy could be shown to have worked badly relative to the actual operations of an authority, such an example would tell little about the relative desirability of the rules, since the whole framework of private decision making would have been different had the rule been in operation instead of the authority. Similarly, empirical studies suggesting the superiority of nonexistent rules can, at best, be broadly illustrative, nothing more.

reveals that group action on many issues may be concluded upon agreement among members of some subgroup smaller than the total group.

In each such arrangement, results will surely be nonoptimal on many occasions. To insure that each position obtained through the process of collective decision making should qualify as Pareto-optimal, all decisions would have to be reached through the unanimous consent of all members of the inclusive group, not some proportion of this number. This requirement need not imply, however, that a constitutional rule dictating the institutional arrangements for ordinary collective decision making need be nonoptimal. It may prove quite impossible, even granted the full use of compensation, to secure the general consent of all members of the group on a constitutional change toward more inclusive voting agreements.

A specific illustration may prove helpful. Assume that the constitutional rule dictates that ordinary group decisions are to be made by simple majority. Assume a three-man group, and assume that each member of the group possesses assets valued at one hundred dollars. Let us neglect purely redistributive transfers and assume that the group, through the exercise of majority decision, can choose to use resources to produce or consume "collective" goods. Is there any assurance that the projects approved will, in fact, be as productive as, or more productive than, the sacrificed private investments? Let us suppose that with a general tax of thirty-three dollars levied on each member of the group a project can be constructed that yields only seventy dollars' worth of benefits, but that these benefits are uniquely concentrated so as to benefit solely B and C. In this case, with simple majority controlling, B and C can carry the decision and insure the expenditure of public funds on the project in question. The result must be classified as nonoptimal. All members of the group could be made better off by some return to the position that existed before approval of the project.[9]

---

[9] One additional and constraining rule must be present to insure these results. If there are no restrictions on vote buying and selling, the political analogue to side payments, those members of a threatened minority could always bribe the members of the majority to refrain from undertaking "wasteful" projects. In this case only purely redistributive transfers would be made through majority voting, and of course Pareto optimality would not be violated. We observe, however, that generally

Must it be concluded in this case that the constitutional rule that allows majorities to carry group decisions is itself nonoptimal? Or is it possible that the group may agree, through an explicit failure to approve any change, on such a rule? Once the costs of reaching agreement are incorporated into the calculus here, there is no necessary contradiction or paradox. The attainment of unanimity in ordinary, day-to-day collective decisions may prove to be extremely costly. Rather than undergo this cost, members of the group may decide, in the constitutional process, to accept the departures from Pareto optimality that less-than-unanimity voting rules may produce. Majority voting is, of course, only one of the many arrangements that might be made.[10]

Other illustrations of what is essentially the same situation may be drawn readily. In ordinary exchange processes potential traders may actually refrain from trading if the costs of bargaining and negotiation promise to be prohibitively high. Or, alternatively, they may choose to adopt conventions or rules that are, in themselves, arbitrary as a means of reducing bargaining costs. In advanced economies it is a conventional rule that the seller of goods shall set the price. This reduces the costs of haggling and bargaining, but, as in the majority voting example, it surely produces nonoptimal results on many occasions, as these results have been traditionally classified by welfare economists using the Pareto classification.

Conclusions

The preceding discussion has demonstrated that the application of the Pareto criterion to organizational rules introduces complexities in prediction and in analysis that have been neglected in the concentration on particular results. The standard procedure, which involves the examination of a position (for example, an "allocation" of resources) with a view to determining whether or not moves from that position are possible that will benefit at least one member of the group without damage to another, is seriously incomplete. When

---

accepted ethical and legal rules prohibit the making of such side payments, that is, vote buying and selling.

[10] For a further elaboration of the ideas sketched here, see Buchanan and Tullock, *Calculus of Consent*.

examined in isolation, many particular positions may be nonoptimal in this narrow sense. And if a single, isolated move could be made, the preferences of all members of the group might, conceptually, be revealed through an agreement to make the indicated change to an optimal position. But group decisions cannot be made in terms of single cases, and for several reasons. Collective decisions must be made in terms of organizational rules or constraints that are expected to prevail over a sequence of results. Nonoptimality in a single case does not imply potential consensus on a change in the organizational rules.

This emphasis on the extension of the Pareto classification to organizational rules does not suggest that its orthodox use in the classification of final positions or results is without value. Surely the operation of alternative rules can only be evaluated in terms of predicted results, and the Pareto construction can be helpful in this process. At the level of application to the social constitution, to the evaluation of the "rules of the game," however, the Pareto criterion serves a function that it cannot possibly serve in the more standard use. Unless the observing economist is assumed to be omniscient, his classification of a final position as nonoptimal can never be more than a conjectural hypothesis that is impossible to test. If members of the group do not explicitly choose among final positions in the appropriately defined welfare space, the hypothesis that some members of the group can be made better off by a change remains empty. By contrast, the classification of an organizational rule as nonoptimal can be considered as a hypothesis that is subject to conceptual testing. If a presumed or apparent nonoptimal rule cannot be changed through agreement among members of the group, the hypothesis stating that the rule is nonoptimal is effectively refuted.

The contrast between the approach suggested here and the more familiar use of the Pareto construction by the welfare economists should not be overemphasized. As suggested earlier, the standard use has, implicitly, defined the Pareto region as that which is limited by the constitutional constraint inherent in the unanimity principle. In addition, the concentration upon final results or positions need not be misleading in those cases where the correspondence between rule and result is reasonably complete. In most cases of economic policy the demonstration of inefficiency in an allocation of resources does imply that there exists some change in the organizational rules upon which all members of the group could agree. Nevertheless, as the situations discussed above have shown, the correspondence need not be present in this sense, and possible errors can always be prevented by an emphasis on the choice among alternative sets of social rules or constraints.

Starting from any existing set of rules, combined with the external or obligatory constraints arising out of technical limitations, the economist has a well-defined Pareto region within which he can bring all of his analytical skills into play. All possible changes in the constitutional structure become admissible as long as these changes may, conceptually, be approved by general agreement. The unanimity principle for changes in the "social constitution" provides the only appropriate facultative constraint.

The alternative approach is, of course, that which involves the introduction of "social welfare functions" or "social value judgments." However, even as the proponents of this alternative approach admit, the economist is no more able to dictate such judgments than is any other citizen. By introducing his constraints in the form of social value judgments, the economist may leave the major part of his appropriate task undone. He may remove himself all too quickly from the area in which he does, in fact, possess some special competence. Instead of closing off discussion through the introduction of such judgments, the economist's function is that of keeping discussion open. He must employ his skills in presenting to the social group hypotheses in the form: "I think that a change from current policy to policy X is one upon which all members of the group can agree." He must try to formulate alternative social compromises as means of testing alternative hypotheses. In slightly different terms, the economist's task is simply that of repeating in various ways the admonition, "there exist mutual gains from trade," emphasizing the word *mutual* and forever keeping in mind that "trade" need not be confined to the exchange of goods and services in the marketplace. Welfare economics can make real progress through such a change in approach, which, quite literally, may be called the introduction of "constructive institutionalism."

16

A Contractarian Paradigm for
Applying Economic Theory

THE object for economists' research is "the economy," which is, by definition, a social organization, an interaction among separate choosing entities. I return deliberately to this element in our primer because I think that it has been too often overlooked. By direct implication, the ultimate object of our study is not itself a choosing, maximizing entity. "The economy" does not maximize, and we may substitute "the polity" here without change in emphasis. No one could quarrel with these simplistic statements. The inference must be, however, that there exists no one person, no single chooser, who maximizes *for* the economy, *for* the polity. To impose a maximizing construction on the models that are designed to be helpful in policy is to insure sterility in results.

Where did economics, as a discipline, take the wrong turn? My own suggestion is that Lionel Robbins's *The Nature and Significance of Economic Science* marks a turning point. That book defined "the economic problem" as the location of maxima and minima. Almost simultaneously, the Chamberlin and Robinson analyses of imperfect and monopolistic competition marked a turning inward, so to speak— a shift toward the maximizing problem of a specific decision-making entity. The economics of the firm was born, to be followed by the Hicksian elaboration of the economics of consumer choice.[1] Paul Samuelson put this all together in his *Foundations of Economic Analysis*, and, importantly, he extended the maximizing construction to welfare economics, extolling the virtues of Bergson's social wel-

---

[1] J. R. Hicks, *Value and Capital.*

fare function as the tool through which such extension was made possible. For four decades we have witnessed many variations on this theme, with economists hither and yon maximizing objective functions subject to specific constraints.

I should not infer that the maximizing models have held monolithic dominance. The institutional economists and their successors have continued their sometimes inarticulate critique of economic theory. Frank Knight and some of his students continued to lay stress on the social-organization aspects of the discipline. Game theory, in its solution instead of its strategy search, offered partial redirection of emphasis. More importantly for my purposes, public choice theory emerged as the positive theory of politics, a theory that necessarily treats individual decision takers as participants in a complex interaction that generates political outcomes.

But let me return to mainstream efforts of economists in the years since World War II. I have no quarrel with the elaborations and refinements of the maximizing models for individual and firm behavior, although I have argued that many of these contributions belong, appropriately, to home economics or business administration instead of political economy. My strictures are directed exclusively at the extension of this basic maximizing paradigm to social organization, where it does not belong. This is the bridge which economists should never have crossed and which has created major intellectual confusion. "That which emerges" from the trading or exchange process, conceived in its narrowest or its broadest terms, is not the solution to a maximizing problem, despite the presence of scarce resources and the conflict among ends. "That which emerges" is "that which emerges," and that is that.

Return to game theory for analogy. The solution to a game with defined rules is not a maximum, and an external observer of the game would not attempt to seek improvements by operating directly on solutions. He would, instead, look at the prospects for changing the rules, and observed solutions would be information to be included in his evaluation of the game. Solutions are not directly "chosen" by a welfare function that embodies the preferences of the players, and solutions are not themselves ordered in terms of such a function. In game theory the attempt to force such a construction would appear, and be, absurd. Yet such forcing of constructions seems to me to be precisely what economists try to do within their analogous domain. Game theorists would indeed be surprised if someone should find that solutions could, in fact, be ordered in any manner that was consistent with the values of individual players. And they would not be profoundly shocked, to say the least, if someone should prove that such an ordering could not be made. Yet is this not what most economists experienced when Kenneth Arrow published his famous impossibility theorem in *Social Choice and Individual Values?*

My own initial reaction to Arrow's work was, and remains, one of nonsurprise.[2] Who would have expected any social process to yield a consistent ordering of results? Only economists who had made the critical methodological error of crossing the bridge from individual to social maximization without having recognized what they were doing would have experienced intellectual and ideological disappointment.

There is no need to limit discussion to Arrow's theorem, although I shall return to this subject. Economists crossed the bridge from individual to social maximization because they wanted to be able to say something about policy alternatives. They desperately needed some instrument which would allow them to play the social engineer, even if they eschewed the explicit intrusion of their own values in the process.[3] With the construction of the social welfare function they could then talk as if their policy statements were operationally meaningful, and this ability provided them with a certain inner satisfaction. They have remained unwilling to use the Pareto criterion as a mere classification scheme, which Ragnar Frisch had advised them to do,[4] and they have not followed my own suggestion (see chapter 15) about shifting the application of the criterion back to the level of institutional choice, where prospects for mutuality of agreement are enhanced.

How would the abandonment of the social maximization paradigm have changed the research thrust of economic theory, and espe-

[2] James M. Buchanan, "Social Choice, Democracy, and Free Markets," *Journal of Political Economy* 62 (1954): 114–123.

[3] I am indebted to Charles Plott for suggesting this explanation of the Bergson-Samuelson approach, which is a more sympathetic explanation than the one which I have elsewhere suggested.

[4] Ragnar Frisch, "On Welfare Theory and Pareto Regions," *International Economic Papers*, no. 9 (1959): 39–92.

cially its potential relevance for social policy? The Pareto criterion classifies all positions into two mutually exclusive sets. Once an initial position is explicitly identified to be "nonoptimal" or "inefficient," we know that there exists at least one means of moving from this position to a position that falls within the optimal or efficient set. The initial position must be dominated, for all persons, by at least one position in the efficient set.

There is no issue here, but what should be the role for the economist who has completed these first steps in applying his expertise? He should neither revert to nihilism nor seek the escapism of social welfare functions. His productivity lies in his ability to search out and invent social rearrangements which will embody Pareto-superior moves. If an observed position is inefficient, there must be ways of securing agreement on change, agreement which signals mutuality of expected benefits. In the limiting case, compensation schemes can be worked out which will achieve Wicksellian unanimity. Yet how many economists do we observe working out such schemes? How many economists bother with proposed compensations (which must, of course, include structural-institutional rearrangements) to those who will be overtly harmed by the effects of a public or governmental policy shift?[5] Instead of this potentially constructive effort we find our colleagues continuing to express opposition to tariffs, quotas, minimum wages, price controls, depletion allowances, monopolies, tax loopholes, and so on, whether these be existing or proposed. And they continue to be surprised when the political process, as it operates, pays little or no heed to their advice. As Wicksell noted eighty years ago, economists act as if they are advising a benevolent despot, in which case their post-Robbins, post-Bergson stance would, of course, be entirely fitting.

There is a place for efficiency in my suggested scheme of things. In this sense, there is little wrong with economic theory per se. Efficiency, as an attribute, is necessarily present when there is a demonstrated absence of possible agreed-on changes. The trading process,

---

[5] An exception is W. H. Hutt. In his much neglected book *A Plan for Reconstruction* he proposed that the postwar British economy be swept clear of all market restrictions through the device of compensating all persons and groups who would lose by the change.

broadly conceived, is the means through which the "potentially realizable surplus" is exploited. But there is no uniquely determinate outcome of the trading process, since exchanges must be made and contracts enforced at preequilibrium, and hence disequilibrium, prices. Under the standard assumptions, simple exchange insures that an efficient or optimal position is attained, but this is only one from among a set containing a subinfinity of possible positions. Economists should be satisfied with this result, and, within theory itself, their search for uniqueness seems to be misguided effort. When the standard assumptions are not descriptive, the simple exchange process will not generate efficient results, and more complex arrangements may be called for. But these arrangements may still be examined in a contractual framework. The specification of these complex contractual arrangements may challenge the skill of the practicing political economist. In facilitating these complex exchanges, which may require the inclusive membership of the whole group, collective and governmental institutions may be necessary. And even though unanimous agreement for change may be conceptually possible, the costs of reaching agreement may be acknowledged to be prohibitively high. This possibility suggests, in turn, that rules or institutions for reaching collective or group decisions may be preselected at some constitutional stage of trade. It becomes possible in this way to apply the basic contractarian paradigm to the discussion of possible agreement on rules, even if it is anticipated that conflict will emerge at some final stage of application.

Whether the contractarian paradigm is applied at the level of simple exchange, within the constraints of well-defined rules, or at the most basic constitutional level where institutions themselves are the objects upon which agreement must be reached, or at any intermediate level, the emergent results of the trading process are properly summarized as a set of optimal positions, each one of which represents a possible outcome and no one of which dominates any other in the set. This statement is enough to suggest my prejudices toward game-theory explorations into mathematics as opposed to the intricacies of complex maximization. The continuing search for solution concepts—the Von Neumann–Morgenstern solution set of imputations and the several cores along with other more sophisticated concepts—seems to me to reflect and in turn to foster an attitude in the theorist that is consistent with, and contributory to, the contractarian approach that I am here suggesting.

The modern efforts to prove that competitive equilibrium exists and lies in the core of an economy are within my own limits for methodological legitimacy. The complementary emphasis here should be placed on the multiplicity of possible equilibria, on the absence of uniqueness. The devices of the Walrasian auctioneer or Edgeworthian perfect recontracting have been required for the proofs here, but I urge those skilled in this particular mathematics to search for theorems that require less stringent assumptions and that incorporate trading at disequilibrium prices.

Now let us return, as promised, to the Arrow impossibility theorem. In his 1973 Nobel Prize lecture Kenneth Arrow offers a lucid summary of modern economic theory, and he concludes with a discussion of his impossibility theorem.[6] Unfortunately, Arrow does not seem to have gone beyond his initial failure to appreciate the inconsistency between his norms for a social welfare function, or choosing process, and the precepts for a society of free men. In his lecture Arrow makes it clear that the Bergsonian requirement of "collective rationality" is prior to the set of reasonable conditions that he lays down for his social ordering. Having long ago proved that these conditions cannot be met, Arrow continues to hold that "the philosophical and distributive implications of the paradox of social choice are still not clear." This statement is both surprising and personally disappointing, since it indicates that Arrow has paid no heed to the arguments which I, along with many others, have made against the whole notion of collective rationality.

The so-called paradox may be used as a single and simple illustration of the profound difference between the maximization paradigm and the contractarian one. There are three voters, A, B, and C, and three alternatives, 1, 2, and 3. The collective choice rule is simple majority voting. Through a series of pairwise comparisons, individual preference orderings may be such that 1 is majority-preferred to 2, and 2 is majority-preferred to 3, while 3 is majority-preferred to 1. This cyclical result is disturbing only to those who seek uniqueness

[6] "General Economic Equilibrium: Purpose, Analytic Techniques, Collective Choice," *American Ecnomic Review* 64 (June, 1974) : 253–272.

in outcome, who seek to impose the maximization paradigm on a social interaction process where it does not belong. By contrast, to those who accept the contractarian paradigm, who seek only to explain and to understand the behavior of persons who interact one with another, there is nothing at all disturbing in the paradox. On the assumptions that all side payments have been made, or that institutional constraints are invariant, the tools of economics enable us to classify all three positions, 1, 2, and 3, as falling within the Pareto-optimal or efficient set, and no one of these positions dominates the other. If individual preferences produce this set of results, we should be content and forego the essentially misleading searches for "philosophical implications" that simply are not there.

In this chapter I have restated a position that I have presented in bits and pieces in several places. Frank Knight's favorite quotation from Herbert Spencer says that, "only by varied reiteration can alien conceptions be forced on reluctant minds." I hope that I have at least varied the reiteration sufficiently to avoid boredom. I would not presume to think that my own views on methodology would convince more than a minority of my professional colleagues, and I am under no illusions about the continued dominance of the maximization paradigm in modern economics. Nonetheless, I think that progress has been made during the last twenty years. Game theory, after a series of disappointing attempts to work out optimal strategies for players, has shifted toward a more comprehensive, and more appropriate, consideration of solution concepts. Public choice has emerged as a subdiscipline in its own right, and one that is currently thriving, both within economics and in political science. But intellectual developments have perhaps been overshadowed in effect by the march of events. As persons from both the streets and the ivory towers observe modern governmental failures, they can scarcely fail to be turned off by those constructions which require beneficent wisdom on the part of political man. And they can hardly place much credence in the economist consultant whose policy guidelines apply only within institutions that embody such wisdom. Something is amiss, and economists are necessarily being forced to take stock of the social productivity of their efforts. When, as, and if they do so, they will, I think, come increasingly to share what I have called the contractarian paradigm.

As I have argued elsewhere,[7] economics comes closer to being a "science of contract" than a "science of choice." And with this conclusion the "scientist," as political economist, must assume a different role. The maximizer must be replaced by the arbitrator, the outsider who tries to work out compromises among conflicting claims. The Edgeworth-Bowley box becomes the first diagram in our elementary textbooks; the indifference curve–budget line construction is relegated to subsidiary treatment. Böhm-Bawerk's horse traders are the basic examples, not the housewife who shops for groceries in the supermarket. Game theory, in its most comprehensive sense, becomes the basic mathematics for the professional, and solutions to n-person games replace the nth-order conditions for maxima and minima. The unifying principle becomes gains from trade, not maximization. These principles merge, of course, at the level of the individual chooser's calculus, but they become quite distinct when attention shifts to the social interaction that we call "the economy."

[7] See my "What Should Economists Do?" *Southern Economic Journal* 30 (January, 1964): 213–222; and my "Is Economics the Science of Choice?" in *Roads to Freedom: Essays in Honor of F. A. Hayek*, ed. Erich Streissler, pp. 47–64.

17

Democratic Values in Taxation

Justice and Democracy

THERE are several ways of approaching the subject matter suggested by the title of this chapter. One projected focus of attention is on the possible inconsistency between ethically derived criteria for imposing taxes and the political process through which taxes must be levied and collected. This approach immediately confronts the philosopher-economist with the question that he often tries to escape or to evade. Many economists, along with other social scientists and social philosophers, enjoy playing God, by which I mean laying out in detail their own private versions of the "good society" without being required to suggest ways and means of implementing their precepts or even to defend the consistency of these precepts with democratic political processes.

Once the question of implementation through democratic politics is raised, however, the possible contradiction between two sets of values becomes apparent. Should we continue to adhere to what we might call "democratic values," even if these values, when institutionally represented, generate results that we do not acknowledge to be "just"? Or do we go along with Plato and drop democracy as a political process if it fails to generate the "just society" that our ethical precepts dictate?

My own position on these matters is at least partially familiar. I think that as economists we spend far too much time worrying about what is "justice" in taxation and far too little time trying to predict the results that will emerge from the political process that we observe to be operating, one which may, in many respects, be labeled as "democratic." My plea is for more positive analysis of taxes and tax institutions, of the taxing process, and for less espousal of personal, private norms for taxes and taxation. In an indirect sense, my position might be interpreted as one that places democratic values above those of "justice" or "equity," putting me in the anti-Plato group. I am willing to accept this classification and, if needs be, to defend the primary role of democratic values in my own scheme of things, provided, of course, that you allow me to use my own definitions.

In my view, democratic values must be founded on the basic Kantian notion that individual human beings are the ultimate ethical units, that persons are to be treated strictly as ends and never as means, and that there are no transcendental, suprapersonal norms. From this idea it follows as a natural corollary that each person counts for one and only one in the determination of collective constraints that are to be imposed on all. This conception of political equality is central to any meaningful definition or formulation of democratic values, but in and of itself it scarcely insures against the coercive treatment of man by man, treatment that could remove all content from such values. Political equality, in its pure form, may mean little more than a right of franchise of all persons in a plebiscitary voting process which is unlimited in range. In such a case democratic values may be of small note to the persons or groups who are subjected to possible majority oppression through the abrogation of rights to life and property. The equal right to the voting privilege, even as an ideal, must surely be complemented by other precepts, which must also find their way into institutional reality. Equality before the law is a necessary condition that must be observed, regardless of how, by whom, and through what process law is made or changed. The majority coalition that imposes its will on the minority must do so within the strict constraints of this precept. The income tax law, for example, cannot be applied differentially to Democrats and Republicans, no matter how much the self-serving bureaucrats of the IRS might want that to be the case. They cannot endorse Lyndon Johnson's actual use of the IRS against Goldwaterites in 1964 while objecting strenuously to Nixon's attempts to use the IRS in 1972. To the extent that observed governmental processes are not bounded by the precept of equality before the law, we have departed from democratic values.

Norms for Taxation

So far, so good. But we must turn more specifically to issues of taxation. Taxes are and must be coercive instruments of the state; they require that persons transfer to the state valued resources or purchasing power. Most of us, save for a few anarchists, recognize the need for the state to exist and also recognize that there are goods and services which can best be provided by the government. Such goods and services must also be financed, and this financing requires taxation in one form or another. Some persons or groups in the economy must give up private command over resources, over values, if the state is to secure the ability to provide public goods and services. But what rules, what precepts, must be followed if the levy of taxes is to satisfy the criterion of equality before the law?

There is no answer to this question that suggests a unique principle for tax sharing. At one level of consideration, only equal-per-head taxes would seem to qualify. At another level, proportional taxes on income or wealth might plausibly be accepted as fulfilling the equality requirement. But what about progressive taxes? The original constitutional requirement for uniformity in taxation was held by successive courts to prohibit the imposition of progressive taxes, and this requirement was written, and interpreted, in the context of the principle of legal equality. As we know, the Constitution was explicitly amended to allow the use of progressive income taxes. But this fact does not answer the philosophical question. Is tax progression, in itself, a departure from "equality before the law," or can such taxation be reasonably interpreted as falling within the constraints of that fundamental precept?

We cannot really begin to answer this basic question until we bring in the public expenditure side of the ledger, until we recognize explicitly that there are benefits to be enjoyed from governmental provision of goods and services, benefits that are of value to the same persons who are taxpayers. Once we look at this side of the fiscal account, however, the applicability of the principle of legal equality to the tax side is called into question. It seems simple enough to talk about taxes in legal terms provided that we forget about public expenditure benefits. If, for example, taxes should in fact represent deadweight losses for the whole economy—if they should be required, let us say, to finance reparations to a foreign country—the simplistic legal criteria of equality might be tolerable. But taxes do not finance reparations payments; they finance public or governmental outlays, and these outlays increase individual utilities. Taxes become a necessary part of a genuine "fiscal exchange," and they become, in one real sense, the public-sector equivalent of private-sector prices.

Taxes and Prices

This analogy between taxes and prices warrants further discussion. What does legal equality mean with respect to prices? This question only becomes relevant under the institutional absence of competition, for example, in the pricing policy of public utilities. But it seems clear that a regulated monopoly would violate this basic legal principle if, say, electric power should be sold to me at a lower rate per kilowatt hour than the rate charged to my neighbor across the street. Nondiscrimination in prices for the same commodity is surely required to satisfy the criteria for legal equality. If this line of reasoning is extended directly to the provision of public goods and services, what is implied about taxes? All persons in the sharing group receive the same quantity of public goods, and this equivalence in consumption is the dominating characteristic for "public goods" in the quasi-technical meaning given to this term. The national defense is equally available to each one of us, as is the whole legal system. Since all receive the same quantity of a public good, would not legal equality require that each person pay the same price, in this case a tax price? Something is amiss here, however, since the equality of consumption need not emerge from individual choices. In the private sector individuals adjust quantities of consumption to uniform and nondiscriminatory prices. But in the public sector, either technologically or institutionally, the equal quantities are not chosen by persons. At a fixed and uniform tax price, different persons would optimally prefer widely differing quantities, but this sort of adjustment is precluded. Equality of tax prices among persons will not, therefore, insure the presence of individual adjustment equilibrium, as is the case in the nondiscriminatory pricing of private goods.

There is no need to elaborate the technical details here, but the discussion is perhaps sufficient to suggest some of the difficulties that arise when we try to put meaningful economic content into simplistic legal norms. Once we abandon uniformity of tax prices among persons, however, how are we to confine the range of tax-price variations or differences? What ranges are appropriate under the plausible limits defined by "democratic values"? Let me return to the two-person setting and consider the comparative tax treatment of me and my neighbor across the street. We secure the same quantity of police services from our municipal government, in this case the town of Blacksburg, Virginia. What set of tax structures will satisfy the criterion of legal equality? If I place a higher value on police services than my neighbor does, it seems reasonable that I should pay more for the same quantity than he does. To tax him more highly than me would seem out of bounds on almost any criterion of reasonableness. Therefore, as long as the basis for taxation offers a good proxy for individual evaluations of the public goods and services offered, serious violation of legal precepts might be kept within broadly acceptable limits. If my property commands a higher market value than that of my neighbor, the assessment of taxes on the basis of property values may correspond roughly to relative evaluations. But how much higher should my taxes be? There seems to be nothing sacrosanct about the rule of proportionality here, and rate structures that are progressive, or even regressive, might be equally tolerated. At base, the ideal here would emerge only from an empirical estimate of relative evaluations for publicly provided services and from the empirical relationships between these and the tax bases under consideration.

How far have we gotten? What sort of taxes can be accepted and what sort ruled out from the somewhat abstract perspective developed? For general-purpose public goods and services, and especially for such services as external and internal defense, the legal system, and the like, the familiar bases for taxation fare reasonably well under our appraisal. Individual evaluations on such services are presumably related directly to individual wealth and incomes. Hence, taxing persons on the basis of these objectively measurable proxies may be justified on broad grounds of legal equality. But what about special-purpose government services? Is there any justification at all in legal principle for the use of general tax revenues, collected from levies based on proxies for evaluations of general-benefit services, to finance the provision of goods and services for special groups, regardless of the means of classification?

Fiscal Asymmetry

Somewhat surprisingly, we find that the application of legal principle to the fiscal structure has been asymmetrical. Uniformity or nondiscrimination in the levy of taxes has been embodied in "the law" as it has developed, but there has been no comparable extension to the expenditure side of the fiscal account. Legally, constitutionally, legislatures are able to provide benefits of public goods to special groups and to finance those benefits from general taxes. Congress has been notorious in its willingness to spend billions on pork-barrel projects. The Arkansas River navigation project is the most flagrant recent example, but regional benefit legislation has been the order of the day for decades. And special benefits for specific occupational and functional groups in the economy are characteristic features of the American fiscal landscape. If the legal principle of equality of treatment is to be applied at all in fiscal matters, symmetry between the tax side and the spending side must be present. Special-benefit and discriminatory spending has no more place in a system reflecting democratic values than does discriminatory taxation.

We have at least come part of the way in our attempt to determine the limits on the fiscal structure that are suggested by consistent adherence to democratic values, as we have interpreted them. The fiscal reforms that would be required to incorporate these limits would be dramatic, but they would not, it seems to me, present issues of conflict with precepts for fiscal "justice." In fact, quite the opposite seems to be the case. The introduction of symmetry between the two sides of the fiscal account should be fully consistent with almost any conception of fiscal justice. But the major issues posed by this subject matter remain unresolved.

Let us suppose that all taxes are levied in a nondiscriminatory fashion on bases such as personal incomes and wealth that do, in fact, serve as reasonable proxies for individual evaluations of general-benefit government goods and services. Suppose further that tax revenues are devoted exclusively to the financing of just such general-benefit goods and services. Within broad limits, as we have suggested, the precepts of legal equality and nondiscrimination would seem to be met.

Transfers

But there seems to be no place in such a fiscal structure for *transfers* of income and wealth among different social and economic groups, whether these transfers be direct or indirect. And when discussions introduce the notion of justice in taxation, these transfers are what the talk is about. Many observers hold that the fiscal system should be used to achieve distributional objectives, quite apart from the provision and financing of public goods and services. In this view, taxes should be levied with the purpose of redressing prevailing differences in incomes and wealth among persons and families in the economy. Great confusion in discussion often arises because the tax structure is simultaneously conceived as serving two separate social functions.

What can be said about the possible incorporation of democratic values in a fiscal structure that is designed primarily to implement real income and wealth transfers? Almost by definition, a fiscal transfer system must be discriminatory in effect. If transfers take place, some persons and groups must be net losers and other groups net gainers. The fiscal exchange paradigm used earlier in the discussion of governmental provision of real goods and services is inapplicable here. Once this fact is recognized, how can we begin to reconcile overt fiscal transfers with any semblance of legal equality? I do not think that reconciliation is possible within the ordinary understanding of democratic polity. To the extent that the fiscal structure comes to be conceived as a transfer mechanism, legal equality must be deliberately sacrificed.

There are several points that may be made here. Once any precept of legal equality is dropped, and once the fiscal system is thought by citizens and by politicians to be a transfer mechanism, how can transfers be restricted to those that might be deemed ethically desirable? It is precisely at this point that the workings of unbounded democratic politics may violate all precepts of fiscal justice. If constitutional constraints are dropped, what is to prevent self-interested political entrepreneurs from carrying fiscal measures far beyond those which might be suggested by ethical criteria, or, more likely, from using the fiscal system to implement transfers that bear little or no relationship to the objectives that might be dictated by norms of equity or of justice? Should social scientists and social philosophers really be surprised when their idealized schemes for income transfers to the demonstrably poor are converted by the legislating process into schemes which produce benefits for members of dominant political coalitions while the poor secure assistance largely as a by-product? If the whole fiscal structure, taxes and benefits alike, comes to be viewed as the instrument through which zero-sum income and wealth transfers can be produced, simplistic economic theory should tell us that attempts will be made to use this instrument to secure political profits. A public-choice approach to politics allows us to make the positive prediction that unconstrained democratic process will generate results that satisfy neither the precepts for fiscal justice nor those which can be meaningfully interpreted as incorporating democratic values.

Is there any way to resolve the dilemma? We can hardly expect political decision makers to become enlightened ethical leaders and, in so doing, to insure their own replacement by others more in tune with constituency preferences. And despite the continuing mythology about liberal education's overriding social values, it is surely naïve to expect that individual citizens, privately or in groups, will voluntarily forego the political and economic profit opportunities that modern fiscal systems appear to offer them.

Constitutional Rules

I think that the dilemma posed can be resolved, at least at the level of conceptual discussion, although practical steps toward resolution may be extremely difficult. Resolution must be based on the introduction of a sharp categorical distinction between what I call the *constitutional* level of collective decision making and the *operational* level. To summarize before I discuss it in detail, "justice," as an attribute of a fiscal structure, must be implemented exclusively at the constitutional level, when institutions that also reflect meaningful democratic values are incorporated into the rules for operational political action. Fiscal institutions that will insure some net redistribution can be constitutionally selected, while at the same time effective constraints can be placed on the range of action taken operationally by dominant political coalitions. Day-to-day exploitation of the fiscal process to seek income and wealth transfers must be abandoned in favor of quasi-permanent and built-in features of the structure which will implement transfers while at the same time restricting legislative authority.

The approach that I take, and have taken, to these matters is essentially contractarian, in the social-contract meaning of this term. Basic decisions on the structural institutions of society, including the limits on governments, must be made in a setting in which, to the maximum possible extent, the identifiable interests of persons and groups are not known. At this genuine constitutional level persons must try to select and to agree upon preferred "rules of the game," and they must use criteria of fairness and efficiency in the selection and evaluation process. The affinity between my general position and that of John Rawls has been discussed in chapter 9.

For purposes of discussing fiscal structure, the Buchanan and Rawls formulations are interchangeable. The question concerns the characteristics of the fiscal structure that would emerge from such genuine constitutional deliberation and agreement. More specifically, how much income and wealth transfer would be built into the structure? As Tullock and I argued in *The Calculus of Consent: Logical Foundations of Constitutional Democracy*, and as Rawls also argues, fiscal transfers would predictably be embodied in the constitutional structure. I think that Rawls, in his book as distinguished from his early papers, made a serious error when he tried to be overly specific and limit himself to predicting the emergence of his so-called difference principle, or maximin principle in the terminology of game theory. It seems to me that any of several institutions of redistribution might emerge from genuine constitutional process, and we should not, it seems to me, be particularly concerned about the uniqueness of our conceptual solution. The important point is not that of describing the specific characteristics of the institutions that would emerge, but that of emphasizing the characteristics of the *process* through which these institutions are chosen—the constitutional process. By this process I refer to the deliberate act of selecting quasi-permanent rules and institutions within which day-to-day operational choices, both private and public, are to be made and implemented. The important practical corollary of this constitutional approach is the implication that once chosen, the fiscal structure should not be subject to year-to-year manipulation and change by shifting coalitions in democratic legislative assemblies. A structure of progressive income taxation, extending over both negative and positive rate ranges, might well be consistent with constitutional process, as here defined, but it must be conceived to be, by public and politicians alike, a quasi-permanent feature of the social setting and not subject to discussion in terms of current operationally determined economic and social policy. Nothing could do more toward promoting nonconstitutional attitudes than continued readjustment of basic income tax rates. Such readjustment surely furthers the view that the political process, as it operates, is after all little more than a complex profit-and-loss system.

In conclusion, a basic structure of rate progression in taxes on incomes and wealth might be plausibly defended on genuine constitutional contractarian grounds. This structure may guarantee some fiscal readjustments in net economic differences among persons in the economy. To this structure there may be appended constraints on the use of tax instruments for financing collective goods and services, constraints that should rule out arbitrary discrimination in both taxation and in the distribution of public goods benefits. Political majorities must be placed within effective constitutional limits, both with respect to the basic institutions of the fiscal system and to the degree of arbitrary discrimination that is allowable. In this conceptual manner "fiscal justice as fairness," to use Rawlsian terminology, may be fully compatible with genuinely meaningful "democratic values."

Honesty forces me to acknowledge, however, that reconciliation in conception is a far different thing from reconciliation in actuality. Anyone who observes American political process today cannot fail to sense the continuing and perhaps accelerating erosion of what I have called the "constitutional attitude" on the part of our legislators, our courts, and, sadly, our legal philosophers. Until we get our thinking straight at the fundamental and even elementary philosophical level, we can hardly criticize working politicians and judges to do anything except carry forward the prevailing attitudes. Honestly described, these attitudes seem to be that, effectively, the government is not really bounded except by the expediently derived gut feelings of the accidentally appointed Supreme Court, which we have allowed to become our supreme legislative authority in a perversion of its historic role. "Constitutional anarchy" instead of "constitutional order" seems characteristic of our time. In my view, "democratic values" have long since been distorted out of all meaning, and anything that might be labeled as "fiscal justice" seems likely to emerge only as a by-product of an ongoing game of political profit and loss.

18

Taxation in Fiscal Exchange

In his paper "Reflections on Tax Reform," delivered as the C. Harry Kahn Memorial Lecture at Rutgers in 1972, Professor Richard A. Musgrave acknowledged that the weakest part of the Henry Simons tradition in the discussion of tax reform policy is its neglect of the expenditure-benefit side of the fiscal account. To assign a predominant role to equity criteria in assessing alternative tax instruments independently amounts to an implicit assumption that taxation represents a net withdrawal of resources from the social economy, a setting which Luigi Einaudi labeled as that of the *imposta grandine*, literally, the "tax as hailstorm." Much the same criticism can be levied against the independent analysis of alternative taxes in terms of their comparative efficiency properties, whether in the older excess-burden form or in the modern and more sophisticated optimal taxation framework.

Even within their acknowledged normative realms of discourse, these conceptions of taxation are seriously incomplete. Even if the objective is limited to advising the social decision maker, whoever that might be, on the implications of a consistent application of either equity or efficiency norms, the two-sidedness of the fiscal approach must be incorporated into the discussion. If a more positive approach is taken, if the objective is that of explaining the emergence of tax institutions in a political setting that is, itself, preferred in an explicitly normative sense, an exchange model becomes a necessary starting point for meaningful analysis. Those who pay taxes and those who receive benefits from services financed by these taxes are members of the same political community; all persons may simultaneously be taxpayers and public-goods beneficiaries.

My purpose in this paper is to examine the implications of apply-ing the fiscal exchange paradigm. I shall demonstrate that only this paradigm offers a fully consistent approach to taxation, and one that is sufficiently flexible to allow both equity and efficiency norms to be incorporated readily into the explanatory framework if and as they are appropriate. To the extent that the political decision-making structure remains "democratic," in any legitimate rendering of the term, only the exchange paradigm offers prospects for the derivation of refutable hypotheses about both the initial selection and the sta-bility of tax instruments. In this treatment I shall not advance the discussion much beyond that of Knut Wicksell in 1896.[1] But modern public finance theory would indeed make great strides if the Wick-sellian level of analysis and understanding could finally be achieved.

In the following section I shall construct a highly simplified ex-ample that is deliberately designed for the simple application of both the equity and efficiency norms for taxation, conceived in the ortho-dox sense. These norms take on a different cast when an exchange setting is imposed. In the third section, "Toward Fiscal Reality," I shall attempt partially to bridge the awesome gap between the ideal-ized results of abstract analytical models and the real world. The fourth section is devoted to a discussion of the fiscal transfer process, an apparent aspect of fiscal reality that seems impossible to bring within the exchange conception under orthodox assumptions. In the fifth section, "The Fiscal Constitution," these assumptions are modi-fied, and the fiscal constitution is distinguished from period-to-period budgetary changes. The final section discusses some of the im-plications of the normative framework for prevailing public attitudes toward political process.

Simplified Illustration

Consider the simplest possible setting in which two persons (fam-ilies), A and B, live side by side in a community. By all objectively measurable standards A and B are identical; both receive the same incomes, and both hold the same claims to assets. Further, revealed information about their potential behavior suggests that A and B

---

[1] Knut Wicksell, *Finanztheoretische Untersuchungen.*

react similarly to the unilateral imposition of taxes, regardless of the form they might take.

The tax policy adviser to the government who has been reared on the familiar slogans will dust off the precepts of horizontal equity —equal treatment for equals—and he will recommend that A and B be taxed alike. Such equality in tax treatment is imbedded in American constitutional law, and, considered in isolation, it seems to reflect a plausible extension of the basic norm of legal equality. To introduce differences in tax liability here would seem to be arbitrarily discriminatory. Regardless of revenue requirements, therefore, A and B would seem to qualify for equal tax treatment, whether the tax be levied on a per-head, income, consumption, wealth, or other basis.

Suppose now that the government asks an economist to advise it concerning the "optimal" means of imposing fiscal charges on A and B. This expert would initially suggest resort to lump-sum levies, and if he introduces a welfare function that assigns an equal "social marginal utility" of income to each person in identical observable economic circumstances, he would suggest that these lump-sum charges be imposed in equal amounts.

In this grossly simplified example, the orthodox equity criterion and the optimal taxation criterion coincide, and the equal treatment of A and B seems to raise little objection, regardless of the revenue needs of the community. But this last proviso, in itself, suggests that the fiscal system remains open in a choice-making context. Neither criterion, as applied here, allows us to say anything at all about the amount of total revenue to be raised, about the quantity of public goods to be provided. This problem was noted by Wicksell, and it was the basis for his argument that the benefits side must be brought into account in any meaningful discussion of the distribution of the tax burden.

In my example I was careful not to assume that A and B are identical in *all* respects. Suppose now that despite the range of identical characteristics, A and B are distinctly different in their demands for public goods and services, with A placing a higher evaluation on such services over all of the relevant levels of possible provision. For illustration, think of a single public service, police protection, and assume that A and B assess the subjective probabilities of criminal damage to life and property differently, despite the equality of objective economic circumstances. If this difference in preferences should exist for a single privately marketed good or service, it would be reflected in differing quantities purchased, with A and B separately adjusting quantities to correspond to their relative evaluations. For the public service, however, such individual quantity adjustment is not possible. Either because of the technology inherent in the service itself (jointness efficiency and/or nonexcludability) or because the institutional setting requires uniformity of provision, both persons will tend to receive the same quantity of the service.

Assume that despite the postulated differences in evaluation of the public service, taxes are imposed in accordance with the equity and/or optimal taxation criterion outlined above; hence, A and B are subjected to equal taxes imposed in a lump-sum fashion. We can discuss this situation under two distinct models for budgetary decision making. In the first, which we can call the planning model, we assume that decisions on the size of the budget, and hence on total tax revenues, are made by an external chooser who is able omnisciently to read individual preference functions. In the second, or public-choice model, we assume that budgetary outcomes emerge from the interactions of citizens themselves operating under some designated decision rules.

Planning Model. If the planner can read individual preference functions, he can simply set the budgetary level so that it will satisfy the necessary Samuelson conditions for public-goods efficiency, the equality of summed marginal evaluations with marginal cost of production.[2] The prior selection of a specific tax-sharing scheme, in our example one that produces equal tax shares, has the effect of designating a "social welfare function" or, more correctly, that of specifying a unique distribution of the posttax, postbenefit fiscal surplus among persons. Under the conditions we have postulated, with equal taxation, both inframarginally and marginally, and with differing marginal evaluations, both persons, A and B, are forced out of "individual equilibrium" at the efficient budget level, but there would be no mutuality of gain to be secured from any change. The solution would, therefore, lie on the Pareto optimality surface.

Let us now suppose that the planner no longer feels constrained

---

[2] I assume that the planner is "individualistic" in the sense that he incorporates individuals' own utilities, rather than his own, in his decisions.

to impose equal taxes on A and B and that he shifts the tax structure to make it conform more closely with public-goods preferences, simultaneously shifting, if and as required, the size of the budget to maintain the satisfaction of the Samuelson marginal condition. He imposes the Lindahl solution, which insures that individual marginal evaluations correspond precisely to individual tax prices. Behaviorally, he now observes that both A and B agree on the budgetary level chosen; both persons are in "individual equilibrium."

The posttax, postbenefit distribution of realizable fiscal surplus is different from that attained under the regime of equal tax shares, and the quantity of public goods may be different. It is necessary to keep in mind the precise definition of the Lindahl solution. In a behaviorally relevant sense, "taxes" have been replaced by "prices." The Lindahl solution converts the public-goods exchange into its closest possible equivalence to private-goods exchange. Individuals are confronted by "prices" (which differ from one person to another), and they are expected to "choose" preferred quantities in a manner that is psychologically equivalent to ordinary market behavior. The "price" of the public good (or public-goods bundle) that an individual faces is invariant with respect to his own behavior. There is no way that a person can modify the "price" with which he is confronted. In this sense the Lindahl price is identical to a lump-sum tax per unit of the public good.[3]

The genuinely omniscient planner could, of course, impose any indicated fiscal charges as lump-sum levies, whether he chooses to do so equally per head or as related to Lindahl evaluations on the public good. If, for purpose of analysis, we assume lump-sum taxes are not feasible, even in this planning model, the required revenues, in either case, may be raised through the use of some standard tax base. Any departure from lump-sum taxes will necessarily introduce "inefficiency" when measured against some idealized criterion. However, given this assumed institutional constraint, either solution qualifies as efficient or optimal.

The shift from the regime of equal tax shares to the regime of Lindahl prices may be interpreted simply as the replacement of one

[3] For further discussion see David B. Johnson and Mark V. Pauly, "Excess Burden and the Voluntary Theory of Public Finance," *Economica* 36 (August, 1969): 269–276.

"social welfare function" by another, with both being, in one sense, "individualistic." A normative argument for the shift toward the Lindahl solution may be based on the presumption that individual utility is influenced by public as well as by private goods and that differences in evaluations placed on public goods are relevant in determining relative tax shares. This presumption suggests that one of the two central attributes of a fiscal-exchange model may be incorporated without difficulty into a nondemocratic decision setting. The two-sidedness of the fiscal account (taxes and benefits) may be fully embodied in the social welfare function that informs the planner's decisions. There is no requirement that externally derived norms for tax sharing be defined independently of predicted or postulated distributions of spending benefits.

The Public Choice Model. The second attribute of fiscal exchange cannot be accommodated in the nondemocratic setting, that which accentuates the voluntary nature of exchange itself. What if no planner exists? And even if one could be invented or imported, would we accept such an implied delegation of decision-making authority? The fiscal exchange approach is derived from Knut Wicksell, who quite explicitly rejected the planning model, even as an instrument for analyzing fiscal alternatives. It is clearly wasteful to devote intellectual resources in proffering advice to a nonexistent decision maker. No social welfare function exists independently of the mutual adjustment process itself. Regardless of how they may be defined, "equity" and "efficiency" will characterize observed results only as they are embodied in the choices made by individual participants.

For such participants, taxes are necessarily treated as prices, as payments that are required for the financing of jointly consumed goods and services provided through governments. If participants make no linkage between the tax and benefit sides of the account, taxes would simply never be observed. In this decision setting it becomes methodologically absurd to lay down norms for tax sharing independent from the distribution of benefits.

Let us return to the two-person example and apply a Wicksellian or public-choice analysis. As before, we postulate that A and B are identical in all objective economic circumstances but that they differ in their evaluations of the single public service that is under consideration. Through some Wicksell-Lindahl type of bargaining process, in which marginal adjustments in tax prices as well as in public-service quantities take place, gains from trade will tend to be eliminated and a position reached that will satisfy the requirements for Pareto optimality. At this "trading equilibrium" individual marginal tax prices will equal individual marginal evaluations, a set of equalities which, in turn, insures the satisfaction of the aggregative condition which requires summed marginal evaluations to equal marginal cost. There is nothing in this model of decision making, however, which allows us to specify the distribution of total tax shares.[4] Any one of a possible subinfinity of distributions of the total fiscal surplus may be achieved in an unrestricted bargaining adjustment, bounded only by the constraint that each party must secure net benefits from the provision of public goods or, in the limit, must undergo no net loss. As the distribution of fiscal surplus changes, income-effect feedbacks may, of course, modify somewhat the quantity of public good or service, the budgetary size, that will be Pareto optimal.

Because the distribution of total tax shares may vary widely over inframarginal ranges, one possible outcome of a Wicksellian process is that A and B, in our example, pay equal total tax bills despite the differences in marginal tax-prices that are required in order that the bargaining process converge toward the frontier of Pareto optimality. To say that this outcome *may* emerge as one from among many possible outcomes of the adjustment process, however, does not imply that such a specific outcome may be "plugged in" as a constraint at the outset, under the expectation that the Pareto frontier will tend to be achieved. For example, suppose that A and B are now constrained in their bargaining behavior by the requirement that at any possible budgetary level total tax shares must be equal. Since the quantity of the public service to be selected is not known, but must instead emerge from the mutual adjustment itself, this requirement amounts to saying that tax shares must be equal for any possible budget size. This rule, in its turn, is equivalent to setting marginal tax-prices to each person at one-half marginal cost. Because individual evaluations differ, the bargaining adjustments in this decision setting may stop

---

[4] If Lindahl tax prices are interpreted to require the uniformity of marginal tax price over varying quantities to each person, the bargaining adjustment need not converge toward the Pareto frontier at all.

short of capturing the full gains from trade and of attaining the efficiency frontier.

To the extent that the Wicksellian adjustment process reaches an equilibrium, which would be indicated by an end of efforts to make further bargains, this equilibrium is clearly Pareto optimal. It follows that there would be no rearrangement of tax shares which could command unanimous consent, even when the possibility of making side payments is allowed. The Wicksellian model requires that potential taxpayers reveal, through their behavior, evaluations on the public good or service even when the strategic motivations for misrepresentation of these evaluations are fully acknowledged. In the fiscal exchange paradigm the necessary condition for efficiency is present when marginal tax prices equal marginal evaluations, but this condition tells us nothing at all about the division of total tax shares.

Toward Fiscal Reality

I have deliberately employed the simplified two-person example because it presents the exchange paradigm in its most favorable and persuasive setting. As we move away from such grossly simplified constructions, however, and as we try to incorporate empirical observations into our analysis, the advantages of adopting the fiscal-exchange perspective seem less apparent. A possible role for using equity and/or optimal taxation norms in shaping tax structure independently of the expenditure side may emerge even within a democratic decision model.

The political unit contains many persons, many potential voters-taxpayers-beneficiaries, and fiscal decisions are made through a very complex political process which involves parties, pressure groups, political entrepreneurs, periodic but sometimes infrequent elections, legislative assemblies operating under complicated rules with ordered committee structures, and bureaucratic hierarchies. The bridge between taxes paid and benefits received, which seems direct in the small-number illustration, may all but disappear in the calculus of the citizen. If taxpayers do not, in fact, make any connection between tax payments and benefits enjoyed, there seems to be a rationale for introducing independent norms. As Wicksell implied, however, the presence of any semblance of democratic decision making requires that in some ultimate sense citizens do construct the bridge. Legislatures are observed to approve the imposition of taxes, however reluctantly, something which could not take place if voting constituencies sensed no return of public-service benefits.

In the strict Wicksellian framework, however, decisions are made by general contractual agreement among all citizens, as illustrated in our two-person example above. In political reality democratic process rarely requires general agreement, even at the level of the legislative assembly. Less-than-unanimity rules are empirically observed to operate in the so-called democratic structures. This departure from the pure exchange paradigm is perhaps more serious than the failure of the individual citizen to construct the bridge between the two sides of the fiscal account. In a real sense, the absence of a unanimity rule implies that for members of some groups there need be no connection between taxes paid and benefits received at all. Consider a political community in which two coalitions, J and K, exist, with each being represented proportionately in the legislative assembly. J is the majority coalition; K is the minority. If the members of J can succeed in imposing all taxes on members of K while at the same time securing for themselves all of the benefits from public services provided through government, there is no fiscal exchange. A member of the majority coalition can secure benefits without paying taxes, and a member of the minority must pay taxes without reckoning on any return of benefits at all.

Once this aspect of political reality is acknowledged, the equity norm for the distribution of tax burdens can be viewed as a constitutional standard designed to prevent the exploitation of minorities through the fiscal process. Under almost any version of the equity norm, taxes should be levied generally on all members of the political community or on some basis that is considered to be nondiscriminatory. If taxes are levied generally on all persons, there are limits to the degree of fiscal exploitation, even if the majority coalition secures all of the benefits from public spending. The political entrepreneurs representing the majority will extend the size of the budget only to the point where marginal benefits to the majority are estimated to equal marginal taxes on the majority, and not to the point at which the majority reaches satiation with public goods.

In this perspective there is no basis for the traditional application of the equity precepts to the tax side alone. The extension of equity norms to public spending, to the distribution of benefits among persons, can even further limit the degree of exploitation that the fiscal process generates. If taxes are imposed only in accordance with general standards, and if public spending is limited to goods that guarantee general benefits to all persons and groups, the power of the majority coalition to secure distributional gains at the expense of the minority may be confined within relatively narrow limits. Differences in evaluations placed on the public goods contained in the budgetary bundle may of course exist, and the majority may be able to insure that its own preferences are more fully reflected in the budgetary mix and levels chosen than are those of the minority. As the earlier two-person example suggested, incorporation of the equity norms into the fiscal structure may prevent the attainment of the Pareto frontier in many cases. But this degree of possible inefficiency may be relatively small when compared with the potentiality for fiscal exploitation that departures from the unanimity rule for decision making might generate without such constraints.

If, in fact, there should exist some reasonably close correspondence or relationship between the individual evaluations for public goods and the general bases for taxation which consistent application of the equity norm might suggest, there might seem to be relatively little conflict between the idealized Wicksellian exchange results and the results which democratic process constrained by equity precepts would generate. If, in fact, income or wealth, properly measured, should prove to be a good surrogate for relative evaluations of public goods, the general taxation of personal income and/or wealth might seem to be both tolerably equitable and tolerably efficient in the sense of Wicksellian fiscal exchange.

The practical achievement of this possible result depends critically, however, on the presumed absence of significant differences in behavioral responses. In reality, the ideally efficient lump-sum taxes are not feasible, and tax liabilities are necessarily related to a base that is subject to some control by taxpayers. This ability to modify the base for tax liability by changing behavior need not introduce a significant problem if all persons are roughly similar in response patterns. Preadjustment income may provide a reasonable proxy for public-goods evaluation or demand, and relative tax prices need not change greatly because of the necessary computation of tax liabilities on the basis of postadjustment incomes. If, however, individuals should differ significantly in their adjustments to the tax, relative tax prices in the postadjustment setting may differ sharply from those anticipated in the preadjustment or planning stage of decision making. Persons whose tastes and opportunities allow them readily to shift away from the base for taxation (for example, measured money income) and toward nontaxable substitutes (for example, leisure) are able to secure differential benefits. In this setting the tax-rate structure applied to postadjustment incomes that would be required to reflect, even if roughly, a possible outcome of a Wicksellian bargaining process might look much different from the tax-rate structure that might be selected on the grounds of orthodox equity norms. Even here some rapprochement is possible through appropriate redefinitions of the tax base, of "income," in the direction of greater generality.

The Fiscal Transfer Process

The reluctance of many tax reform advocates to accept the exchange paradigm may be based on their unwillingness to abandon explicit normative argument supporting what they consider to be at least a subsidiary if not the primary function of the fiscal process, namely the *transfer* of real income and wealth among persons and groups within the political community. The taxing and spending process seems to offer a means through which the distributional results of the market may be modified in the direction of results that command more ethical legitimacy.

At one level of analysis the introduction of a specific distributional role for the fiscal process requires a departure from the exchange paradigm. If real income is to be transferred from one set of persons to another, there is no exchange, save in the limited degree allowed by utility interdependence. And the distributional role assigned to the fiscal process in this discussion of tax reform is not that which may emerge from positive predictions about the workings of less-than-unanimity rules for collective decision making, which may be designated as "imperfect" fiscal exchange. As envisaged by participants in this discussion, the distributional objectives of the fiscal process must be laid down from outside the decision structure itself, presumably by the benevolent despot against whom Wicksell raised such formidable objections.

Let us isolate the pure distributional or pure transfer aspects of fiscal process from both the allocational aspects and from those transfers which might plausibly be explained by the existence of utility interdependence. For the pure transfer aspects the decision process becomes fully analogous to a zero-sum game which which players must continue to play. In this context, political equality, as signaled by universality of the voting franchise, will generate predictable transfers, but these need not be heavily weighted in favor of the very poor as envisaged in the discussions of reform.[5] In recognizing this fact, as they must, what do the distributionally motivated advocates of tax reform consider themselves to be doing? Are they trying to persuade citizens to incorporate the utility of others in their preference functions? Are they advising political entrepreneurs to take up positions that are contrary to those reflected in their constituency interests?

I do not think that these reformers are consciously engaging in persuasion of this sort. They consider themselves to be articulating value judgments that "should" be universally held by all informed persons. But what is the basis for such an attitude? Here we must, I think, examine the fundamental conception of society and the place of individuals relative to each other in the society. In its short-term context, the fiscal exchange paradigm is based on the presumption that persons are well-defined entities, defined in terms of rights encompassing spheres of allowable and enforceable activities, both with respect to each other and to physical objects. In one sense the exchange paradigm requires an acceptance of the status-quo distribution of rights. An unwillingness to attribute "justice" or "equity" to the status quo may suggest grounds for a rejection of the exchange paradigm for the fiscal process. There has been, and remains, much ambiguity here which is again absent from Wicksell's discussion, which contains a categorical distinction between the distribution of

---

[5] I have examined some of the implications of universality in franchise for fiscal transfers in my article "The Political Economy of Franchise in the Welfare State," in *Essays in Capitalism and Freedom*, ed. Richard Selden.

rights and the complex exchange that the fiscal process represents.[6] Whether at the level of intellectual discourse or of political reality, attempts to force the fiscal process into the dual roles of redressing differences in endowments and capacities among persons and of implementing complex exchanges for public goods among persons with defined rights can only create confusion. Even in the purest model of fiscal exchange, the Wicksellian unanimity setting, there exists individual motivation for strategic behavior, for the investment of resources in socially wasteful attempts to secure relatively large shares of the gross gains from trade. As we depart from the unanimity-rule setting, the motivation for behaving strategically falls, but it is offset by incentives offered for successful fiscal exploitation of minorities by majorities, even if no direct transfers are made. If, appended to and mixed up with this complex political exchange, the fiscal process is viewed by participants, and by political entrepreneurs, as an instrument for effecting direct transfers of incomes and wealth, the waste of resources involved in attempts to capture and to control collective decision making may swamp the potentially realizable surplus that may be promised by the provision of public goods. Furthermore, as suggested above, there is no assurance at all that the net transfers which would take place in such a setting would come close to those dictated by ethical precepts of "justice."

The Fiscal Constitution

In the earlier discussion of the equity norm as a possible constraint on the political exploitation of minorities there was an implicit distinction made between constitutional rules and decision making under defined rules. In much the same manner we can now reinterpret the exchange-contractarian approach in a way that will account for observed fiscal transfers. To accomplish this reinterpretation, however, it is necessary to shift away from the implicit assumptions underlying the several orthodox models of fiscal process which proceed from a setting in which individual claims to income flows and/ or asset values are well defined.

Once we recognize, however, that the assignment or distribution

---

[6] For my attempts to explore the questions concerning the basic distribution of rights, see my *The Limits of Liberty: Between Anarchy and Leviathan*.

of endowments and capacities among persons has some time dimension, and that identification of any person's specific position in future periods can be predicted only under uncertainty, it becomes possible to discuss the conceptual emergence of fiscal institutions in a contractarian framework, which is equivalent to the exchange framework except for the level of decision. In earlier work I have referred to this level of collective decision as "constitutional," as opposed to collective choice under conditions when the distribution of rights is fully specified, which I have referred to as "postconstitutional."

Fiscal institutions may be analyzed in a constitutional setting. The distinguishing feature of genuine constitutional choice lies in the recognized permanent or quasi-permanent nature of the alternatives that are considered. The individuals who participate in such choices are necessarily uncertain, at least to some degree, about their own roles during the periods through which the chosen alternative will remain operative. To the extent that such uncertainty exists, they will be led to select among alternatives in accordance with generally applicable criteria of "fairness," "equity," and "efficiency" instead of fully identifiable self-interest. Uncertainty about income and wealth positions in future periods can produce a general contractual agreement on a set of fiscal institutions, a fiscal constitution, that may incorporate protection against poverty and which may seem, when viewed in a short-term perspective, to produce pure transfers among individuals and groups.[7]

[7] This insurance approach to fiscal redistribution, based on a contractarian model, was developed in some detail in James M. Buchanan and Gordon Tullock, *The Calculus of Consent: Logical Foundations of Constitutional Democracy*. There is an obvious affinity between this approach and the basic contractarian approach taken by John Rawls, both in his earlier papers and in his book *A Theory of Justice*. One difference lies in our imposition of genuine uncertainty regarding individual positions as the device that insures motivation for a person to adopt the attitude required. Rawls, by comparison, suggests that even when an individual's own position is clearly defined, a person should act as if he is choosing behind the "veil of ignorance." A second difference in the two approaches lies in Rawls's attempt to describe specifically the distributional principle that would tend to emerge from the original contract, namely, the difference principle. By contrast, in our view the contractarian framework must allow for the possible emergence of many alternatives. And indeed, the emphasis must be placed on the process instead of the specific outcomes.

This contractarian approach to distribution is fully consistent with, and possibly complementary to, Musgrave's analytical separation between the allocation and distribution branches of the budget. Cf. R. A. Musgrave, *The Theory of Public Finance*

The philosophical advantage of the contractarian-constitutional approach lies in the fact that it enables us to derive fiscal institutions from individual choices independently of externally imposed ethical criteria. There is no logically necessary contradiction between pure fiscal transfers and procedures of democratic choice, provided that the latter are bounded by constitutional constraints. Whether or not the pure transfers that we do seem to observe represent some embodiment of such a constitutional choice calculus is, of course, strictly an empirical question, along with the determination of the genuine exchange content in the observed provision of public goods and services. These are questions worthy of research effort, but they can scarcely be examined until and unless there is first some understanding of the necessity for making the constitutional-postconstitutional distinction. This distinction tends to be blurred in political reality when long-range structural reforms which may properly be classified as "constitutional" are discussed simultaneously with period-to-period allocative decisions.

Conclusions

Critics may properly object by suggesting that the exchange-contractarian paradigm, as I have interpreted it here, may be used to explain everything and hence to predict nothing. To a limited extent this objection has merit, although testable implications of the approach may readily be derived. But the purpose of presenting the exchange-contractarian model of fiscal process here is not primarily to facilitate the making of scientific predictions. The charge of non-operationality may be levied, much more effectively, against the alternative approaches to taxation under consideration, those which embody either the traditional equity objectives or the efficiency-optimality norms. In my interpretation we are examining alternative paradigms of the fiscal process, different windows through which the actual institutions which exist and those which might exist are viewed. The methodological alternative that is selected will determine both the predictive hypotheses to be derived and tested and, perhaps more important,

---

The contractarian approach suggests the possible advantages of formal institutional separation, with quite differing temporal perspectives informing the political deliberations in the two cases.

the evaluative judgments to be made concerning prospects for "improvements."

In my view, one that I think was shared by Wicksell, the exchange-contractarian paradigm is the only one that is wholly consistent with what we may legitimately call "democracy" or with a social order that embodies "democratic values." The alternative visions of fiscal order depend, in some ultimate sense, on the presence of a decision maker for individuals in the community, and reform proposals are aimed at modifying results. Observed outcomes are evaluated against normative criteria that apply to outcomes. For example, a tax system is given low marks if it is "regressive." By contrast, the normative evaluation that emerges from the exchange-contractarian paradigm applies to *process* instead of results. In this approach it matters relatively little whether a tax system is regressive or progressive. What does matter is whether or not the tax structure, along with the pattern of budgetary outlays, is generated through a decision-making process that reflects, even if imperfectly, individual values in a regime where all persons are given roughly equal weights.

This difference in perspective leads to differing objects or targets for improvement. The traditional proponent of equity objectives worries about the erosion of the income tax base, for example, evaluating what he sees in political reality against his idealized general income tax. The exchange-contractarian, on the other hand, finds relatively little to disturb him in the presence of tax loopholes, per se, if he conceives these loopholes to reflect plausible outcomes of a political bargaining process that he evaluates to be the "least bad" among possible decision structures. He is much more likely to get exercised about the inflation-induced increases in real rates of income tax, which reflect departures from explicitly legislated rate structures and which foster instead of dispel fiscal illusion.

Finally, the differences in approach to tax and fiscal institutions are important for the promulgation of attitudes of citizens as ultimate voters, taxpayers, and beneficiaries of public outlays. The exchange framework tends to promote a constructive attitude toward governmental process, an attitude that accentuates the cooperative aspects, that underlines the prospects for mutuality of gain for all citizens. The alternative framework may lead citizens and their political spokesmen to accentuate the profit-and-loss aspects of political competition, to promote a willingness on the part of a dominant coalition to impose its will on its minority opposition, and, conversely, to generate in the minority an acceptance of a quasi-Marxist and exploitative view of governmental process. These public attitudes become more significant as the size of the public or governmental sector grows relative to national product. To this point in the history of the United States the relatively limited scope of overt fiscal exploitation can, I think, largely be explained by a generalized and widely shared sense of fiscal exchange which has informed public thinking about both the constitutional and postconstitutional decision processes. To the extent that the fiscal process, and politics generally, comes increasingly to be viewed as a source of profit opportunities, unrestricted by constitutional precepts, we must predict decreasing fiscal equity along with further departures from efficiency, almost regardless of how these objectives are defined.

19

Pragmatic Reform and Constitutional Revolution

None of thy wholesome counsels have escap'd me,
but nature's force subdues my better reason.
                                                Chrysippus

WHEN ventured at all, predictions of permanence and stability in sociopolitical institutions are now made with caution. General malaise
seems to characterize modern attitudes about civil order. The aging
positivist idol, the benevolent nation-state, neither commands obedi-
ence nor inspires respect, and men search for a new god. Materialist
ideals are challenged by young and old alike, and the clichés of
middle-aged and liberal politicians are treated with near-contempt.
The individual suffers alienation, social claustrophobia, and frustration in a congested, collectivized civilization that he feels powerless to
control. Democratic process seems out of kilter, and faith in political
leaders seems almost wholly extinguished. Fundamental values are
being questioned, even by those who do not claim to be philosophers;
yet policy making and policy advising move piecemeal along prede-
termined and predictable patterns.[1]

There is no need to expand this familiar description of the age, a
description that is itself riddled with facile images. Description is at
best only a faltering first step toward the intelligent understanding
that is required for improvement. We propose to contribute to such
understanding by applying the professional tools and the approach of
economists. These provide an explanation of historical experience

---

[1] Cf. C. E. Lindblom, "Policy Analysis," *American Economic Review* 48 (June,
1958): 298–312.

which may complement other explanatory hypotheses. We claim neither exclusive nor primary causal significance for the models that we develop.

Our hypothesis has its foundation in economic theory, but it is not economic in the restricted sense that denotes a preeminence of materialistic motivation in man. The analysis has three sources: the theory of opportunity cost, the theory of externalities (of public goods, of common-property resources), and the theory of collective decision making. The basic methodology is individualistic. We examine the behavior of an individual who participates in a sequence of collective or political choices over a finite period of time. We demonstrate that patterns of behavior that seem privately rational at each point in time may produce results that generate inefficiencies over time. Somewhat differently from orthodox analysis, however, our model does not necessarily converge to an inefficient equilibrium. Indeed, one of the more interesting aspects of our model is its ability to explain the major swings in political organization that may take place upon recognition of inefficiency or nonoptimality. Quantum changes in organization, derived from the behavioral choices of individual participants, are not inconsistent with our model. The results of choices made over a whole sequence of time periods may be reversed at one fell swoop, and the cyclical pattern of events may be repeated only after such "revolutions."

Although developed in a broader framework, our analysis is related to the incremental approach to policy analysis and policy making developed by C. E. Lindblom.[2] In a positive sense, we accept Lindblom's proposition that political changes normally take place incrementally and in small stages. Our hypothesis, however, does not produce the normative or quasi-normative implications suggested by Lindblom, because the genesis of nonincremental or quantum changes is to be located precisely in the cumulation of distortions that piecemeal policy making generates. In fact, our hypothesis allows no room for an "invisible hand" that insures either efficiency or stability from evolutionary step-by-step political reforms.

In a general sense, the argument is very simple. The state extends its control over society through a gradual process of usurpation,

2 Ibid., p. 302.

stretching over a long period. Society reverses this process and reestablishes its freedom from the state only through "revolution."[3] The cycle is nonsymmetrical. Our analysis grounds this general argument in the choice behavior of individuals who participate simultaneously as citizens of the state and as members of society. Our analysis does not invoke hypotheses of differential power structure; we do not discuss usurpation of power by particular groups or "active" minorities. On the contrary, we attempt to map one possible "democratic" road to revolution.[4]

Specifically, we develop a model of rational choice behavior in which the individual pragmatically approves the collectivization of a series of activities over a sequence of time periods. As he takes these separate decisions, one at a time and separately, he fails to include relevant intertemporal and interpersonal externalities in his cost-benefit calculus. At some critical stage, however, the environmental changes imposed by the decisions of earlier periods begin to exert influences on behavior. At this point, instead of remaining in an inefficient and overcollectivized equilbrium, the individual may support political reforms aimed at dramatically reversing the collectivization process. Under some conditions, paradigmatic or constitutional revolution may ensue. Again, overadjustment is possible, and the whole cycle may be recommenced.

The next section of this chapter develops the framework of an extremely restricted model within which the pattern of results suggested is not possible. Following it, the section "Imperfect Foresight, Opportunity Cost, and Institutional Rigidity" begins the progressive relaxation of the extreme assumptions. In the fourth section the relaxation is continued, with the emphasis on the indivisibility of freedom. The fifth section, entitled "Interpersonal Externalities and Collective Decision Making," introduces the peculiar problems emergent from collective decision processes. Our summary conclusions are presented in the final section.

[3] For a provocative treatment of the current situation, along with some discussion of prospects, see Ignazio Silone, "Rethinking Progress, II," *Encounter*, April, 1968, pp. 27–40.

[4] For some introductory remarks about limitations in the rationality of democratic choice in a dynamic setting, see Clement A. Tisdell, "Some Bounds upon the Pareto Optimality of Group Behavior," *Kyklos* 19, fasc. 1 (1966): 81–105.

The Symmetrical Community of Equals

We shall initially describe a pattern of rational choice behavior that will embody no trace of the effects that we emphasize in this paper. The extreme assumptions that are required to generate such a result negatively illustrate the generality of our explanatory hypothesis. First of all we assume that the person whose decision calculus we examine has perfect knowledge of all the alternatives that he confronts, both at present and in all future periods, and that this knowledge includes information about external events as well as his own utility function. Second, the individual behaves in terms of an infinitely long planning horizon; he acts as if he will live forever. Third, he is hypersensitive; his choice behavior exhibits no threshold phenomena. The individual cannot, of course, be considered in isolation, since our whole purpose is to analyze collective action. We add the restrictive assumption that the community is made up exclusively of persons who are identical in all respects. Collective decisions are made upon agreement among all citizens.

In this rarefied setting, no relevant externalities are produced by collective community action, either intertemporally or interpersonally. To show this, assume that initially all activities are in the private sector; no collective goods are provided. Members of the community will recognize that net efficiency gains are promised through joint production and consumption of some goods. They will unanimously agree to collectivize these activities. Since all persons are identical, agreement will be reached easily on both quantities and cost sharing.

The collectivization of any activity will reduce to some extent the individual's freedom of action. Collectively imposed results must be applicable to everyone, which is the obverse way of saying that the options open to anyone are diminished.[5] In each case, however, the individual's private cost-benefit calculus suggests to him that the efficiency gains from joint effort outweigh these restrictions on freedom as well as the more explicit costs that he must bear under collectivization. When he casts a positive "vote" for shifting an activity to the

---

[5] Emphasis here is on what Sir Isaiah Berlin calls "negative freedom": "the area within which a man can do what he wants." This is to be distinguished from what Berlin calls "positive freedom," which is centered on the idea of self-realization. On these definitions see Berlin, *Two Concepts of Liberty*.

public sector, the individual is, of course, aware that he is participating in a collective or group choice. In so doing, he is generating a potential external economy or diseconomy on his fellow citizens. He is "voting" to impose costs on all others, including restrictions on their freedom of action. This inherent externality in collective decision making is not eliminated even in this extreme model. This situation does not, however, generate inefficiency in results because of the precise symmetries that the restrictive assumptions guarantee. The individual who "votes" for the collectivization of an activity faces a decision alternative in which the Pigovian divergencies between private and social marginal cost and private and social marginal benefit are large, indeed. His calculus leads him to efficient results, however, because proportionately his share in community costs is symmetrical with his share in community or social benefits. There are no differentials among individuals on either the cost or the benefit side of the account.

The organization of activities that will emerge from collective decision making in this model will be fully efficient. All interdependence among separate activities will be taken into account, and no individual will experience regrets about any organizational decision that has been taken. The organization need not, of course, settle to an unchanging equilibrium, descriptively speaking. Individual utility functions may change over time, but as long as the shifts here are predicted in advance, the appropriate adjustments in structure will be made, again on the basis of unanimous agreement.

Imperfect Foresight, Opportunity Cost, and Institutional Rigidity

Only when we relax our restrictive assumptions do we begin to approach realistic choice situations. Initially, we drop only the assumption of perfect foresight on the part of the individual; other conditions of the model, including that of the world of equals, are retained. Imperfections are now allowed to emerge in the foresight of events in future periods, including foresight about the individual's own utility function.[6] This change dramatically converts the model

---

[6] Even in the simplest of decision models, complexities arise when individual utility maximization over time is introduced. On some of these complexities see

into one in which decision made in one period can exert relevant externalities on individuals in other periods. In effect, unless he has perfect foresight, the individual becomes a different person in each period. Choices made at one time may not reflect the preferences of another time.

If we could assume with any degree of plausibility that organizational decisions could be made anew at the onset of each time period, that individuals could start from *tabula rasa* with unbiased choice alternatives before them, the absence of foresight in the still-restricted model would not create major difficulty. But such an assumption would make the whole analysis absurd. Individuals do not participate in a "social contract" that involves organizing everything from scratch. They do participate in social decision processes that involve changes in organizational structure, changes from what exists to what might be. Once this simple fact is acknowledged and the notion of opportunity cost is fully grasped, the bias of all organizational choice toward nonreversibilty becomes evident.[7] The cost of making any change in structure from what was to what is has been borne *in past periods*. The cost involved in making a change to something different must be borne *at the time of decision*. There is always a bias toward the status quo, toward continuing in existence the set of organizational rules that exist.[8]

To illustrate, let us assume that after careful consideration of the alternatives, the individual "votes" for a shift in the organization of some activity from the private to the public sector. He does so rationally; the anticipated benefits at the time of decision exceed anticipated costs. Since all persons in the community are identical, the collective decision is made unanimously. Consider, now, in some time period after that during which the organization choice was made and the collectivization of the activity was implemented, that either the course of external events or the individual's own utility function is different

Robert H. Strotz, "Myopia and Inconsistency in Dynamic Utility Maximization," *Review of Economic Studies* 23 (January, 1956): 165–180.

[7] James R. Schlesinger and Almarin Phillips, "The Ebb Tide of Capitalism? Schumpeter's Prophecy Reexamined," *Quarterly Journal of Economics* 73 (August, 1959): 448–465.

[8] This argument has been developed in relation to the familiar fiscal adage, an old tax is a good tax, in James M. Buchanan, *Public Finance in Democratic Process*, pp. 68–71.

from that which was foreseen in the initial period. Further, let us specify that the subjective "terms of trade" have shifted against collectivization, and that this shift is significant enough that the individual would have reversed his initial-period decision if the new information had been properly anticipated. Note, however, that the alternatives confronted in the later period will not be the same as those initially faced. Therefore, the individual may not actually reverse the organizational decision that has been made. The reason is that the opportunity cost involved in collectivization was borne at the time of the initial choice; the opportunity cost of reversing that decision remains to be borne in the later period. Clearly, the value placed on the anticipated stream of benefits may fall substantially before an organizational decision of an earlier period can rationally be reversed, even if the earlier-period decision should have been precisely marginal in that anticipated benefits barely exceeded the anticipated costs. The individual's choice behavior, as observed, would exhibit characteristics that are analogous to threshold-sensitive responsiveness despite the assumed hypersensitivity in his cognition pattern.

It is perhaps useful to contrast the relevance and importance of "bygones" or "sunk costs" as features of organizational decision, whether private or collective, and as features of the standard decisions discussed in economic theory. In the latter the consumer or entrepreneur is faced with given choice alternatives in a specific period. The commitments made can, of course, extend over a time sequence. But there takes place, in each instance, a using-up process over time that makes resort to new decisions necessary. Goods purchased are consumed; the consumer must return to the supermarket each week. Capital goods wear out; the entrepreneur must replace his old equipment. The continuing necessity for making new or replacement choices through time produces a quickly and smoothly adjusting convergence toward long-run equilibrium even in the face of constantly changing environmental conditions and utility functions. Long-run equilibrium may never be achieved, of course, but where choices are *by their nature* bounded in time, the system is described by a continuing process of readjustment.

With organizational choice, or the choice of rules more generally, there is no "using up"; there is no "natural" or "behavioral" time limit placed on commitments that are made when a rule is modified.

There is no physical necessity which requires the explicit making of new or replacement decisions; constitutions do not wear out. The choice of an organizational form modifies the environment and does so permanently. In the light of imperfectly foreseen events, therefore, the individual must look on the organizational structure inherited from past-period choices as embodying externalities analogous to the ordinary sort. Previous choices have affected his level of utility, and even if he made these choices himself, he still experiences regrets even though, given the environment that he confronts, it remains irrational to change. But he muses over what might have been.[9]

To this point we have relaxed only one of the central assumptions of our extremely restricted model—the one that requires perfect foresight. It is evident that the effects noted will be enhanced in significance as relaxation proceeds. If we impose limits on the planning horizons of individuals and no longer assume that they act as if they live forever, the intertemporal externalities become intergenerational. For any existing generation the environmental structure will seem to have been imposed by others than themselves. This will surely produce an even greater sense of frustration than any sense of regret over past mistakes that were of one's own choosing. While it may remain fully rational for existing organizational structure to be continued instead of being overthrown, individuals may be acutely sensitive to the distance of this structure from that which we may call the "long-term equilibrium," by which we mean the constitutional pattern that would be optimally desired.

Nor does it seem probable that the departures from optimality in organizational structure will fall symmetrically on either side of the arbitrary and existing private-sector, public-sector line of division. If the subjective terms of trade have shifted against collectivization for one activity, they seem likely to have shifted in the *same* direction for

<hr/>

[9] The features of organizational choice that exert the bias toward the status quo and that allow the intertemporal externalities to be introduced even in our still-restricted model apply to individual private choices as well as to group collective choices. There is a categorical difference, however, in the significance of organizational rules of individual private behavior and of group collective behavior. An individual may, and often does, institutionalize his own behavior over time by adopting rules to which he more or less routinely conforms. To the extent that he does so, the analysis sketched here holds. When groups of individuals are concerned, however, organizational rules become essential.

other activities, and vice versa. This suggests that the discontent experienced by the individual may have important implications for political reforms that might be observed to take place. If the departures from long-term equilibrium are in the same direction over a whole set or range of "goods," and if the changes in external events or in utility functions are also unidirectional over some reasonable time span, the effective decision threshold may be crossed sequentially, even if not simultaneously, for a whole set of activities. Hence, even in this near-perfect world of equals, the absence of foresight alone, supplemented by some limitation on planning horizons, may generate broad and general shifts between private and collective organization in the supply of goods and services. The line of division between the political and the market sectors may not remain at or even near the long-term equilibrium position, which will itself, of course, be changing. The equilibrating forces set in motion by departures from equilibrium here operate only with significant time lags and then only when significantly large thresholds are surmounted.

Freedom as an Indivisible but
Exhaustible Good

In this section we examine more carefully one element of cost that arises from joint or collective action, the restriction on personal freedom to which the individual must submit when his behavior is subjected to community controls. The indivisible nature of personal freedom, the difficulty of making specific imputation of this cost to particular collective activities, may produce an interdependence among separate individual decision that cannot be fully incorporated in the results of a sequential choice process where foresight is imperfect.

Consider the person who must make an organizational choice when the line of division between individual and collective activity (between the private and the public sector) is on the noncollectivist extreme of the scale. Rational consideration may suggest that the limitation on personal freedom that collectivization might involve is not sufficient to warrant either careful estimation or undue value weighting. Individual freedom of action may remain open over so wide an area, over such a large number of options, that the restricting of only one of many avenues for private behavioral expression becomes insignificant for choice. As more and more activities are subjected to collective control, however, the limitations on personal freedom are cumulative. At some stage, they become relevant in any rational consideration of cost, and this cost may increase exponentially as the range of collectivization is extended. Because of the indivisibility of personal freedom, however, the individual may find attribution of this cost to separate activities difficult. In one sense he may feel schizophrenic when he confronts new organizational choice alternatives. If he neglects the limitations on personal freedom embodied in collectivization of an activity, the anticipated benefits may substantially exceed anticipated costs. If, on the other hand, he tries to include this aspect of cost, he will recognize that he is really loading the one activity with the burden arising from the general narrowing of his options and not with the specific closing off of one avenue of free behavior. More importantly, the individual may feel that the activity in question offers considerably higher net efficiency gains from collectivization than many activities that were organized governmentally during earlier periods when the added cost element seemed irrelevant. For reasons already discussed, however, these now inefficient activities may not be rationally decollectivized. In the struggle here, the Galbraithian elements seem likely to dominate the Goldwaterian, at least until some substantial departures from an ideally desired state of affairs are made. At some critical stage, however, the individual will begin to attribute the cost in personal freedom to all activities that are collectivized, and again because of the indivisibility of freedom itself he will neglect the interdependence among separate activities. As a result, he may support drastic political reforms that amount to constitutional revolution.

An economic analogue is provided in the behavior of a person who exploits a natural resource that he considers initially to be inexhaustible. He proceeds to use the resource as if the supply were infinitely large with respect to his own demands. At some stage, however, the individual discovers that the resource is exhaustible; he then recognizes that his earlier exploitation rate has been inefficient and that he has wasted a scarce resource. He may at this point dramatically reduce his rate of use, and if he thinks it possible, he may also take measures that are aimed at renewing the stock. At the point of recognition the individual may be observed to undergo a revolution in his behavior. The analogy with freedom does not seem farfetched here.

As more and more avenues for free individual behavior are closed, the individual may quite suddenly realize that his options are not limitless.[10] Collective controls become stifling at this point. Not only will the person refuse to support further collectivization; he may actively support measures aimed at reversing the organizational pattern. Hence, this feature of choice behavior tends to reinforce the more general features discussed in the preceding section.

Interpersonal Externalities and Collective Decision Making

To this point, discussion has been deliberately restricted to the extreme world-of-equals model, which has been designed to emphasize that even if interpersonal externalities of the familiar sort could be wholly disregarded, intertemporal externalities may arise when a historical sequence of organizational choice behavior is examined. It should be clear, however, that the whole analysis becomes much more plausible and its results more meaningful when we drop the assumption of a world of equals and allow for collective decisions under some nonunanimity rule.

If persons differ, they will not exhibit similar preferences about the organization of an activity. Some will prefer collectivization; others will prefer to leave the provision of the "good" in private hands. Differing attitudes will prevail about any demarcation line between the private sector and the public sector. In the face of such individual differences, the requirement of unanimity in collective decision making may create unacceptable delays. The community may, with general agreement on the part of all members, settle for some less inclusive rule, and of course democratic process is normally analyzed as if its institutions embody majority rule.

If a nonunanimity rule is operative, however, political decisions inherently embody externalities, even if we now limit attention to one period of time. The dominant majority, the members of an effective coalition for any particular decision, imposes net costs on the dissident minority. Therefore, even before the intertemporal changes in the

---

[10] For a corresponding view as regards sequential market choices, see A. E. Kahn, "The Tyranny of Small Decisions: Market Failures, Imperfections and the Limits of Economics," *Kyklos* 19, fasc. 1 (1966): 23–47.

choice situation take place, a minority of citizens may disagree with decisions that have been made collectively. This disagreement tends to reinforce and to strengthen the probability of wide swings in organizational structure that we have already derived from the choice behavior of the individual decision maker. As more and more members of a dominant majority coalition become disaffected, as these persons come to experience regrets over past-period organizational choices, the possible attractiveness of their shifting to a new coalition increases. At some point the exploited minority is converted into a majority, and a new value pattern typifies the average or representative decision maker for the community. There is, in one sense, a quantum difference in the utility function of the effective chooser in two periods of time surrounding this critical switching point. For reasons noted, there will remain a bias toward the status quo in organizational structure, but once the effective threshold is crossed, shifts in the composition of the majority coalition may generate quantum variations in constitutional patterns.

Conclusion

Our general hypothesis is that dominant majorities will choose one decision at a time and piecemeal to collectivize activities over a wide constitutional organization range from rather extreme reliance on spontaneous interaction processes to substantial conscious collectivism. At some critical point in this historical sequence, the limitations on individual freedom that collectivism embodies will be sensed by a majority of the community. Equilibrium in the marginal sense may be established, and the disadvantages of further colletivization may be held to offset the advantages. However, this equilibrium will be inefficient; it will tend to embody an excess collectivization due to the forces that we have discussed. The potential exhaustibility of freedom has been neglected, and the political decision process itself may have imposed relevant external diseconomies. "Long-term disequilibrium" may be suffered for a considerable period of time due to the bias toward nonreversibility of organizational decisions, but during this period frustrations will increase and a new majority coalition will come into being. At a critical stage in this sequence a proposal for a genuine constitutional housecleaning will command widespread support.[11] Because of the indivisibility of freedom itself, there may be an abrupt and dramatic shift away from collective controls and an attempt to start again from an institutional *tabula rasa*. This constitutional revolution may not take on violent form, but it will be revolution nonetheless.

Social scientists have often used the pendulum in discussing historical change, and especially in their discussion of collective controls. The swing between extreme laissez faire and collectivism has been interpreted in this manner. In the early part of the nineteenth century signs were evident that the end of a noncollectivist swing was being approached. At first intellectual discussion and later public policy began the swing back; the collectivization process was commenced. In this pendulum analogy, we may now be in the stage where the end of the collectivist swing can be foreseen. A turning back and gradual reversal might be predicted over the remaining decades of this century. Our analysis does not depend on specific predictions about identifiable stages in the historical cycle. Our hypothesis does involve a rejection of the pendulum analogy. The symmetry is absent, although the cyclicity remains.

Analysis of individual and collective choice behavior is greatly fa-

---

[11] The possibility of quantum changes in behavior when the environmental challenges exceed certain critical limits is discussed briefly in Arthur Koestler, *The Act of Creation*, p. 554. In theoretical welfare economics, private or independent behavior in the presence of external effects will generate an equilibrium. As the theorems prove, however, this independent adjustment equilibrium is inefficient or nonoptimal. It becomes relatively easy to demonstrate that all persons may be made better off in terms of their own preferences through some collectivization of the activity if certain costs of organization are neglected. In this literature, however, relatively little attention seems to have been given to the quantum jump from individual adjustment behavior to collectivization that must take place when the externalities are internalized. Presumably welfare economists consider that such "revolutions" take place through the ordinary collective decision processes when and if the externalities are widely sensed by individuals and when they are of significant importance. The analogy between this quantum jump from independent adjustment to collectivization in the context of a single activity that embodies externalities and the quantum jump from excessive collectivization over a whole range of activities that have been collectivized over a historical sequence seems close. The point is that collectivization itself embodies external diseconomies which, at some critical state, will come to be recognized.

cilitated when it can be limited to instantaneous or one-period models. We have discussed choice phenomena that extend over a long historical sequence. Of necessity, therefore, the analysis is less rigorous and more heuristic than that which can be more appropriately restricted. Nonetheless, the economist's approach yields a hypothesis that is conceptually testable. With three-fourth of the twentieth century behind us, societies in both East and West seem to be characterized by persons who are in the process of awakening to the realization that collective controls have been allowed to exhaust dangerously the scarce stock of personal freedom. If this description is relevant, our hypothesis predicts first a slowing down of the collectivization process, the signs of which may be already apparent. More importantly, we should expect to witness a growing disaffection with the institutions of collective control, a disaffection with bureaucratic procedures generally, and an increasing discussion of major constitutional changes. If our hypothesis remains valid, this process may produce genuine constitutional revolution, which, it is hoped, may take place nonviolently but which will, regardless, represent genuine revolution. There is, of course, nothing in our analysis which leads us to predict the paradigmatic content that such revolution might embody.

20

Criteria for a Free Society: Definition, Diagnosis, and Prescription

IN this book, as well as in other works, I have examined basic issues of political, legal, and social philosophy from the perspective of a political economist. From this discussion should emerge an internally consistent position, although I do not claim that ambiguities are absent. It may be useful, in this final chapter, to bring apparent loose ends together and to try somewhat more explicitly than before to lay down criteria that must be met for a society to be legitimately classified as free. In the process I can assess the America of the late 1970's against these criteria and suggest conceptual requirements for meaningful prescription. I shall develop the following arguments:

1. Freedom is possible only under rules, under law.

2. The choice of rules, the constitution of society, must be categorically separated from the choices made within rules, private and public.

3. The choice of rules which define the structure of social order must be conceived as endogenous to and inclusive of all members of the community.

4. Pragmatic drift, along with inattention to structural change, may produce and, in my view, has produced, with consequent dangers to the maintenance of individual freedom, grossly inefficient results that may have been designed by no one, intended by no one, and, in some ultimate sense, desired by no one.

5. This diagnosis suggests that improvement is conceptually possible; general prescription for improvement may be made, but major difficulties arise in making specific prescriptions for change.

In shorthand, and with the required qualifications, these separate arguments may be summarized as (1) the rule of law, (2) constitutionalism, (3) contractarianism, (4) the social dilemma, and (5) prospects for constitutional revolution. These may be used as subheadings for the sections of this chapter.

The Rule of Law

There should be relatively little dispute about the proposition that individual freedom, in any meaningful sense, is possible only under law, along with the implied consequence that the rules, "the law," must be enforced by some collective entity, some state. Only the anarchists, of either the romantic or the libertarian variety, would question this proposition. Dispute may, of course, arise over the origins of law, of the rules, and I shall discuss the matter of origins briefly in the contractarian section below. But the alternative to a society with law is one without law, that is, anarchy. In order, therefore, to establish the validity of the proposition here, we need only to examine anarchy as the universal principle for organizing social life.

In some ultimate sense, anarchy must always represent a utopian ideal for anyone who places a high value on freedom of the individual. The idealized society is one peopled by beings who have somehow come to share a common set of definitions concerning the assignment of claims to scarce resources and who behave with mutual respect in regard to these universally acknowledged claims. In such a setting there could arise no conflicts among putative individual claims and no invasions or "boundary crossings" among claims. But we scarcely recognize the people in such a world. Human nature, as we observe it or even as we might imagine it, forces us to allow both for the emergence of conflicts among claimants and for violations of acknowledged claims. Reality requires that we reduce our sights, even when discussing first-best institutional arrangements, and discard anarchy as a self-sufficient organizing principle.

While we should never overlook the wide and varied range of human interactions that are essentially organized by principles of anarchy and that do not, for that reason, necessarily degenerate into chaos, for discussions of social philosophy generally my own procedure is to commence analysis from a model of Hobbesian anarchy in which nature is "red in tooth and claw," in which there is an acknowledged "warre" of each against all, and in which the life of solitary man is indeed "poor, nasty, brutish, and short." This model is helpful because it accentuates the possibility that the dilemma created in a world without law may be all-inclusive. Each and every person in the group may be in the worst possible position; agreement upon law, upon general rules for behavior, may, if adopted and enforced, be expected to improve the lot of everyone. From this it follows that unanimous agreement should be possible, agreement on any one from among alternative sets of rules or alternative sets of assignments among claims. This derivation of agreement does not require the introduction of some transcendent moral or ethical code or some imposition of the privately preferred values of a self-anointed person or group.

Agreement on a set of rules, on a legal arrangement, is not, however, in itself sufficient to remove the Hobbesian dilemma. Rules must be enforced; violations of agreed-on standards must be punished; this punishment must be anticipated. This enforcement-punishment role must be assigned to an agent on behalf of the whole community of persons. This agent or agency then becomes what I have called "the protective state."

Constitutionalism

The enforcement of an assigned set of claims, a set of defined rights of persons to do things, along with the appropriate punishment of those who violate these claims and rights must not be confused with the decision process in which these claims and rights are established. The latter may be called the constitutional stage of decision, the outcome of which is the whole set of legal-political arrangements, including the definitions of the rights of persons, groups, and the state. It is the constitution, in the broad meaning of the term, which establishes the limits or constraints within which the whole range of post-constitutional choices or decisions takes place, whether they be the decisions of private persons, those of the enforcing agent in the form of a state, or those of persons acting collectively through what I have called the productive state.

The constitution defines the rules of the game, and the choice of these rules is categorically distinct from the enforcement of these rules and must be conceived as such both by the players and by the referees or umpires. The agent who is appointed as referee does not himself participate in the choice of rules, at least in his role as referee, and in an abstract logical sense he makes no choices in carrying out his assigned task. He is ideally limited to finding fact. He asks the questions: What rules are in existence? Have these rules been violated? What punishment rules are to be applied? The enforcing agent or referee is *not* allowed to ask, and indeed it is wholly inappropriate for him to ask the questions: What would be a good set of rules? How might the existing rules be reformed to make for a better game? What criteria (justice, efficiency, and so on) should be employed to assess alternative rules?

I stress these very elementary points, and I do so in a game setting because it is precisely at this level that profound and ultimately dangerous confusion emerges about the role of the state in making constitutional law and in modifying the whole set of legal arrangements, including the assignment of individuals' rights and claims. In its most blatant form this confusion emerges in the form of legal positivism, which states that "the law" is what the state determines it to be and that individual rights are, and must be, defined by the state and, as a consequence, are necessarily dependent on the state. In this vision of reality the state itself, along with its various arms and agencies, is subject to no rules beyond its internal limits. Individuals are vulnerable to the whims and fancies of those persons who wield power on behalf of the state. There is no meaningful constitution in this construction.

It is, nonetheless, relatively easy to appreciate the tendency to slip into this mode of conceiving state activity. In the real world the existing set of rights and claims contains many areas where precise boundaries are unclear. Conflicts emerge among persons and groups over these disputed boundaries, and the arms and agencies of the enforcing agent, the protective state, are observed to be drawing clear lines of demarcation among claims where none seemed to exist before. In such actions the state is clearly "making the law." But its own conception of what it is doing and the conception of those affected by its actions are extremely important in the sense of establishing some normative limits on state power. As long as the fiction is maintained that the agency of the state is discovering those boundaries that may have been obscured or hidden and over which conflict has emerged, there is no tendency for the agency or its clients to invade the domain where "the law" is clearly established and understood or to claim powers to rewrite existing law independently of prior obscurities and potential conflict.

The confusion between the constitutional stage of decision, in which the choice of basic rules takes place, and private or public action taken postconstitutionally, or within the chosen set of rules, emerges in a more subtle and ultimately more pernicious form under what we may call legal normativism. In this form, as in the most general legal positivism, "the law" remains what the state determines it to be. But in this normative variant the state is to be guided in its determination by externally evoked criteria. Judges can "make law"; this is acknowledged. But they are supposed to do so on the basis of precepts for justice, efficiency, or like criteria. "The law," in this conception, is the instrument for social reform; its meaning as a set of rules within which the game is played out is lost in the process.

This conception of "the law" as the instrument for reform is now pervasive among American law schools and among members of the American judiciary. The essential meaning of the constitution has been perverted, and I am personally more pessimistic about a reversal of these particular ideas than I am about almost any other of the many shifts in attitude that seem to be required for the maintenance of a free social order. And here the particular features of the American constitutional structure and constitutional history are relevant and important. The judicial branch of the United States national government throughout much of our history did stay within its role as the enforcing agent for the rules, as defined in the initial constitutional document. Its powers of enforcement extended also to cover the boundary crossings made by the government itself, through its legislative and executive arms and agencies.

It is for this reason that the traditional and more familiar variant of what I have called legal normativism has never been so important in America as elsewhere. Even in the America of the late 1970's we find common reference to the inappropriateness and inability of either Congress or the president to modify "the law of the land," as defined by the judiciary. Within certain areas (although not in others, as I shall note below) the public political philosophy of America today embodies severe limits on the powers of legislative assemblies or elected executives to change the rules—to change the constitution itself. These limits are not, however, extended to apply to the judiciary. The public political philosophy in other Western democracies is, I think, quite different in this respect. And the more relevant confusion is presumably that between the making of law, in the basic constitutional sense, and the activity of elected representatives through parliamentary assemblies in legislating, a distinction which Hayek stresses, I think correctly.

At base, of course, the confusion is the same in the two cases. The American judiciary views law as an instrument to promote the "social good," as this good is defined by the judges, and it also allows, in its "majesty," the legislative bodies to promote the "social good" in those areas where the judiciary has chosen to remain aloof, and notably in so-called economic legislation. In matters of economic policy the effective American constitution is what Congress determines it to be; the judiciary adopts a hands-off attitude here. With the other western democracies the range of legislative or parliamentary determination of the basic rules, of the effective constitution, is presumably wider and that of the judiciary more limited than in the United States. But some variant of the confusion between the constitutional stage of choice, where law is made, and collective actions taken within "the law" will almost necessarily arise as long as the objectives of the state are seen as those of promoting "social good." To the extent that the institutions of law and government, along with the prevailing public attitudes toward these institutions, reflect this teleological conception of the state, constitutional order is necessarily undermined. In its most elemental meaning a constitution is a set of rules which constrain the activities of persons and agents in the pursuits of their own ends and objectives. To argue directly or by inference that the constitution in itself embodies or should embody a "social purpose" is to negate its very meaning.

Contractarianism

In the preceding discussion I have implicitly defined "constitutionalism" broadly, and in my interpretation the basic conception becomes equivalent to one that elevates to center stage criteria for process or procedure as opposed to criteria for end states.[1] That which is to be evaluated is the process through which the rules are made instead of the content of the rules, per se. That which emerges from an acceptable process is, by inference, acceptable, and indeed, acceptability has no independent meaning beyond this.

It is interesting to note that all of the major protagonists in the philosophical discourse of the 1970's are constitutionalists in the sense herein defined. Hayek, Nozick, and Rawls share with me an emphasis on the relevance of process criteria in evaluating the basic legal-constitutional framework. All of us are constitutionalists in the sense that we separate categorically the basic rules," the law," from actions taken within these rules. Beyond this point of conceptual agreement, however, there arises a distinct divergence among us concerning how the rules should be conceived as being made and changed. Both Hayek and Nozick may be classified broadly as evolutionists in their positive explanations of how "the law" emerges. They go further, however, and make normative inferences to the effect that explicit efforts toward constructive reforms are not desired. Law emerges spontaneously, as if by an "invisible hand," as the result of the adjustments made by many persons to the localized choice situations they confront. The development of the English common law is the archetype or, more generally, the spontaneous order produced by the decentralized process of the competitive market.

By contrast and comparison with the evolutionists both John Rawls and I can, I think, be classified as contractarian. In this position we do not necessarily reject the evolutionary explanation of how the basic rules in fact emerge. But something akin to a contractarian position seems to be essential if we are to go beyond explanation, if we are to be able to evaluate existing elements of the constitutional order with any prospect of securing improvement. This is true quite independently of how the existing rules might, in fact, have been generated through history. There seems to be no basis for the presumption that whatever may have emerged that we may now observe is necessarily "efficient" or "just."

But how are criteria for "efficiency" or "justice" to be introduced

---

[1] Robert Nozick's discussion of the differences between process and end-state criteria in *Anarchy, State, and Utopia* is to be recommended here.

without reference to end states? It is precisely at this point that the notion of agreement, of quasi-contract, becomes critical in the argument. That rule is acceptable which is itself defined by agreement among all participants in the game. We may, if desired, substitute *fair* for *acceptable* here, and if we want to go one step further semantically, we may replace *fair* with *just*. Or, perhaps more eloquently, we may follow John Rawls in defining justice as fairness. Note carefully that the attribute assigned to the rule in this way is derived from the agreement instead of any independent quality or property of the rule itself. (Of course, in choosing among rules upon which they might conceivably agree, persons will necessarily examine the predicted working properties of alternatives.) There is no notion of some intrinsic "goodness" involved in the argument at all.

This contractarian argument may be accepted in its idealized version. If there is observed agreement among all persons affected, a rule so chosen might be acknowledged to be acceptable. But we live in time; there exists a set of legal rules, a constitutional order, and persons in the here and now have not been observed to agree, and have not so agreed, on this order in whole or in part. There has been no explicit act of consent to the particular set of institutions in existence. The contractarian response to this situation is subject to much misinterpretation. The individual who finds himself as a participant in a social order defined by legal rules that he had no part in choosing must ask the question: Are these rules within the set of alternative possibilities that might have emerged from an agreement among all persons who are now participants in the game? To even begin to answer such a question, the individual cannot look merely at his own well-identified position in any time-dated end state. He must look at the pattern of positions and also at the changes in these positions over a sequence of rounds of play, over time. He must account for probabilistic elements in the results. Something like "the original position" behind the "veil of ignorance," made familar by Rawls, must be introduced to make evaluation possible.

Misunderstanding tends to arise in moving from this process of individual evaluation toward inferences for constitutional reform—for changes in the rules that are in existence. There has been some tendency to interpret the contractarian position as implying that conceptual consent or agreement offers a criterion for *imposing* constitutional change, independently of agreement on change itself. That is, the argument has been advanced that a judge (or a legislator), considering himself to be empowered to change the law, should, on the contractarian logic, make his own Rawlsian assessment of an existing rule and act accordingly. This argument represents, however, a gross perversion of the contractarian position, properly understood. Once again the central importance of agreement must be stressed. Change in an existing rule, or changes in a set of rules, finds a contractarian justification only on agreement among all participants.

This necessary consequence of the contractarian position tends to generate the criticism that, so interpreted, the position amounts to little more than a dressed-up justification for the status quo, for whatever set of rules might exist, regardless of the historical origins of such rules. This criticism must be squarely faced. If existing rules are to be changed without agreement, some external criteria for change must be introduced. Beyond agreement there is simply no place for the contractarian to go.

We may, however, respond more positively to the status quo restrictiveness by pointing out that the prospects for achieving consensus on basic changes in rules are much wider than a simplistic application of the unanimity requirement might suggest. In the first place we must keep in mind that we are concentrating on genuine constitutional rules, which are known to be quasi-permanent and which, once changed, are predicted to remain stable over a whole sequence of time periods. To the extent that the modifications under consideration are treated as quasi-permanent by those who participate in the discussion and debates, the position of any one person is necessarily uncertain. An individual cannot know just what specific rule will benefit him under a particular set of future circumstances. He will, therefore, be forced under precepts of rationality to move toward an attitude akin to that described by Rawls.[2] In the second place, there may be more prospects for general agreement on a whole set of changes in the basic rules, in the whole constitutional order, than there would be on any one change taken singly. The packaging of several prospective changes

---

[2] The uncertainty concerning the particularized application of the rules in future periods was the device used by Gordon Tullock and me in *The Calculus of Consent* to accomplish the conceptual agreement on efficient rules for making collective choices. This device serves the same purpose as Rawls's original position.

allows for trade, for compromise, for compensation, for side payments. These are all instruments of agreement which allow the differing intensities of preference to be weighted by the individuals affected. A person may well agree to a modification of an existing rule that
seems to impose limited damages to his own position in exchange for
some reciprocal agreement by others for another change or set of
changes that will greatly benefit him.

The Social Dilemma[3]

I have referred to the present situation in the United States as one
of "constitutional anarchy." The effective constitution has been allowed to erode to the extent that the predictability that should be inherent in a legal structure is seriously threatened. In part this situation
is the result of what might be called "pragmatic drift," the piecemeal
adjustments made to situations as they are confronted without attention to the design of the structure as a whole, either in a backward-
looking or a forward-looking direction. Indeed, my primary critique
of those philosophers who hold up the evolutionary process as ideal is
based on my reading of what this process has now produced. But the
situation is also attributable to intellectual error of monumental pro-
portions. The basic confusion noted above, in its several forms, has
destroyed our understanding of "the constitution of freedom," an
understanding that the American founding fathers did possess.

My central diagnostic hypothesis is that the status quo is not
"efficient," that it does not qualify as "fair" or "just" even in the
most limited application of the contractarian precepts. The legal-
constitutional order (or disorder) that we now observe places us *all*
in a dilemma that is akin to the one described in the Hobbesian jungle, where the privately rational behavior of each person produces a
result which all persons find unsatisfactory. (This diagnosis explains
my own interest in analysis of the means for escaping from this setting.) Continued drift will worsen the situation for all, or substantially all, participants. We shall, slowly but surely, be swallowed up by
an insatiable Leviathan. The freedoms that we now possess will be

---

[3] In his book under this title Gordon Tullock discusses several applications of
the more general dilemma that I examine briefly here.

continually eroded by an enveloping array of bureaucratic regulation.

This scenario which is unfolding around us, and in which we are unwilling and, for the most part, unwitting participants is *not* the working out of some grand design aimed at the destruction of a social order based on freedom of the individual. In making this statement I am explicitly rejecting the significance of any "march through the institutions" that may be present in Western democracies. Rejection of the significance of such a march is not, however, equivalent to denying the possible existence of such efforts which may, of course, complement in some small way the more important underlying forces for change. But it would indeed be tragic if attention comes to be unduly concentrated on minuscule destructive conspiracies to the neglect of the obvious fact that what we see is explainable as the unintended consequence of individual actions, taken pragmatically, locally, and with no sense of overall design or purpose, either destructive or constructive. In a real sense my diagnosis turns those of the evolutionists, of Hayek, Oakeshott, and Nozick, on their heads; we can adequately explain what is happening to us by an "invisible-hand" logic. And who can, even by inference, label this as desirable or acceptable?

But precisely because we can employ such a logic to explain and to understand what we see, we are also able to identify a rational basis for improvement, which again can be consistently defined by agreement, allowing us to hold fast to contractarian precepts. If my diagnosis is correct, there should exist means of securing very general agreement, genuine consensus, on change. We are, on this diagnosis, all trapped in what we may properly call a "constitutional dilemma," in which the basic rules of the game have been eroded, forgotten, and allowed to wither away.

Prospects for Constitutional Revolution

The prescription that follows from my diagnosis is straightforward. Genuine constitutional revolution should be possible. All, or substantially all, persons and groups in the United States of 1978 should be able to reach agreement on a carefully designed and properly orchestrated set of legal-institutional arrangements which could then replace those that are in existence and in disarray. As we move beyond such general statements, however, major difficulties emerge. How is such a constitutional revolution to be organized? How are the rules of the game to be changed while the game continues to be played under the old rules?

I shall acknowledge my own inability to offer satisfactory answers to such questions as these. I have called for the adoption of a "constitutional attitude," by which I mean an appreciation and understanding of the difference between choosing basic rules and acting within those rules. But this does not get me far. Suppose, by some miracle of the educational process, the prevailing public philosophy should shift rapidly toward that which I would personally prefer. In this setting let us presume that each and every person would come to share the basic constitutional attitude suggested, and further, let us presume that each person independently arrives at a diagnosis roughly equivalent to that outlined above.

This imagined world of rational beings, all of whom recognize the dilemma confronted, would still face the problem of getting a constitutional revolution organized. The public-goods problem would necessarily emerge to make individual action toward promotion of such change unlikely. Why should a single person make the investment of time and effort required in evaluating alternative proposals for constitutional change, in discussing these alternatives with his fellows, and in arranging for some means of collective choice among alternatives?

It is easy to become extremely pessimistic about prospects for effective constitutional revolution when such questions are raised. But economists tend to overlook the interests of men that extend beyond the narrow confines of *homo economicus*. Men who are excited by the grand design of the new constitutional order that is possible may, in fact, be willing to overcome the public-goods threshold noted above. That some men will do this may be admitted. But will these same persons be willing to design and to propose rules changes that are not aimed to further their own interests or those of their social group? More importantly, will these persons be willing to accept agreement among all participants as the test, even when they recognize that the large majority of their fellows have not, and will not, undertake the effort necessary to understand and to appreciate the alternatives offered to them?

I raise these questions rather than answer them. But lest this chapter, and this book, end on an overly pessimistic note, let me recall that in 1976 we celebrated two bicentennials. In addition to the American Declaration of Independence, 1776 was also marked by the publication of Adam Smith's *Wealth of Nations*. What did this book accomplish? I think that it does not exaggerate to say that a genuine constitutional revolution did take place in Great Britain during the half-century that followed. Is it too much to hope that after 1976 we are on the verge of a renewed faith in and an understanding of the strengths of a society in which men are free? Is the current mistrust of governmental solutions, surely an increasingly relevant part of the prevailing public philosophy in the West, the first step toward a genuine constitutional revolution that may take place without our recognizing explicitly what has happened?

Bibliography

BOOKS

American Economic Association. *Readings in Price Theory.* Homewood, Ill.: Richard D. Irwin, 1952.

Arrow, Kenneth. *Social Choice and Individual Values.* New York: John Wiley, 1951.

Banfield, E. C. *The Unheavenly City.* Boston: Little, Brown & Co., 1970.

Beck, Lewis White. *A Commentary on Kant's Critique of Practical Reason.* Chicago: University of Chicago Press, 1960.

Berlin, Isaiah. *Two Concepts of Liberty.* Oxford: Clarendon Press, 1958.

Bickel, Alexander. *The Morality of Consent.* New Haven: Yale University Press, 1975.

Breton, Albert. *The Economic Theory of Representative Government.* Chicago: Aldine Publishing Co., 1974.

Buchanan, James M. *Fiscal Theory and Political Economy: Selected Essays.* Chapel Hill: University of North Carolina Press, 1960.

———. *The Limits of Liberty: Between Anarchy and Leviathan.* Chicago: University of Chicago Press, 1975.

———. *Public Finance in Democratic Process.* Chapel Hill: University of North Carolina Press, 1967.

———, and Gordon Tullock. *The Calculus of Consent: Logical Foundations of Constitutional Democracy.* Ann Arbor: University of Michigan Press, 1962.

Friedman, David. *The Machinery of Freedom.* New York: Harper & Row, Publishers, 1973.

Friedrich, Carl J., ed. *Rational Decision.* Nomos Ser. No. 7. New York: Atherton Press, 1964.

Hayek, F. A. *The Mirage of Social Justice.* Vol. 2. *Law, Legislation, and Liberty.* Chicago: University of Chicago Press, 1976.

———. *Rules and Order.* Vol. 1. *Law, Legislation, and Liberty.* Chicago: University of Chicago Press, 1973.

Hicks, J. R. *Value and Capital*. Oxford: Clarendon Press, 1939.

Hutt, W. H. *A Plan for Reconstruction*. London: Kegan Paul, 1943.

Knight, Frank H. *Risk, Uncertainty, and Profit*. Boston: Houghton Mifflin Co., 1921.

Koestler, Arthur. *The Act of Creation*. New York: Macmillan Publishing Co., 1964.

Leoni, Bruno. *Freedom and the Law*. Princeton: D. Van Nostrand, 1961.

Musgrave, R. A. *The Theory of Public Finance*. New York: McGraw-Hill Book Co., 1959.

Niskanen, William. *Bureaucracy and Representative Government*. Chicago: Aldine Publishing Co., 1971.

Nozick, Robert. *Anarchy, State, and Utopia*. New York: Basic Books, 1974.

Olson, Mancur. *The Logic of Collective Action*. Cambridge: Harvard University Press, 1965.

Polanyi, Michael. *Knowing and Being*. London: Routledge & Kegan Paul, 1969.

————. *Science, Faith, and Society*. Riddell Memorial Lectures, University of Durham. London: Oxford University Press, 1946. (With new introduction) Chicago: University of Chicago Press, Phoenix Books, 1964.

Posner, Richard. *Economic Analysis of Law*. Boston: Little, Brown & Co., 1972.

Rawls, John. *A Theory of Justice*. Cambridge: Harvard University Press, 1971.

Robbins, Lionel. *The Nature and Significance of Economic Science*. London: Macmillan Publishing Co., 1932.

Robertson, D. H. *Economic Commentaries*. London: Staples, 1956.

Rothbard, Murray. *For a New Liberty*. New York: Macmillan Publishing Co., 1973.

Samuelson, Paul. *Foundations of Economic Analysis*. Cambridge: Harvard University Press, 1947.

Schelling, Thomas C. *The Strategy of Conflict*. Cambridge: Harvard University Press, 1960.

Singer, M. G. *Generalization in Ethics*. New York: Alfred A. Knopf, 1961.

Smith, Adam. *The Wealth of Nations*. New York: Random House, Modern Library Edition, 1937.

Stevenson, Charles L. *Ethics and Language*. New Haven, Conn.: Yale University Press, 1944.

Tullock, Gordon. *The Logic of Law*. New York: Basic Books, 1970.

——. *The Politics of Bureaucracy*. Washington, D.C.: Public Affairs Press, 1965.

——. *The Social Dilemma*. Blacksburg, Va.: Center for Study of Public Choice, 1973.

——, ed. *Explorations in the Theory of Anarchy*. Blacksburg, Va.: Center for Study of Public Choice, 1972.

Wicksell, Knut. *Finanztheoretische Untersuchungen*. Jena: Gustav Fischer, 1896.

CONTRIBUTIONS TO BOOKS

Buchanan, James M. "Is Economics the Science of Choice?" In *Roads to Freedom: Essays in Honor of F. A. Hayek*, ed. Erich Streissler. London: Routledge & Kegan Paul, 1969.

——. "The Political Economy of Franchise in the Welfare State." In *Essays in Capitalism and Freedom*, ed. Richard Selden. Charlottesville: University Press of Virginia, 1975.

——. "Political Equality and Private Property: The Distributional Paradox." In *Markets and Morals*, ed. G. Dworkin, G. Berwent, and P. Brown. Washington, D.C.: Hemisphere Publishing Co., 1977.

Bush, Winston C. "Individual Welfare in Anarchy." In *Explorations in the Theory of Anarchy*, ed. Gordon Tullock. Blacksburg, Va.: Center for Study of Public Choice, 1972.

Hammond, Peter. "Charity, Altruism or Cooperative Egotism." In *Altruism, Morality, and Economic Theory*, ed. E. S. Phelps. New York: Russell Sage Foundation, 1975.

Letwin, Shirley. "The Achievements of Hayek." In *Essays on Hayek*, ed. Fritz Machlup. New York: New York University Press, 1976.

Mansfield, Harvey C., Jr. "Rationality and Representation in Burke's 'Bristol Speech.'" In *Rational Decision*, Nomos Ser. No. 7, ed. Carl J. Friedrich. New York: Atherton Press, 1964.

Moss, Laurence. "Private Property Anarchism: An American Variant." In *Further Explorations in the Theory of Anarchy*, ed. Gordon Tullock. Blacksburg, Va.: Center for Study of Public Choice, 1974.

Wicksell, Knut. "A New Principle of Just Taxation." In *Classics in the Theory of Public Finance*, ed. R. A. Musgrave and A. T. Peacock. London: Macmillan Publishing Co., 1958.

ARTICLES

Adelman, M. A. "The Antimerger Act, 1950–60." *American Economic Review* 51 (May, 1961): 236–244.

304 BIBLIOGRAPHY

Alchian, Armen A. "The Economic and Social Impact of Free Tuition." *New Individualist Review* 5 (Winter, 1968): 42–52.

——, and Harold Demsetz. "Production, Information Costs, and Economic Organization." *American Economic Review* 62 (December, 1972): 777–795.

Alexander, Sidney. "Social Evaluations through Notional Choice." *Quarterly Journal of Economics* 88 (November, 1974): 597–624.

Arrow, Kenneth. "General Economics Equilibrium: Purpose, Analytic Techniques, Collective Choice." *American Economic Review* 64 (June, 1974): 253–272.

Auspitz, Josiah Lee. "Libertarianism without Law." *Commentary* 60 (September, 1975): 76–84.

Banfield, Edward C., and James Q. Wilson. "Public-Regardingness as a Value Premise in Voting Behavior." *American Political Science Review* 58 (December, 1964): 876–887.

Brennan, Geoffrey. "Pareto Desirable Redistribution: The Non-Altruistic Dimension." *Public Choice* 14 (Spring, 1973): 43–68.

Buchanan, James M. "The Institutional Structure of Externality." *Public Choice* 14 (Spring, 1973): 69–82.

——. "The Justice of Natural Liberty." *Journal of Legal Studies* 5 (January, 1976): 1–16.

——. "Positive Economics, Welfare Economics, and Political Economy." *Journal of Law and Economics* 2 (October, 1959): 124–138.

——. "Rawls on Justice as Fairness." *Public Choice* 13 (Fall, 1972): 123–128.

——. Review of *The Machinery of Freedom*. *Journal of Economic Literature* 12 (September, 1974): 914–915.

——. Review of *Rational Decision*, Nomos Ser. No. 7. *The Annals* 359 (May, 1965): 189–190.

——. "Social Choice, Democracy, and Free Markets." *Journal of Political Economy* 62 (1954): 114–123.

——. "Utopia, the Minimal State, and Entitlement." *Public Choice* 23 (Fall, 1975): 121–126.

——. "What Should Economists Do?" *Southern Economic Journal* 30 (January, 1964): 213–222.

Bush, Winston C., and L. S. Mayer. "Some Implications of Anarchy for the Distribution of Property." *Journal of Economic Theory* 8 (August, 1974): 401–412.

Coase, Ronald. "The Nature of the Firm." *Economica* 4 (1937): 386–405.

———. "The Problem of Social Cost." *Journal of Law and Economics* 3 (1961): 1–45.

Davis, Otto, and Andrew Whinston. "Externalities, Welfare, and the Theory of Games." *Journal of Political Economy* 70 (June, 1962): 241–262.

Dewey, Donald. "Mergers and Cartels: Some Reservations about Policy." *American Economic Review* 51 (May, 1961): 255–262.

Frisch, Ragnar. "On Welfare Theory and Pareto Regions." *International Economic Papers* 9 (1959): 39–92.

Gellner, Ernest. "The Last Pragmatist: The Philosophy of W. V. Quine." *Times Literary Supplement* 25 (July, 1975).

Gordon, H. Scott. "The New Contractarians." *Journal of Political Economy* 84 (June, 1976): 573–590.

Hochman, Harold, and James Rodgers. "Pareto Optimal Redistribution." *American Economic Review* 59 (September, 1969): 542–547.

Johnson, David B., and Mark V. Pauly. "Excess Burden and the Voluntary Theory of Public Finance." *Economica* 36 (August, 1969): 269–276.

Kahn, A. E. "The Tyranny of Small Decisions: Market Failures, Imperfections and the Limits of Economics." *Kyklos* 19, fasc. 1 (1969): 23–47.

Knight, Frank. "Virtue and Knowledge: The View of Professor Polanyi." *Ethics* 59 (July, 1949): 271–284.

Lindblom, C. E. "Policy Analysis." *American Economic Review* 48 (June, 1958): 298–312.

MacCallum, Spencer. "The Social Nature of Ownership." *Modern Age* 9 (Winter, 1964–1965): 49–61.

Nisbet, Robert. "The Pursuit of Equality." *The Public Interest* 35 (Spring, 1974): 103–120.

Olson, Mancur, and Christopher Clague. "Dissent in Economics." *Social Research* 38 (Winter, 1971): 753.

Phillips, Almarin. "Policy Implications of the Theory of Interfirm Organization." *American Economic Review* 51 (May, 1961): 245–254.

Plattner, Marc F. "The New Political Theory." *The Public Interest* 40 (Summer, 1975): 119–128.

Rawls, John. "Reply to Alexander and Musgrave." *Quarterly Journal of Economics* 88 (November, 1974): 638.

Samuels, Warren J. "Interrelations between Legal and Economic Processes." *Journal of Law and Economics* 14 (October, 1971): 435–450.

————. "The Myths of Liberty and the Realities of the Corporate State: A Review Article." *Journal of Economic Issues* 10 (December, 1976): 923–942.

Samuelson, Paul A. "Diagrammatic Exposition of a Theory of Public Expenditure." *Review of Economics and Statistics* 37 (November, 1955): 350–356.

————. "The Pure Theory of Public Expenditure." *Review of Economics and Statistics* 36 (November, 1954): 387–389.

Schelling, Thomas C. "Game Theory and the Study of Ethical Systems." *Journal of Conflict Resolution* 12 (March, 1968): 34–44.

Schlesinger, James R., and Almarin Phillips. "The Ebb Tide of Capitalism? Schumpeter's Prophecy Reexamined." *Quarterly Journal of Economics* 73 (August, 1959): 448–465.

Silone, Ignazio. "Rethinking Progress, II." *Encounter*, April, 1968, pp. 27–40.

Stigler, George J. "Director's Law of Public Income Redistribution." *Journal of Law and Economics* 13 (April, 1970): 1–10.

Strotz, Robert H. "Myopia and Inconsistency in Dynamic Utility Maximization." *Review of Economic Studies* 23 (January, 1956): 165–180.

Tisdell, Clement A. "Some Bounds upon the Pareto Optimality of Group Behavior." *Kyklos* 19, fasc. 1 (1966): 81–105.

Tuerck, David G. "Constitutional Asymmetry." *Papers on Non-Market Decision-Making* 2 (1967): 27–44.

Tullock, Gordon. "The Charity of the Uncharitable." *Western Economic Journal* 9 (December, 1971): 379–391.

Wick, Warner. "Generalization and the Basis of Ethics." *Ethics* 72 (July, 1962): 288–298.

UNPUBLISHED WORKS

Cooter, Robert. "What is the Public Interest?" Mimeographed. Cambridge: Harvard University, 1974.

Davis, Otto A., and Andrew Whinston. "Some Foundations of Public Expenditure Theory." Mimeographed. Pittsburgh: Carnegie Institute of Technology, 1961.

Polanyi, Michael. "The Creative Imagination." Mimeographed. Oxford, 1965.

————. "The Republic of Science." Lecture delivered at Roosevelt University, January 11, 1962.

Tuerck, David. "Uniformity in Taxation, Discrimination in Benefits: An Essay in Law and Economics." Ph.D. dissertation, University of Virginia, 1966.

Author Index

Subject Index